TREATING PATIENTS WITH ALCOHOL AND OTHER DRUG PROBLEMS

Psychologists in Independent Practice

Leon VandeCreek, Series Editor

Ethical Practice in Small Communities: Challenges and Rewards for Psychologists
    Janet A. Schank and Thomas M. Skovholt

Treating Patients With Neuropsychological Disorders: A Clinician's Guide to Assessment and Referral
    Jeffery B. Allen

Treating Patients With Alcohol and Other Drug Problems: An Integrated Approach
    Robert D. Margolis and Joan E. Zweben

Treating Patients With Memories of Abuse: Legal Risk Management
    Samuel J. Knapp and Leon VandeCreek

Treating People With Chronic Disease: A Psychological Guide
    Carol D. Goodheart and Martha H. Lansing

Michal J. Murphy, Series Editor

Couple Power Therapy: Building Commitment, Cooperation, Communication, and Community in Relationships
    Peter L. Sheras and Phyllis R. Koch-Sheras

Treating Patients With Alcohol and Other Drug Problems: An Integrated Approach, Second Edition
    Robert D. Margolis and Joan E. Zweben

TREATING PATIENTS WITH ALCOHOL AND OTHER DRUG PROBLEMS: AN INTEGRATED APPROACH

SECOND EDITION

ROBERT D. MARGOLIS

AND

JOAN E. ZWEBEN

AMERICAN PSYCHOLOGICAL ASSOCIATION
WASHINGTON, DC

Published by
American Psychological Association
750 First Street, NE
Washington, DC 20002
www.apa.org

To order
APA Order Department
P.O. Box 92984
Washington, DC 20090-2984
Tel: (800) 374-2721; Direct: (202) 336-5510
Fax: (202) 336-5502; TDD/TTY: (202) 336-6123
Online: www.apa.org/pubs/books
E-mail: order@apa.org

In the U.K., Europe, Africa, and the Middle East, copies may be ordered from
American Psychological Association
3 Henrietta Street
Covent Garden, London
WC2E 8LU England

Typeset in Minion by Circle Graphics, Inc., Columbia, MD

Printer: Maple-Vail Books, York, PA
Cover Designer: Minker Design, Sarasota, FL

The opinions and statements published are the responsibility of the authors, and such opinions and statements do not necessarily represent the policies of the American Psychological Association.

Library of Congress Cataloging-in-Publication Data

Margolis, Robert D.
   Treating patients with alcohol and other drug problems : an integrated approach / Robert D. Margolis and Joan E. Zweben. — 2nd ed.
      p. cm.
   Includes bibliographical references and index.
   ISBN-13: 978-1-4338-0965-1
   ISBN-10: 1-4338-0965-6
   1. Substance abuse—Treatment. I. Zweben, Joan E. II. Title.

   RC564.M29 2011
   362.29—dc22
                                      2010042152

British Library Cataloguing-in-Publication Data
A CIP record is available from the British Library.

Printed in the United States of America
Second Edition

doi: 10.1037/12312-000

To all our wonderful patients, clients, and colleagues who have made this work meaningful for so many decades.

To those who are sober and to those who still struggle.

Contents

Preface   ix

Introduction   3

1. Psychologists in the Substance Abuse Field   13

2. Models and Theories of Addiction   27

3. Assessment of Substance Abuse and Dependence   59

4. Determining Appropriate Treatment   83

5. Individual Psychotherapy   117

6. Family Therapy   145

7. Group Therapy and Self-Help Groups in   173
    Addiction Treatment

8. Relapse Prevention   199

References   225

Index   251

About the Authors   269

Preface

This book was written for clinicians as well as those who are preparing to become practitioners in the field of mental health and substance abuse problems. It is intended to be a text that introduces students to the field of alcohol and other drug (AOD) problems and that focuses on theory, assessment, and treatment from a variety of different perspectives. In presenting different theoretical models and approaches to assessment and treatment we have attempted to point out commonalities as well as controversial issues that inevitably arise from the intersection of different perspectives. The book is also written for a range of practitioners, from clinicians in a variety of treatment settings to those in specialty addiction treatment settings. The latter may benefit from the articulation of the rationale for practices taken for granted.

We believe that knowledge of these issues is especially important today because of the increased demand by professionals, third-party payers, and consumers for demonstrated evidence of proficiency in these areas. The certificate of proficiency offered by the American Psychological Association's College of Professional Psychology is a prime example of the recent focus on documented proficiency.

This second edition of *Treating Patients With Alcohol and Other Drug Problems: An Integrated Approach* incorporates the highlights of new research and treatment methods as they are evolving in this field. In this new edition, to focus on more current developments, we have eliminated some historical material that appeared in the first edition. We have tried to be comprehensive without writing a research tome. At a certain point the decision has to be made to stop writing even though much remains to be covered and new information is constantly developing. We hope that this book will help readers to think innovatively about their treatment approaches, to interact more effectively with the AOD treatment system, and to relate more compassionately with individuals experiencing these problems.

As clinicians, we are continuously engaged in teaching and writing. As such, we have endeavored to address complex clinical issues by drawing on whatever research is available, offering, when possible, clinical opinions on which there is widespread consensus and offering our own views on matters that are controversial or on which there appears to be no prevailing consensus.

We thank the following people and organizations for their assistance with the preparation of this book. Robert Margolis thanks Sandy Cohen for his invaluable help in locating articles and in drafting and editing certain sections, especially regarding the neurobiology of addition. He also especially thanks his wife, Karen, for her expertise in editing and rewriting sections of the book.

Joan Zweben thanks the Center for Substance Abuse Treatment and the National Institute on Drug Abuse for the resources provided to the East Bay Community Recovery Project and for the unparalleled learning opportunities associated with each of these federal agencies. They exemplify public service at its best.

TREATING PATIENTS
WITH ALCOHOL AND
OTHER DRUG PROBLEMS

Introduction

For several decades, epidemiological studies have demonstrated that alcohol and other drug (AOD) use is so widespread in clinical populations that practitioners can assume it may be an issue even in the absence of warning signs. AOD use needs to be ruled out, not in. Yet the more experienced the clinician, the less likely he or she has any systematic training in addressing these problems. Mild to moderate problems with alcohol and drugs in patients can be handled even by the therapist who is not a specialist in alcohol and drug treatment; typically these patients present for problems that are completely unrelated to substance abuse. For many of these patients, a little attention to the problem goes a long way because the therapist is in a prime position to do early intervention. It is especially important for those in supervisory roles to update their knowledge to ensure that those in training will be adequately prepared for the clinical populations they will face.

For patients with severe problems (i.e., those who experience profound loss of control over their alcohol and drug use), effective referral requires knowledge of the treating agency to which the therapist is directing the patient. In this book, we describe the major addiction treatment modalities and the types of patients appropriate for them. We also describe the basic assumptions and operating principles of treatment modalities in an effort to minimize miscommunication that occurs when professionals from differing "cultures" attempt to collaborate on the patient's care.

We hope that this book will broaden the perspective of psychologists already working in addiction treatment settings. It is typical even for practitioners in the field to be unfamiliar with major modalities other than those with which they regularly interact, particularly if the populations served, basic assumptions, and clinical practices are different from their own. For example, it is common for those working in hospital-based inpatient settings treating insured patients to be unfamiliar with methadone maintenance, despite the fact that it is one of the major treatment modalities for opiate use. Such lack of familiarity can result in inappropriate recommendations and at best makes it less likely that the patient will actually connect and engage with an appropriate treatment modality. Broader knowledge of the available resources will assist the therapist in helping the patient become more "treatment ready," even as the therapist becomes more skilled at dealing with alcohol and drug issues in ongoing therapy.

Addiction treatment settings are designed for those with severe problems who arrive relatively willing to acknowledge that they have a problem and to begin to address it. Although patients are usually ambivalent, addiction treatment settings start from the premise that a focus on AOD use is appropriate. In other settings (e.g., private therapists' offices, mental health programs, employee assistance programs, homeless shelters, criminal justice settings, social services agencies), patients arrive with minimal awareness of the relationship between alcohol and drug use and their other problems, or they arrive with some awareness and a resistance to focus on it. AOD use influences feeling states and behavior long before people meet criteria for addiction. When patients have a coexisting mental disorder along with substance use issues, that disorder is often magnified, and therapists are often unaware of the potential influence on premature dropout and failure to progress in treatment. When they do become aware that AOD use might be a problem, they seek to refer the patient to self-help meetings and/or specialty treatment settings. Many clinicians resist the idea of learning to address such problems themselves, striving instead to increase their effectiveness at referral. Although referral is certainly appropriate for some, it is our hope that this book will enhance the confidence and skill of psychotherapists and other practitioners in addressing alcohol and drug use in the context of their ongoing work.

THERAPEUTIC ORIENTATIONS: ABSTINENCE AND HARM REDUCTION

It is important to clarify some of our basic positions and biases on issues for which some controversy exists. We believe that AOD use disorders are best understood from a biopsychosocial model. There are a variety of factors from genetic vulnerabilities to traumatic life events to family and social dynamics that can help to propel the individual into a drug-using lifestyle (see Chapter 2, this volume). Furthermore, we believe that AOD use disorders can correctly be considered as existing along a continuum from use to dependence, a continuum characterized by increasing loss of control and increasing functional impairment. We also believe, however, that once individuals reach a certain stage in their chemical abuse, they move beyond a point at which their AOD use is voluntary (or at least potentially under their control) to a point at which it is involuntary and beyond their control. This is the point that the *Diagnostic and Statistical Manual of Mental Disorders* (4th ed., text revision; *DSM–IV–TR;* American Psychiatric Association, 2000) defines as *dependence* (see Chapter 3, this volume), the point that others might label as *addiction* or *alcoholism,* and the point that Alcoholics Anonymous (AA) refers to as "crossing the wall."

We agree with the previous and current directors of the National Institute on Drug Abuse, Alan Leshner and Nora Volkow, respectively, that addiction is a brain disease—but not *just* a brain disease. It moves from a state in which drug use is under some degree of voluntary control to a state at which it is compulsive and not under dependable control. Physical dependence, characterized by the presence of tolerance and withdrawal, is often present but not required to meet criteria for substance dependence. We have learned much about processes within the brain that lead to the addictive behavior that can so mystify onlookers. Fundamental brain changes, brought on by AOD use, are being revealed by new techniques such as brain imaging. Understanding the genetic, biological, and environmental underpinnings will allow psychologists and others to develop increasingly effective prevention and treatment strategies.

The fundamental point, in the authors' opinion, is not whether addiction stems from brain changes, psychosocial factors, or a combination of factors but that addiction is a primary disorder. This primary disorder is characterized by a loss of control and increasing use despite negative consequences. Our position results from our understanding of the scientific evidence as well as our extensive clinical experience with these individuals. Our position has profound implications for our work with patients who use AOD.

In most of what we do, we operate from an abstinence-based model, but we are willing to start wherever the patient is prepared to begin. Our recommendation to patients who meet the criteria for dependence is complete abstinence from alcohol and illicit drugs and use of psychoactive medications only as prescribed by physicians familiar with the patient's history and knowledgeable about addiction. This does not mean that we terminate those who cannot or will not become or remain abstinent but, rather, that we endorse abstinence as the goal offering the widest margin of safety and the greatest potential benefit.

This emphasis grows out of our work in specialty addiction treatment, in which most of our patients are those who have spent significant portions of their lives conducting personal experiments on controlled AOD use— to the detriment of school and work performance, relationships, and health. Encouraging the patient to prolong this experiment serves no useful purpose and may place the therapist at some risk of liability. However, even with patients whose history is less clear-cut and whose use appears mild to moderate, the abstinence model allows the therapist to bypass many ambiguities. Is the patient minimizing his drinking or drug use? Is moderate alcohol consumption exacerbating her depression? Is the patient's difficulty accessing feelings related to his weekly marijuana consumption? Is the intractable marital bickering related to the moderate but nonetheless disinhibiting amount of wine the couple consumes when they reunite after work and begin to try to talk? Given the individual variability in response to alcohol and drugs, these are questions that have no unequivocal answer. At minimum, complete abstinence (even for a relatively brief period) provides an opportunity for patient and therapist to understand the impact of alcohol and drug use more clearly. Certainly, many will object to this suggestion, even for the short term. However, it appears to us that those patients most highly invested in some form of controlled use are precisely those with attachments and vulnerabilities that make it unlikely that they will succeed in moderating their consumption.

Harm reduction models are increasingly in the spotlight, with good reason. Harm reduction is a public health approach intended to reduce the harm done to AOD users, their loved ones, and their communities. It acknowledges that many people are unwilling to give up their alcohol and drug use or unable to access addiction treatment and that there is merit in helping them reduce the damage caused to themselves and others. One of the coauthors of this book offers harm reduction activities oriented to these public health goals in a public sector treatment program in Oakland, California: harm reduction services for street drug users unable or unwilling to access treatment, outreach and education (clean needles, safer sex) to reduce HIV transmission, and supportive housing on the "housing first" model. For almost 3 decades, an affiliated program offered methadone maintenance not only for patients who were committed to full recovery but also for those who were merely seeking to reduce some of the negative consequences of using drugs. In this context, abstinence is seen as the highest form of harm reduction, but not the only form. There are many public health benefits even if complete abstinence is not fully achieved.

Abstinence-oriented addiction treatment, with all its failings, has been well documented to reduce or eliminate illicit drug use and associated crime and improve health status (including psychological status), employment, and family functioning. These improvements occur despite the fact that many people do not achieve long-term continuous abstinence but, rather, have lapses and relapses, perhaps for years. An orientation toward abstinence accomplishes harm reduction goals even when it does not achieve the gold standard of continuous abstinence. In this sense, harm reduction coexists naturally within an abstinence-oriented approach, particularly when clinicians appreciate that improvement is fostered by retaining the patient in treatment, not terminating him or her prematurely. It is not possible to blend these approaches within all settings. Staff in residential treatment facilities have the responsibility to maintain safety in the facility, and allowing active drug users to remain in residence has a contagion effect that is unacceptable. Outpatient treatment, however, offers greater flexibility to move the patient in and out of activities, thereby continuing treatment for the individual while reducing the negative impact a serious relapse has on others.

Debate about harm reduction continues, with proponents typically polarized on which approach is superior. We do not wish to enter the fray here. However, we do view abstinence as the preferred goal, not only for those with severe problems but also for those with lesser problems. This does not mean that we take a punitive approach toward those who continue their alcohol and drug use, but neither do we suggest that moderation goals can achieve the same benefits. Moderation management approaches (for alcohol) are enjoying a resurgence of interest, but they have not been subjected to extensive, long-term, careful study using criteria that allow comparison with abstinence-oriented approaches. (It is also relevant that the amounts of alcohol designated as "moderate" in these approaches are typically well above those considered to be devoid of negative health consequences.) Other harm reduction approaches, such as HIV education and counseling, are valid in their own right, but we prefer to offer them with encouragement to become fully abstinent and with access to resources to assist in doing so.

The research base in many areas of the addiction field is enormous, but in other significant areas it is sparse. For example, it would be difficult to report the exhaustive work done on the genetics of alcoholism, efficacy and safety of methadone maintenance, or the biomedical factors involved in cocaine dependence; these topics have been extensively studied over a long period of time. Other factors are more difficult to study rigorously. *Recovery* is defined as more than the absence of AOD use; it is also the progressive achievement of physical, emotional, and relational health (White, 2008). What produces successful recovery? We know a great deal about specific interventions that are effective in the short term, but what are the essential ingredients of that complex process by which some succeed and others do not? Currently, emphasis is shifting to the concept of recovery-oriented systems of care, reflecting the recognition that treatment is only one component of a long-term recovery process. Research funding is always limited, and the emphasis on psychosocial factors has varied over time. Clinicians, as always, must often make decisions based on the information they have available and on their clinical instincts honed by experience.

TERMINOLOGY

We use a number of different terms in discussing the spectrum of AOD abuse disorders. In addition to *AOD abuse disorders,* we use *substance abuse, substance-related disorders, substance dependence, addiction, alcoholism, alcohol or drug abuse,* and *alcohol or drug dependence.* Some points should help to clarify the meaning of these terms. The term *abuse* is broad, referring to any maladaptive use of a psychoactive substance. The term *substance abuse* encompasses dependence. The term *dependence* refers to a more severe form of abuse characterized by a habitual use of a substance that is taken more frequently and in larger amounts over time, leading to increasingly negative consequences. The line between abuse and dependence is often difficult to discern, but an individual is generally considered to be dependent on a substance when attempts to quit or cut back have been unsuccessful, even in the face of increasingly negative consequences. This is explained in more detail in Chapter 3 along with the associated information from the *DSM–IV.* The terms *alcoholic, addict, alcoholism,* and *addiction* all refer to individuals or conditions related to dependence. Thus, an alcoholic is by definition substance dependent. In deciding which terms to use in which context, we have tried to be consistent with terminology that is most commonly used in a given context. For example, when discussing private treatment centers, we do not refer to AOD abuse treatment centers but, rather, to addiction treatment centers. When discussing public sector and/or psychological treatment approaches, we are more likely to use terms such as *AOD abuse* or *substance abuse.*

The reader will find a variety of terms used to describe those providing treatment: *practitioners, clinicians, therapists, addiction specialists, professionals.* We do not use the term *counselors,* but we certainly view them as clinicians. Although some of these are considered to be more highly trained, in practice the role boundaries have become more ambiguous. Cost-cutting pressures have greatly broadened the scope of practice for many types of practitioners. Managed care panels often distinguish between *physicians* and *therapists* but do not make distinctions within the category of therapists. Therefore, we address a broad group of those who may need to address AOD use in their practice.

OVERVIEW OF CONTENTS

In Chapter 1, we discuss our view of the lack of participation of psychologists in mainstream addiction treatment. We discuss the medicalization of the field, the lack of education and training, and the hopeless views of addiction that can hold psychologists back. In addition, we discuss some of the problems of doing traditional psychodynamic therapy with these types of patients.

In Chapter 2, we review five models or theories of addiction: the disease model, the psychoanalytic model, the family theory model, the learning model, and the biopsychosocial model. Each of the models has strong and weak points. It is our belief that effective treatment for patients who use AOD requires an integrated biopsychosocial approach so that the therapist can maintain great flexibility in dealing with AOD use problems.

In Chapter 3, we discuss the process of assessing AOD use problems and disorders. We discuss the *DSM–IV–TR* classifications, the diagnostic interview, questions to ask, signs to look for, the importance of the use profile and the family and developmental history, the importance of drug screens, and various questionnaires that can be used for testing. We also review the stages of change and judging a person's readiness for change.

In Chapter 4, we describe the treatment modalities and continuum of care available in substance abuse, summarizing research data on efficacy when available and describing models and approaches for both residential and outpatient treatment. We then offer a variety of ways to determine appropriate treatment, ranging from the problem–service matching approach to the patient placement criteria developed by the American Society of Addiction Medicine to select levels of care. In this chapter, we also look at a rapidly expanding treatment associated with the criminal justice system, with increasing attention to careful evaluation.

In Chapter 5, we introduce therapists to a recovery-oriented model, in which treatment is modified to address the changing tasks of the patient. These tasks begin with making a commitment to change alcohol- and drug-using behavior, breaking the pattern of drinking and/or using, and consolidating changes to achieve a comfortable and satisfying sobriety. These tasks can be integrated into ongoing psychotherapy, providing the therapist is willing to shift the nature of his or her activity to best achieve the recovery task of the patient. In cases where the addiction treatment occurs as a parallel activity, it is important that the therapist appreciate certain vulnerabilities of the patient so as not to undermine creating the foundation of abstinence that makes other therapeutic efforts more productive.

In Chapter 6, we write about family therapy, an essential component of treatment. We review the reasons for its popularity and the tasks of a family therapist as they apply to AOD use problems specifically: joining with the family, stabilizing the family, educating them about AOD abuse, analyzing family systems, helping with alternative coping skills, and helping to prevent and handle relapses.

Group activities form the cornerstone of addiction treatment, and in Chapter 7, we describe a variety of these structures. Professionally led groups include motivational enhancement groups and recovery groups as well as network therapy and harm reduction group activities. In the chapter, we describe the characteristics and distinctive issues of recovery groups in some detail. Self-help groups, particularly 12-step groups descended from AA, constitute a powerful resource with no financial barriers; hence we give special attention to how therapists can facilitate their use.

Relapse prevention is embedded in good treatment; however, the variety of approaches and issues merits separate consideration, particularly because these have a strong research base. In Chapter 8, we describe common relapse precipitants and effective strategies for addressing them. We also cover medications, both as tools and as relapse hazards. Addiction treatment at its best is multidisciplinary, and it is important that all practitioners have some comfort with these medical aspects of treatment. In the chapter, we also describe other forms of addiction-like behaviors associated with relapse: eating disorders, gambling, and compulsive sexual behaviors. These areas frequently emerge as part of a reciprocal relapse pattern in which compulsive or disturbed behavior precipitates relapse to alcohol and drugs and vice versa.

1

Psychologists in the Substance Abuse Field

Alcohol and other drug (AOD) abuse is a major public health problem in the United States. The combined economic cost to society of alcohol, nicotine, and other drug abuse is estimated to be upwards of half a trillion dollars a year (National Institute on Drug Abuse, 2007, p. 3). AOD use has been implicated as a factor in many of the nation's most serious and expensive problems, including high-risk sexual behavior, HIV/AIDS and other sexually transmitted diseases, teen pregnancy, school failure, car crashes, violence, and death from injuries (U.S. Department of Health and Human Services, 2007).

As the understanding of AOD problems has evolved, the treatment field has also undergone dramatic changes. In the 19th and early 20th centuries, AOD problems were dealt with as a moral or spiritual condition best handled by religious organizations. Alcoholics and drug users were considered sinners who needed to exercise willpower in choosing not to consume the particular substances. In the early 20th century, alternative views of addiction began to emerge. The psychiatric community began to offer psychodynamic explanations of addiction. An example is the early psychoanalytic view of alcoholism as a regressive phenomenon or a return to infantile fixations such as oral dependency needs (Frances, Franklin, & Borg, 1994, p. 239). The psychiatric approach to addiction dominated treatment centers until the 1970s, but the success rates were dismal. The founding of the National Institute on Alcohol Abuse and Alcoholism (NIAAA) and the National Institute on Drug Abuse (NIDA) in the early 1970s fostered the development of new approaches, with evaluation and other types of research included. This permitted better identification of approaches that worked.

In 1935, Bill Wilson began the Alcoholics Anonymous (AA) movement after his treatment needs were unmet by the professional community and his own efforts at sobriety failed. The AA program taught that alcoholics had a disease in which their response to alcohol was different from that of other people. The AA program is based on the belief that the alcoholic must abstain from mood-altering chemicals and develop a connection to a power greater than him- or herself. AA members believe that stopping drinking is a first step to recovery. Developing a sober state of mind or serenity, however, is what separates an individual who is merely dry from one who is in recovery. To aid the alcoholic, AA has developed a series of 12 steps based on spiritual and behavioral principles. Applying these 12 steps in all of the individual's daily affairs is the core of a good recovery program (Alcoholics Anonymous World Services, 2001). The program became popular as alcoholics found supportive, understanding help and learned coping skills for living without alcohol. In the 1960s, treatment centers based on AA principles were established. The centers were often deliberately located away from major metropolitan areas, in places such as Center City, Minnesota (Hazelden), and Statesboro, Georgia (Willingway), in an attempt to avoid pressure from the psychiatric community. Eventually, mainstream psychiatric treatment centers began to adopt the AA program. AA programs were understandable to the average person, the disease concept seemed to alleviate the moral stigma, and the programs provided practical solutions for the problems that recovering individuals faced. This model still prevails in the majority of treatment centers today.

In the 1970s, as the AA-based disease model of addiction became more widely incorporated into mainstream addiction programs, psychologists questioned this view of addiction in part because scientific research was not available to support its efficacy. They developed other approaches to addiction, such as cognitive–behavioral modalities, relapse prevention, and motivational enhancement. These approaches are supported by efficacy research.

THE RIFT BETWEEN PSYCHOLOGISTS AND THE MAINSTREAM ADDICTION TREATMENT FIELD

For many years there has been a practical and philosophical rift between the psychological community and the mainstream addiction treatment community. The practical rift occurred because the mainstream addiction treatment field was dominated by physicians who were not receptive to psychologists' work in the field. For many years treatment centers did not allow psychologists to be primary therapists, and the physicians did not welcome them to the environment. During the past decade, however, this rift has changed, as psychologists have published more in mainstream medical journals, presented at medical addiction conferences such as the American Society of Addiction Medicine annual conferences, and participated more in treatment.

The philosophical rift has been more divisive. It resulted from differing beliefs over the nature of addiction. The majority of addiction treatment centers subscribe to the disease model of addiction (see Chapter 2, this volume). Briefly, this model states that addiction is a biochemical disorder in which the individual cannot consistently control his or her alcohol and drug using behavior outside of total abstinence. The disorder is not curable because the individual will never escape the biochemical condition, but the individual can live a normal, rewarding life without the use of alcohol and/or drugs if he or she accepts his or her powerlessness over the alcohol and/or drugs; strives for abstinence; and adopts the support, values, and methods of a new social group, AA (Wallace, 1996, pp. 15–21). The treatment centers believe that without abstinence the disease is progressive: It gets worse over time. They believe that even though the methods may not work for everyone every time, their methods do provide the best available way to live with the disease of addiction.

Psychologists generally have approached addiction as a behavior that has been learned in the same way other behaviors are learned—through positive and negative rewards (Marlatt, 1985; McCrady, 1994; W. R. Miller & Hester, 1995, p. 5). Because the behavior has been learned, it can also be unlearned, changed, or controlled through these same methods. Controlled trials have not shown to their satisfaction the effectiveness of the methods used by the mainstream treatment community. However, controlled trials have shown to their satisfaction that methods based on learning and behavioral models are effective in treating addiction. In addition, psychologists point out that the 12-step approach does not work for everyone (Sobell & Sobell, 1993). Some patients do not mesh with the 12-step approach, and these people need other treatment methods that are not found in mainstream treatment centers. They believe that individuals should have different treatment goals and that controlled drinking may be a satisfactory goal of treatment for some substance abusers. Finally, they believe in enhancing self-efficacy and self-control rather than admitting powerlessness over the substance use.

The philosophical and practical rift resulted in several unfortunate consequences detrimental to everyone in the field, including the patients (Wallace, 1989, pp. 267–306). First, the mainstream addiction community downplayed the psychosocial factors of addiction and ignored some of the advances that psychologists have made in techniques to help these patients. Major advances such as W. R. Miller and Rollnick's (1991) motivational interviewing, Marlatt's (1985) relapse prevention techniques, or O'Farrell's (1993; O'Farrell & Fals-Stewart, 2006) behavioral marital therapy were underused in the mainstream treatment community.

Another unfortunate consequence has been psychologists' investigation into controlled drinking as a proper goal for alcoholics. If addictive behavior can be changed by conditioning and skills training, then it should be possible to learn controlled drinking through the same methods. For many years prominent learning theorists did research trying to support the notion that alcoholics can learn to drink in a controlled social fashion (Sobell & Sobell, 1978, 1993). However, controlled drinking procedures that use broad definitions such as "problem drinker" may be placing patients at risk.

These procedures rely heavily on self-report data, which are not consistently reliable (NIAAA, 1993, p. 327). They also fail to take into account that for a sizeable subgroup of individuals, this disorder is progressive and that what is defined as problem drinking today could well be alcoholism in a few months. For example, women have a telescoped course and typically incur damage far more quickly and at lower levels of consumption than men (Blume & Zilberman, 2005). Controlled drinking discussions also do not address the data indicating progressive physical and social harms once relatively small amounts of alcohol levels are exceeded (Ashley, 1996).

The mainstream community, after many years of clinical experience, concluded that alcoholics cannot drink or use drugs in any kind of controlled fashion. The mainstream community knew that many substance-dependent individuals try their own efforts at controlled alcohol and drug use for many years before they enter treatment (Schuckit, 1989; Vaillant, 1983). They make their own rules for drinking or using on certain days or certain hours or in certain situations. Typically they find that the rules give way and the drinking or drug use increases until a crisis develops. Even though substance-dependent individuals may have temporary periods of controlled use, the overall trend in their life is typically toward greater loss of control and escalation of use. Research is now supporting the treatment community's position that controlled drinking is an inappropriate goal for substance-dependent alcoholics (Goldsmith, 1997, p. 393; Leshner, 2001; Schuckit, 1994, p. 4; Wallace, 1989, 1996).

It is important to be clear about the precise nature of this controversy. Many therapists, especially in an outpatient setting, may work with an alcoholic who refuses to acknowledge the need for abstinence. They may use motivational strategies to help the client move through the stages of change. This is a perfectly appropriate and effective approach to take. It is a far different issue, however, to have a treatment goal of moderation management strategies for clients who have little or no chance of being successful with these strategies.

Since the publication of the first edition of this book, the situation has improved. Many psychologists who formerly supported controlled drinking have recognized that it does not work for substance-dependent individuals (Hester, 1995; Sobell & Sobell, 1993). A variety of researchers have examined the literature and do not find support for controlled drinking interventions with patients who meet the criteria for dependence (Goldsmith, 1997, p. 393).

Both sides are recognizing that the other side has something of value to offer. Addiction is a complex multivariate disorder. Simple reductionist theories on either side do not work. The addiction treatment community is adopting the psychologists' learning and behavioral techniques for changing behavior. Psychologists are coming to understand the biochemical and genetic bases for the disorder. Treatment centers now facilitate psychologists working as primary and family therapists. Psychologists and the field of psychology played a major role in the design, implementation, and analysis of the largest alcohol treatment outcome study ever undertaken, Project MATCH (Project MATCH Research Group, 1997). Project MATCH demonstrated that of three treatment methods studied—12-step facilitation, cognitive–behavioral intervention, and motivational interviewing—no one approach was markedly superior to the others, and all approaches tested proved to be efficacious.

The American Psychological Association (APA) established a division on addictions (Division 50). There is now an American College of Professional Psychology that offers a certificate of proficiency in alcohol and other drug disorders. In addition, both authors of this volume have observed that some of our colleagues just emerging from graduate school are more knowledgeable about basic addiction theories and concepts than we were at the early stages of our careers. This suggests that graduate programs are including more information about the treatment of addictive disorders in their curricula.

DIFFICULTIES IN WORKING
WITH ADDICTED INDIVIDUALS

Anyone who attends AA meetings is almost sure to hear horror stories in which alcoholic individuals share how they were undiagnosed by a psychologist or other mental health professional and how their addiction was allowed to progress unnoticed and unchecked until it became a crisis. Addicts can be difficult to work with, especially when the therapist does not have the necessary specific education or personal experience. Most psychologists have not personally craved alcohol or other drugs. They do not tell themselves after a night of outrageous drinking that they will never do that again, only to repeat the same behavior the next night. They have not hidden bottles of alcohol or other drugs around the house so their spouse would not find them. They have not lied to their spouse about where they were going as they headed out to a bar. They have not stolen to get money for drugs, or traded sex for drugs, or gone to jail for drugs. Yet these psychologists with little training about addiction or addicts' behavior are attempting to diagnose and treat these individuals in a non-judgmental, compassionate, and effective manner. Zweben and Clark (1991) pointed out that many of the symptoms of borderline personality disorder, such as unstable interpersonal relationships, impulsivity, affective instability, anger control problems, suicidal behavior, identity disturbance, and feelings of emptiness or boredom, are also characteristic of patients with substance abuse problems. These symptoms often disappear or markedly lessen after the cessation of substance abuse, suggesting that they are secondary to the addictive process and not symptomatic of underlying character pathology. "Those who work with patients for long periods during their recovery observe a gradual shift in many behavioral patterns once abstinence is solidly established, an impression which is supported in the empirical literature (Vaillant, 1981, 1983)" (Zweben & Clark, p. 1439).

The importance of this differential diagnosis is twofold. First, to the degree that one views addictive disorders as a reflection of impaired character pathology, the treatment will necessarily focus on those underlying intrapsychic conflicts that produce the character pathology rather than on a cessation of the alcohol and drug use itself. Yet this pathology frequently tends to lessen or disappear as the individual remains abstinent of mood-altering chemicals. Without a focus on abstinence, however, the practitioner is likely to feel frustrated because the same set of maladaptive behavior patterns will continue.

Second, the view that addiction is a reflection of underlying character pathology is significant because such disorders are considered less amenable to psychotherapeutic interventions. Whether it is the antisocial character pathology alluded to by the presenter at the addiction seminar or the borderline/narcissistic features suggested by Imhof, Hirsch, and Terenzi (1983), ingrained character pathology is generally regarded as more difficult to treat and thus more likely to evoke negative or countertransference reactions from the therapist (Imhof et al., 1983).

Imhof et al. (1983) described some of the countertransference reactions that the therapist may have in treating patients who are addicted to drugs. He or she may assume the role of the "good parent rescuing the bad impulsive child" (Imhof et al., 1983, p. 503). The overinvolvement of the therapist initially is an attempt to rescue the addict, but it may lead later to disappointment and resentment when the addict continues to act out despite the therapist's best efforts. "The therapist often then becomes both furious and hurt at this betrayal, labels the drug addict as 'resistant and acting out' and may proceed with plans to discharge the patient as untreatable in an outpatient basis" (Imhof et al., 1983, p. 503).

Amodeo (1995) summarized some of the frustrations that all therapists feel in treating this most difficult population as she wrote about power struggles between addicted individuals and their therapists:

> Because alcoholism and drug dependence are conditions character-ized by impulsive and compulsive behavior, therapists are repeatedly confronted with control related issues. Clients may come to sessions high or intoxicated and fail to respond to the therapist's limit setting. They may report drinking and drug use between sessions or describe behavior such as violence against family members, unprotected sex with strangers, taking tranquilizers and alcohol together or using dirty needles. These experiences are likely to stimulate the therapist's anxiety and feelings of being out of control, especially for those therapists for whom control was a difficult early life issue. Common therapist responses to this behavior, which can undermine the relationship and potential success, are rigid limits, emotional distancing, feelings of betrayal and adopting a moralistic attitude. (p. 110)

A familiar scenario is a young and idealistic therapist who secures a position at an addiction treatment center with dreams of helping those who are truly in need. Over time the therapist becomes frustrated when patients who are addicted tell lies, relapse on a regular basis, and manipulate therapy sessions. The therapist may feel like a failure and a bad therapist. These feelings are expressed as frustration, anger, and eventually burnout. The once eager psychotherapist develops

> a self-protecting, narcissistic distancing which manifests itself as indifference, tiredness, boredom and in general, separation from the therapeutic interaction. Such burnout features are not uncommon when considering the consistent and intense demands that the patient makes and the recidivistic and chronically relapsing manifestations of the addictive disorders. (Imhof et al., 1983, p. 504)

These burnout reactions closely parallel society's moralistic and pejorative view of alcohol and drug abuse. Often addicts are viewed as weak-willed or even as sinners. Although this moralistic stance is not often overtly found among psychologists, it is common in the larger society. To the extent that the psychologist moves from idealism to boredom and burnout, the attitude is perceived by the addicted patient as judgmental and rejecting. As the psychologist moves from a posture of rescue into a posture of anger, resentment, and burnout, he or she may begin to chastise the patients for not being able to achieve sobriety or, even worse, for not being able to control their drinking. This behavior only reinforces the addict's sense of shame and self-loathing, further increasing the chances that he or she will continue to drink and use drugs to medicate these feelings. Addicts and alcoholics are intensely sensitive to shaming messages of condemnation because they have received these types of messages for many years.

In contrast, the more experienced therapist will view this same behavior in a different light. For some patients, the desire to use has become so compelling from both the physiological and psychological standpoints that not using, in the early days of abstinence, appears to be overwhelming. Abstinence is the major goal of early stage recovery–oriented psychotherapy. Experienced therapists will acknowledge that relapses are a frequent, if not inevitable, component of this disorder. They will be less likely to view these frequent relapses as an expression of acting out than as a reflection of the loss of control that the addict experiences, which is driven by the overwhelming physiological and psychological demands of the drug dependency itself.

In this way, more experienced therapists can join with patients in acknowledging their sincere, if not always successful, attempts to achieve sobriety. They can offer specific motivational and behavioral techniques to help patients achieve and maintain sobriety and abstinence. They will make this struggle the major focus of early stage recovery. In so doing, they can achieve an alliance with the patient that is more compassionate and more effective in helping the patient to achieve their desired goals.

REWARDS OF WORKING WITH ADDICTED INDIVIDUALS

Even those psychologists who do not specialize in addiction need a thorough knowledge of its signs and symptoms. Any psychologist with direct patient contact will be confronted with alcohol and drug disorders. Substance abuse disorders can and do mimic virtually every other psychiatric diagnosis. Not knowing the signs and symptoms of the substance abuse disorder can lead to misdiagnosis and poor outcomes, as well as legal vulnerabilities for therapists who incorrectly diagnose the problem.

In outpatient therapy settings, therapists should be capable of addressing mild to moderate cases of alcohol and drug abuse in the context of ongoing work. Therapists can facilitate recognition of the problem, enhance motivation to address it, and cultivate patients' readiness to engage in specialized addiction treatment when needed. In many cases, a clinician with some specialized training such as that defined by the APA College of Professional Psychology in its certificate of proficiency in substance abuse can manage AOD abuse in an outpatient setting. Managed care organizations are increasingly aware that untreated substance abuse is costly in health terms alone and are requiring documentation of proficiency by licensed professionals.

Given the difficulties in working with this population, one might legitimately ask why any professional would specialize in the treatment of addictive disorders. As people recover to an abstinent lifestyle, they experience enormous life-giving changes. It is an exhilarating experience to participate in their rebirth as they emerge from their drug- and alcohol-addicted lifestyle into the clean air of sobriety. Patients report that these changes touch not only behavior and attitude but also every aspect of their life. Physical health, family relations, vocational matters, social relations, and spiritual life can be dramatically improved with recovery. Many go on to make outstanding contributions once they regain command of their positive resources. The therapist who invests the effort, patience, and time to learn about the experience of addiction from the inside finds that empathy and a positive therapeutic alliance with these patients become much easier to attain. These are the rewards that make it all worthwhile.

The heartening news is that many problems are not intractable and some yield to relatively modest intervention. The literature has documented that giving advice is effective for some patients. Clinicians are often pleasantly surprised by how therapeutic strategies such as motivational interviewing yield rapid results in some patients. Successfully addressing AOD use enhances the effectiveness of all other clinical interventions, such as in the following case:

> Sam came to treatment with general malaise and dissatisfaction with his marriage. His wife, Nancy, was frustrated by his emotional inaccessibility and avoidance of conflict and felt she was beginning to outgrow him. Feeling disadvantaged by her greater articulateness in couples therapy, he refused to participate further but was willing to try individual work with his own therapist.
>
> During the initial meetings, the therapist elicited the fact that Sam had been smoking marijuana since he was 15, like others in his middle class suburban community. He did not view it as a problem. He reported being bored at work, and it emerged he was vaguely dysphoric most of the time. He felt discouraged in his efforts to stand up to his wife and was frustrated by the important dead ends in his life.

Without asking him to alter his behavior, the therapist raised questions about his marijuana use. During the first 3 months of the treatment, she commented on how his marijuana use may have been affecting his symptoms. The dysphoria and malaise he described are accompaniments of marijuana use for many, but not all, people. Its deadening effects lead to both loss of vitality and conflict avoidance in relationships. The amotivational syndrome often produces a sense of boredom at work, and a lack of capacity for initiative exacerbates the boredom. Because the effects of this drug are subtle, most people underestimate its negative potential, but abstinence reveals negative consequences more clearly.

To the therapist's surprise, Sam agreed rather readily to her suggestion of an "experiment with abstinence," and over the next 6 months changes began to unfold. His apathy dissipated, bringing irritability and insomnia initially, then renewed interest in work. His comfort level decreased as he became more in touch with his feelings. These changes rendered his therapy much more productive. His dissatisfaction with his marriage came more into the foreground, and he began to respond more assertively to his wife's criticisms. After several months of work with his individual therapist, he expressed willingness to tackle couples therapy again.

There is often no way to precisely determine the effect of alcohol and drug use until it is eliminated. Individuals vary a great deal in their response to the drugs, so relatively small amounts can have large effects. Alcohol and drug use imitates every other entity found in clinical practice. Anxiety and depression are often exacerbated. The disinhibiting effects of even small amounts of alcohol can escalate marital bickering. Thus the clinician who is comfortable raising and addressing alcohol and drug use is in a much better position to ultimately assist the patient in making meaningful changes.

CONCLUSION

Addictive disorders are complex, and we believe that they cannot be reduced to simplistic theories based on biological or psychosocial imperatives alone. We believe that only through an integration of these factors can one truly understand the totality of this disorder. Therapists who can remain flexible and open to new ideas are likely to be the most effective in helping addicts move from abusive drinking and drug use into sober lifestyles.

To the extent that our patients will allow us, we can participate in the liberating struggle of their recovery. At times the role closely resembles that of a parent who is willing to both nurture and to set limits. At other times we are more like a coach offering advice and support, encouraging the patient to try new cognitive and behavioral strategies. At still other times we are more like guides, helping patients explore the inner world of their thoughts and emotions as they struggle with the answer to deeper questions such as, "How could my behavior have gotten so out of control?" Like other mental health professionals, this process of behavior change and self-exploration is one that we are privileged to observe. A significant differentiating factor is that with addicted populations the rate of change is so rapid and the nature of the change so profound. Watching this transformation motivates and sustains us to keep working with addicted individuals.

2

Models and Theories of Addiction

Understanding alcohol and other drug (AOD) abuse disorders can be complex and confusing. Addicted individuals compulsively consume alcohol and drugs despite increasingly negative consequences. The majority of drinkers are able to regulate their intake of alcohol without loss of control. However, alcoholics and addicted individuals, like passive spectators watching their lives career out of control, seem helpless to alter the course of this downward spiral.

Through the years, psychologists and psychiatrists have developed a variety of theoretical models that try to explain the complexity and paradoxical nature of addictive behavior. What would motivate individuals to act in such a seemingly self-destructive manner? Is it a genetic susceptibility? Is it a learned behavior caused by dysfunctional thoughts and behaviors? Is it a disorder of self caused by early childhood trauma? Is it an attempt to restore homeostasis to a dysfunctional family system? Recent research has brought new knowledge that is leading to the coalescing of the models. The research now shows that addiction is a "biobehavioral disorder" (Leshner, 2001, p. 2) for which some individuals have a genetic susceptibility and that alcohol or drug abuse can cause physical changes to the brain structure. These physical changes lead to compulsive use. In addition, the disease is complicated by learning or conditioning factors, social factors, family dynamics, and developmental factors as well as the presence of comorbid disorders such as anxiety and depression (Volkow & Li, 2005). Accordingly, in this chapter we talk about the various elements of and contributing factors to the disease of addiction.

THE DISEASE MODEL

The idea that alcoholism or addiction is a disease dates from the 1800s but became popularized through the development of Alcoholics Anonymous (AA) through the efforts of Bill Wilson in the late 1930s. In the 1970s, the medical community and treatment professionals incorporated the disease concept into treatment programs. The disease model became known as the *Minnesota model* (White, 1998, pp. 207–212).

The disease model states that addiction is a primary disorder, independent of other conditions, with a biologically inherited susceptibility to the effects of alcohol and drugs. Addiction is not a result of psychological or emotional problems; psychological impairments are often consequences rather than causes of addiction. The disease model views addiction as similar to other diseases such as essential hypertension, which have an inherited biochemical component combined with environmental exposure factors.

The key characteristics of addiction are loss of control over alcohol or drugs, denial, continued use despite negative consequences, and a pattern of relapsing (N. S. Miller, 1995, pp. 84–85). The first goal of treatment is abstinence from alcohol and drugs.

Research Evidence

There is now a large body of research supporting the view that vulnerability to addiction can have strong genetic influences, depending in part on the drug of choice. In the 1960s, researchers began studies into the genetics of alcoholism.

> The genetics evidence has been developed in much more detail
> for alcohol dependence than for other chemical dependencies. . . .
> This is because the research on drug dependence evolved rather late
> compared to that of alcohol dependence. . . . It is estimated that 60%
> of the variability in explaining the causes of alcohol dependence is
> due to a genetic vulnerability or susceptibility to the effects of alcohol.
> As is typical of many medical and psychiatric disorders, "alcoholism"
> is genetically heterogeneous (multiple genes and alleles are involved).
> (Erickson, 2007, pp. 75, 83)

Studies of twins, adopted children, sons of alcoholic fathers, and animals all supported the idea that addiction is a genetically based disorder leading to a vulnerability to developing the disease of addiction. The reader is referred to the *Tenth Special Report to the U.S. Congress on Alcohol and Health* by the National Institute on Alcohol Abuse and Alcoholism (2000) as well as the first edition of this book for further investigation.

In 1989, the National Institute on Alcohol Abuse and Alcoholism started the Collaborative Study on the Genetics of Alcoholism (COGA; Bierut et al., 2002). This study involves 3,000 individuals in 300 families with voluminous data. The COGA has moved from trying to determine whether genetics plays a role to trying to determine which specific genes are responsible. As a result of in-depth analyses of psychological, physiological, electrophysical, and genetic characteristics of subjects, researchers have identified several traits or phenotypes that seem to be associated with alcoholism. "These phenotypes include the presence of alcohol dependence, the level of response to alcohol, the presence of coexisting depression, and the maximum number of drinks a person consumes per occasion" (Erickson, 2007, p. 84). Scientists are in the process of linking these phenotypes to specific chromosomes.

Neuroimaging Studies

As a result of neuroimaging studies, we now know that all drugs of abuse activate the brain's natural reward pathway, which is the same pathway that is activated by food and sex; however, the drugs of abuse act in a much more powerful way than natural reinforcers (Childress, 2006). Over time, compulsive drug use changes the structure of the brain, resulting in a compulsive desire for, and out-of-control use of, drugs. This process is referred to as *neuroadaptation*. "Drugs of abuse are known to act through the brain's circuitry for natural rewards, but they activate the system in a much stronger, supranormal way" (Childress, 2006, p. 50). Erickson (2007) pointed out that drugs of abuse offer "special 'advantages' over other forms of stimuli such as the release of dopamine, serotonin, and endorphin after intense exercise because of the amount of neurotransmitter chemicals released" (p. 57). Although an increase in brain endorphins can be substantial following exercise (e.g., "runner's high"), this increase is still much smaller than the changes in brain morphine levels produced by a dose of heroin. Such dramatic differences in the magnitude of effect can lead to qualitative differences in the types of adaptation that occur (Erickson, 2007).

Alan Leshner (2001), former head of the National Institute on Drug Abuse (NIDA), stated that just as we now know that depression is more than a lot of sadness, addiction is more than a lot of drug use. Prolonged drug use causes brain changes that affect functions such as brain metabolic activity, receptor availability, and responsiveness to environmental cues. The brain changes persist long after the cessation of drug use. These changes, along with new memory associations, are responsible for the cognitive and emotional characteristics of addictive behavior, especially the compulsion to seek and use drugs:

> It is as if drugs have hijacked the brain's natural motivational control circuits, resulting in drug use becoming the sole, or at least the top, motivational priority for the individual. Thus the majority of the biomedical community now considers addiction, in its essence, to be a brain disease: A disease caused by persistent changes in brain function. (Leshner, 2001, p. 75)

The brain changes occur mostly within the brain's natural reward pathway, the mesolimbic dopamine system (MDS). All drugs of abuse activate the MDS. The dysregulation of neuronal activity over time is the defining characteristic of chemical dependence disease (Erickson, 2007, p. 56).

Physical Versus Psychological Addiction Misconception

Research also supports the disease model in proving false other common misconceptions about addiction. The distinction between physical and psychological addiction is no longer considered useful. Physical withdrawal can be medically treated, and many addicting drugs do not produce severe physical dependence symptoms.

> What really matters is whether or not a drug causes what we now know to be the essence of addiction: uncontrollable, compulsive drug craving, seeking, and use, even in the face of negative consequences. . . . Compulsive craving that overwhelms all other motivations is the root cause of the massive health and social problems associated with drug addiction. (Leshner, 2001, p. 76)

The Use-to-Addiction Continuum Misconception

Another misconception is that "use, abuse, and addiction are points along a continuum" (Leshner, 2001, p. 76) on which an individual can move back and forth. Instead, addiction is a very different state from use and abuse. "It is as if a threshold has been crossed. Very few people appear able to successfully return to occasional use after having been truly addicted" (Leshner, 2001, p. 76). About 50% to 70% of the variability in one's vulnerability to becoming addicted can be accounted for by genetic factors. Environmental and contextual cues are frequent causes of relapse and explain why it is so hard for individuals to leave the controlled environment of the treatment center and return home.

Research on Relapse

Other researchers have highlighted the addicted individual's propensity to relapse, even after years of abstinence and effective treatment, as evidence of pervasive and long-lasting changes in brain function (Kalivas & Volkow, 2005). Research on the neural basis of motivation, conditioned learning, and behavior activation has provided a new understanding of relapse.

Kalivas and Volkow (2005) accordingly identified relapse prevention as an area in which pharmacological advances may prove effective.

Childress et al. (1999) used brain-imaging studies to demonstrate that exposure to cue-induced cocaine craving can trigger activation of brain structures within the limbic region that are associated with motivation and affect, offering an explanation for the relationship between environmental cues and craving, potentially resulting in relapse. Essentially, although an addicted individual is actively seeking and achieving his or her primary motivation (i.e., obtaining the high), the stimuli in the surrounding environment are conditioned to the reinforcing effects of the drug. Even long after cessation of drug use, encountering such stimuli, which had previously preceded and predicted the behavior of drug use, continues to trigger dopamine release (Kalivas & Volkow, 2005). This dopamine activation, given its involvement in drug reward, affects the brain similarly to a small drug dose and can easily activate the old pattern of behavior of compulsive drug seeking and use.

> Drugs . . . act as "instrumental reinforcers" . . . That is, they increase the likelihood of responses that produce them, which results in drug self-administration or "drug-taking." Stimuli in the environment that are closely associated in time and space with the effects of self-administered drugs gain "incentive salience" (meaning "connected to the incentive to take the drug") through Pavlovian conditioning and later become cues for relapse. (Erickson, 2007, p. 64)

Another researcher who has relied heavily on brain imaging studies is Nora Volkow, current director of NIDA. In results from neuroimaging studies, Volkow and her colleagues (Volkow, Fowler, & Wang, 2003; Volkow et al., 2002) have proposed a model of drug addiction that implicates areas of the limbic system, the prefrontal cortex, and the orbitofrontal cortex. Kalivas and Volkow (2005) determined that the prefrontal cortex is involved in the regulation of motivational importance ascribed to the drug and in the intensity of the behavioral response, which both affect the activation of behavior. Certain areas of the limbic system have been associated with drug reward (i.e., nucleus accumbens), and others with memory and conditioned responses linked to craving (i.e., amygdala, hippocampus; Goldstein & Volkow, 2002). The research disclosed significant increases in dopamine levels during intoxication, which coincide with activation of the prefrontal cortex and anterior cingulate gyrus (Goldstein & Volkow, 2002). Research findings indicate that the orbitofrontal cortex is mainly involved in motivation; the cyngulate gyrus is associated with cognitive control; and the prefrontal cortex is linked to one's perception of intoxication, enhanced mood, and a drug's reinforcing properties. During withdrawal and after chronic abuse, however, dopamine function decreases, and these decreases are associated with dysfunction in the prefrontal region. For individuals with previous drug exposure, craving, without drug administration, can be sufficient to increase activation in the prefrontal cortex and anterior cingulate (Goldstein & Volkow, 2002). Because dopamine also regulates sensitivity to natural reinforcers (e.g., food, sex) and affects other frontal cortical functions such as inhibitory control and salience attribution, these are likely to be disrupted as well. Volkow et al. (2003) proposed the following:

> In drug addiction the value of the drug and drug-related stimuli is enhanced at the expense of other reinforcers. This is a consequence of conditioned learning and of the resetting of reward thresholds as an adaptation to the high levels of stimulation induced by drugs of abuse. In this model, during exposure to the drug and drug-related cues, the memory of the expected reward results in over-activation of the reward and motivation circuits while decreasing the activity in the cognitive control circuit. This contributes to an inability to inhibit the drive to seek and consume the drug and results in compulsive drug intake. (p. 1444)

In accordance with the findings that heredity and environment, along with repeated drug exposure, play a role in drug addiction, imaging studies have revealed that having fewer dopamine receptors may influence susceptibility to drug responsiveness (Goldstein & Volkow, 2002; Volkow et al., 2003). Individuals with low quantities of dopamine receptors appeared to be more responsive to the effects of certain drugs. "Subjects with low numbers of DA D2 (dopamine) receptors tended to describe the effects of the stimulant drug methylphenidate as pleasant, whereas subjects with high numbers of DA D2 receptors tended to describe it as unpleasant" (Volkow et al., 2003, p. 1449). This study is significant because it sheds light on both genetic and psychological aspects of addiction. From a genetic perspective the findings suggest that individuals with a genetically determined lower level of dopamine receptors may in fact be more susceptible to drug liking, drug taking, and, ultimately, addiction (Childress, 2006).

Finally, a number of studies indicate that dopamine levels and/or receptors vary across individuals and are affected by factors such as genetic vulnerability (Thanos et al., 2001), social dominance (Morgan et al., 2002), and stress (Papp, Klimek, & Willner, 1994). These findings are important because they suggest that dopamine levels and/or receptors and consequently vulnerability to chemical dependence are influenced by more than just genetics; they are also influenced by psychosocial factors. Hence brain research supports the findings of psychological research that interventions designed to address social skill deficits and stress reduction are productive ways not only to alter brain chemistry but also to treat this disease.

Conclusion on the Disease Model

Current thinking regarding the disease model of addiction postulates that there is a subgroup of the population that is genetically more vulnerable to developing addictive diseases. In addition, psychosocial factors can affect brain function and, in turn, one's propensity to abuse drugs. However, addiction itself is a result of an altered brain state secondary to a chemical assault on the brain by extensive drug use. Often, but not always, this chemical assault is potentiated by a genetic vulnerability. Leshner (2001) compared this altered brain state to a biochemical switch that gets turned on in the brain. Once the switch is thrown, it cannot be undone. Once individuals become addicted, it is neither advisable nor realistic to suggest that they can return to moderate or controlled use.

Prolonged alcohol and drug use can alter areas of the brain that control memory, cognitive control, and primary drive states. These areas change in such a way that impairs the individual's ability to exercise cognitive control over those primary drive states. As a result, the individual's clinical characterization corresponds to what brain imaging studies reveal (Childress, 2006; Volkow et al., 2003). Individuals begin to use and to experience the reinforcing properties of drugs. Some individuals report increasing difficulty controlling their use. Some people report intense craving, whereas some simply report that they began to lose all volitional control.

The term *craving* has been controversial in the literature (Kozlowski & Wilkinson, 1987; Tiffany, Carter, & Singleton, 2002; Tiffany & Conklin, 2000) because the concept is hard to define and hard to measure. Also, some studies have shown a less than robust association between drug craving and drug taking or relapse in addicted individuals (Sayette et al., 2000). To some degree these criticisms miss the larger question of why addicted individuals compulsively use drugs in the face of negative consequences. The answer can be found in the neurochemistry of addictive drugs and how this neural activity interacts with psychosocial factors to impact human behavior, specifically drug seeking and drug taking.

We now know that all drugs of abuse activate the MDS. Dopamine is a neurotransmitter that is associated with both a sense of euphoria and well-being as well as with motivation. In other words, one function of the MDS is to attribute "incentive salience" (Robinson & Berridge, 1993) to any behavior (i.e., drug taking) or ancillary, related behavior (i.e., drug cues) that activates this system. Eventually, in some individuals, drug taking leads to "incremental neuroadaptation" (Robinson & Berridge, 1993), or brain changes. These brain changes persist for a long time and may even be permanent.

The effect of these brain changes is to sensitize the brain to drugs and drug cues, to imbue these things with a sense of meaning or salience, and ultimately to dramatically increase the probability that the addicted individual will use drugs, especially when under psychological duress and/or in the absence of appropriate coping skills. Sometimes this phenomenon is consciously experienced, and this is what is meant by craving. At other times the individual may not be aware of these neurological imperatives that are shaping behavior. Reasons for this lack of awareness may be memory biases, misattributions, or self-consciousness (Sayette et al., 2000, p. 192). Differences in awareness of neural processes may account for the lack of robust association between self-reports of craving and actual drug taking or relapse in addicted individuals. Ultimately, however, these neuroadaptive changes lead to enhanced salience of drugs and drug-related cues, which increases the probability that the individual will take drugs whether or not the underlying processes are conscious (in which case we call it craving) or occur on an unconscious level.

It is important to emphasize that the neuroadaptive changes leading to loss of control do not absolve the addicted individual of responsibly for managing the disease. Just as the person with diabetes must manage that disease with diet, exercise, and medication, people who face addiction must manage their disease with an abstinence-based program of recovery.

LEARNING THEORY MODELS

Learning theory provides deep insights into the nature and treatment of addictive behaviors. Social learning theory (SLT) postulates that people's life experiences and conditioning not only affect behaviors but also lead to the development of thoughts and emotions that drive future behavior. "A central concept in SLT is reciprocal determinism, which states that people both influence and are influenced by their environments" (Rotgers, 1996, p. 184). Thus, changes can be initiated both by changing the environment and by changing the self-control processes that shape the individual's response to the environment. SLT suggests that an individual's alcohol or drug use begins and continues through modeling, positive and negative reinforcement, expectancies, conditioned responses (cue reactivity), and his or her own sense of self-efficacy (Monti, Kadden, Rohsenow, Cooney, & Abrams, 2002, p. 3).

Modeling Behavior

Modeling behavior involves observing other people's behavior to develop concepts of appropriate behavior and to learn how to successfully perform such behaviors. Bandura (1977) believed that the individual develops a process of cognitive mapping, in which aspects of behavior are stored and can be reproduced at a later time. Modeling behavior has been used to explain the initiation of AOD abuse, especially in adolescents (Rotgers, 1996). Parent and peer models influence all individuals, especially young people, by promoting appropriate standards of behavior and modeling the behaviors themselves. The media also influences attitudes toward alcohol and other drugs.

Positive and Negative Reinforcement

Psychologists have shown that people choose their behaviors based on the positive or negative reinforcements they have experienced in the past. AOD-use behaviors are influenced by the positive reinforcement of euphoria and the negative reinforcement of relief from anxiety and tension. Negative reinforcement occurs when unpleasant physical or psychological states are removed.

Reinforcing properties that are closer in time to the actual behavior exert greater influence on future behavior than reinforcing factors that occur later. Thus, an alcoholic person who drinks in the morning to avoid withdrawal symptoms achieves an immediate reinforcing effect. This effect is greater than the negative consequences that may occur later, such as getting in trouble at work for smelling strongly of alcohol. In addition, even though people know that alcohol is a central nervous system depressant, they associate it with euphoria and may not be aware of its connection to their depression.

Negative reinforcement may explain why AOD abusers continue to use: They are trying to relieve negative affective conditions. Although these conditions may be due to withdrawal symptoms, they may also be caused by internal or external stressors, such as pressure at work, marital discord, or arguments. Individuals learn early in their drug use to detect internal cues and act preconsciously to prevent the onset of aversive symptoms. Individuals may be aware of wanting to take drugs, but they may be unaware of the "motivational impetus" (Baker, Piper, McCarthy, Majeskie, & Fiore, 2004, p. 35).

Expectancies

Most people expect that they will have positive reactions to using alcohol. Examples of such expectancies include increases in social assertiveness and pleasure, relaxation and tension reduction, enhanced sexual experience and performance, and feelings of physical pleasure (S. A. Brown, Goldman, Inn, & Anderson, 1980). These expectancies frequently develop at a young age and strongly influence how one reacts to using alcohol and beliefs about what alcohol is meant to do for the drinker.

Results of a series of studies suggest that expectancies can be a more powerful determinant of drug effects than the actual physiological properties of the drug itself (Marlatt & Gordon, 1985; Marlatt & Rohsenow, 1980). This research used a balanced placebo design in which the expectancy of the amount of alcohol being administered was viewed independently of the actual amount of alcohol being administered. Participants' expectation of the potency of the drink and likely effect of the alcohol (e.g., tension reduction, euphoria) was a greater factor in patient ratings regarding the potency of the drink than was the actual alcohol content. Those participants who were erroneously told that they were receiving a high potency drink tended to expect a significant alcohol effect and said that they had received a large alcohol effect regardless of the potency of the drink (Monti, Rohsenow, Abrams, & Binkoff, 1988). This type of research shows that these ideas and behaviors are learned and therefore are subject to change through learning theory. Treatment should focus on making these behavior changes rather than on physiological causes.

Self-Efficacy

A key part of the cognitive mapping mentioned previously is the concept of self-efficacy (Bandura, 1999). *Self-efficacy* refers to a person's confidence and self-assurance that he or she will be able to deal effectively with a difficult situation. The greater his or her self-efficacy, the less likely a person will respond inappropriately in a given situation. Substance use may serve a compensatory function, alleviating stress experienced in situations in which individuals lack, or believe that they lack, the coping skills necessary to diffuse their feelings of stress. As a result, individuals in treatment learn how to effectively deal with the stresses created by their problems. They also learn to anticipate future stresses to avoid situations that may trigger negative affective states because these situations can increase the desire to use AOD. Increasing self-efficacy is essential for maintaining long-term abstinence.

Conditioned Responses and Cue Reactivity

The progression and maintenance of AOD behaviors can also be explained with classical conditioned responses. Cue reactivity studies have shown that exposure to external stimuli previously conditioned with drug use (e.g., drug use paraphernalia) can trigger the release of dopamine through the same neural pathways as the drug itself effects (Phillips, Stuber, Heien, Wightman, & Carelli, 2003; Schultz, 1998; Sutton & Beninger, 1999, cited in Kalivas & Volkow, 2005). This dopamine release can begin an uncontrollable cycle of drug craving and drug seeking. For this reason, exposure to environmental cues that were previously paired with drug use can seriously endanger an addicted individual's attempts at achieving sobriety.

Cue reactivity studies focus on the responses of AOD-dependent individuals to internal cues, such as negative mood states, in addition to external cues. Childress and her colleagues (Childress, Ehrman, Rohsenow, Robbins, & O'Brien, 1992; Childress, Hole, Ehrman, & Robbins, 1993; Childress et al., 1999) have extensively studied the significance of one's reactivity to conditioned drug cues in cocaine- and opiate-dependent persons. The experiments focused on differential physiological and subjective responses of these individuals to neutral versus opiate- or cocaine-related cues (S. J. Robbins, Ehrman, Childress, Cornish, & O'Brien, 2000; S. J. Robbins, Ehrman, Childress, & O'Brien, 1999; Volkow et al., 2008).

Childress and others (Childress, 2006; Childress et al., 1999) have also focused on internal cues such as mood states and the way that they interact with external cues to become powerful drug signals themselves. Although no mood state was found to solely increase one's susceptibility to cue reactivity, a more general correlation was found between having more negative mood states prior to the session and reporting greater levels of high, craving, and withdrawal symptoms both before and after exposure. Thus, negative mood states contribute greatly to the pattern of substance abuse by increasing craving and withdrawal symptoms (S. J. Robbins et al., 2000).

Cognitive–Behavioral Therapy

Two models for AOD abuse treatment, rational emotive therapy developed by Albert Ellis (Ellis, McInerney, Di Giuseppe, & Yeager, 1988) and cognitive therapy developed by Aaron Beck (Beck, Wright, Newman, & Liese, 1993), are derived from a cognitive–behavioral framework. In both of these theories it is postulated that irrational thoughts and feelings contribute to the development of AOD abuse. They are used in the attempt to reprogram or change these thoughts and feelings in a more functional direction, so the individual does not buy into the belief that using alcohol or drugs is a reasonable option (Rotgers, 1996, p. 185). Cognitive–behavioral treatments are concerned with teaching techniques that aid in the development of one's self-efficacy (e.g., assertiveness training, anger management, relaxation techniques).

Conclusion on Learning Theory Models

Learning theory models have contributed an extensive body of data and theory to our understanding of the initiation and development of addictive disorders, highlighting the role of neural adaptations, environmental factors, contextual variables, and social interactions in this process. When used in conjunction with one another, learning model theories can explain much of the developmental process leading to the destructive cycle of drug seeking and use that characterizes addiction. A person's decision to start using drugs or alcohol is determined by both past modeling of behavior and expectations of drug or alcohol use. Following the initiation of AOD use, neural adaptations combined with the behavioral principles of conditioning and other cognitive influences take precedence and determine a great portion of the variance in how individuals will use drugs differently in the future.

Psychological research has led to treatment interventions designed to assist the individual in developing a sense of self-efficacy, as well as to specific techniques to avoid situations for which coping skills are lacking. Relapse prevention work has assumed an ever increasing and important role in all treatment environments, including traditional 12-step programs. Marlatt's (1985) work on relapse prevention is used in these programs through the work of others, such as Gorski (1989), who have adapted Marlatt's concepts to be compatible with a 12-step model.

In the past, learning theorists have held that AOD dependence is a purely behavioral disorder and can be entirely reversed. Some have unwisely asserted that those who meet criteria for substance dependence can return to controlled use of substances. This criticism is not meant to undermine the major contributions of learning theorists but simply to point out that reductionist thinking can lead to serious problems in the field of addiction theory and treatment and ultimately complicate recovery efforts. Although there is a place for controlled drinking for those clients who meet the criteria for abuse, in our view such approaches are not appropriate for clients who have crossed the line into addiction. An integration of the contributions from the various learning theories with the disease model would help practitioners move toward a more effective model of how to provide addicted individuals with comprehensive treatment that can teach them coping skills to help them function successfully in their newfound abstinent lifestyle.

PSYCHOANALYTIC THEORY

Early psychoanalytic theories focused on addiction as a regressive attempt to return to an infantile, pleasurable state. In contrast, contemporary psychoanalytic theories, based on ego and object relations theory, view addiction as a progressive response to deficits of self-regulation. Contemporary theorists view the addictive use of alcohol and drugs as an adaptive mechanism by which the individual attempts to cope with self-regulatory deficits arising from early infantile deprivation and maladaptive parent and child interactions. This theory has been labeled the *self-medication hypothesis* and has primarily been associated with Edward J. Khantzian (1981, 1982, 1985, 1997).

The self-medication hypothesis states the following:

> Rather than simply seeking escape, euphoria, or self-destruction, addicts are attempting to medicate themselves for a range of psychiatric problems and painful emotional states. Although most such efforts at self-treatment are eventually doomed, given the hazards and complications of long-term, unstable drug use patterns, addicts discover that the short-term effects of their drugs of choice help them to cope with distressful subjective states and an external reality otherwise experienced as unmanageable or overwhelming. (Khantzian, 1985, p. 1263)

The theory evolved in the course of Khantzian's extensive clinical experience working in public-sector outpatient substance abuse programs, a Massachusetts inpatient facility for patients who were severely mentally ill, and private practice (Khantzian, 1997). After creating an empathic bond with the patient in recovery and helping the patient establish abstinence, Khantzian explores the issue of how the patient experienced the drug in the initial period of use, before tolerance developed (Khantzian, 1997).

Khantzian's (1997) theory is supported by the clinical opinion of other writers. Gerard and Kornetsky (1954) viewed adolescent addiction as an attempt to escape the overwhelming anxiety of preparation for the adult role. Weider and Kaplan (1969) viewed addiction as a pharmacological attempt to reduce stress by the addicted individual. They emphasized that "individuals self-select different drugs on the basis of personality organization and ego impairments" (Khantzian, 1985, p. 1260). Thus, drugs are not selected indiscriminately; they are chosen to act as "prostheses" (Khantzian, 1985, p. 1260). The work of Milkman and Frosch (1973) suggested that heroin users prefer the calming effects of opiates whereas amphetamine addicts use the stimulating action to enhance their sense of self-worth and grandiosity (Khantzian, 1985, p. 1260). Alcohol and other central nervous system depressants minimize feelings of isolation, emptiness, and related anxiety and tension. "Patients experiment with various classes of drugs and discover that a specific one is compelling because it ameliorates, heightens, or relieves affect states that they find particularly problematic or painful" (Khantzian, 1997, p. 232).

The idea that addicted individuals select specific drugs of choice on the basis of unmet intrapsychic needs has not been validated through research. It should perhaps be viewed as a clinically useful topic of discussion to draw clients out about what they are seeking when they use drugs but not to make assumptions or connections between drugs of choice and unmet needs.

Addiction as an Attachment Disorder

Flores (2004) recently presented a more integrative psychoanalytic theory of addiction. Potentially indicating the current and future trends of prominent psychoanalytic theory, Flores posited that addictive behaviors are driven by an underlying disorder in attachment patterns and that this attachment disorder results from unmet developmental needs. With a foundation in unfulfilling relationships and undeveloped interpersonal skills, the individual is left with an impaired or fragmented sense of self. Vulnerable individuals are unable to regulate their emotions or even to be aware of what they are feeling. Unable to draw on their own internal resources, individuals with this disorder turn to external objects for sources of support. Because they do not have the ability to form healthy attachments with others, fewer options are available to them that sufficiently meet their needs. Having been deprived of their needs for nurturance and support, which causes them to feel "object hunger and . . . intolerable affects" (Flores, p. 83), they turn to alcohol and drugs as a means of dealing with these painful experiences.

According to Flores, psychoanalytic theory lays the basis for attachment theory. Kohut (1977) stated that addictions are "misguided attempts at affect regulation and self-repair generated by inadequate psychic structure" (cited in Flores, 2004, p. 84). This is a common thread throughout all psychoanalytic theory as it relates to addictive disorders. Kohut went on to state that "in all of these disorders, the afflicted individual suffers from a central weakness; a weakness in the core of his personality. He suffers from the consequences of a defect in the self" (cited in Flores, 2004, p. 85).

Thus, substance abuse is perceived as one's way of trying to repair this disorder of self. However, in so doing, the substance abuser only increases stress on his or her already frail psychic structures. "Substance use, which originally started as a way to help the individual manage the difficulties generated by interpersonal relationships, gradually impairs an already fragile capacity for attachment" (Flores, 2004, p. 2). The chronic use of mind-altering substances ultimately causes the abuser's interpersonal skills to diminish even further, gradually increasing reliance on the substances as use continues.

Attachment theory is consistent with the disease model of addiction in that they both maintain that certain individuals cross over into the state of addiction at some point in time and can never safely use mind-altering chemicals in any form without setting in motion again the terrible cycle of chronic alcohol and drug use. Flores (2004) also acknowledged that addicted individuals will be completely incapable of addressing the issues driving their addictive behavior while they continue to use AOD. Intrapsychic conflicts are no longer seen as the cause of addiction but more likely as the result of addiction. Therefore, the conflicts should be addressed after abstinence has been achieved.

Treatment Implications

Attachment theory holds many implications for successful treatment of AOD disorders. Because addictive behavior is driven by a social and interpersonal deficiency in the core of the addicted individual's being, treatment emphasis is on the social aspect of recovery. Therefore, Flores (2004) endorsed the support an individual finds in 12-step groups such as AA, Narcotics Anonymous (NA), Cocaine Anonymous, Crystal Meth Anonymous, and so forth.

Parallel to attachment theory, Flores cited Kurtz (1979), saying that it is the alcoholic's denial of his or her need for people that leads to his or her eventual denial that he is an alcoholic (cited in Flores, 2004, p. 99). Recovery is thus dictated by an effort to reverse this process. The alcoholic must first admit that he or she is an alcoholic and ultimately confess that he or she needs people. As the person exchanges destructive ways of getting needs met (e.g., substance use) for more mature means of establishing close human contact (e.g., the removal of "character defects" by working through the recovery program's steps), he or she is able to internalize more self-care and monitoring of affective states. The central issue is the addicted person's acceptance of who his or her real self is, which requires dealing with the shame about the self that was previously denied, followed by an earnest effort to better align one's behaviors with a concept of self that produces esteem.

Conclusion on Psychoanalytic Theory

Khantzian (1981, 1982, 1985, 1997) and Flores (2004) have gone a long way toward reintegrating psychoanalytic thought into the mainstream of addiction treatment. The theory is supported by many clinical observations, though it has not been studied in a methodologically rigorous manner. The lack of empirical support is generally considered to be a weakness. In addition, there are alternative explanations to the self-medication theory. Individuals who are beginning their drug use may be responding to genetic vulnerabilities. Substance abusers may be trying to medicate withdrawal or avoid facing the consequences of their use. The concept that individuals dealing with addiction are attempting to address early disorders of the self arising out of impaired object relations does, however, have clinical utility. Many therapists will verify that addicts speak about wanting to "feel normal" or avoid painful affective experiences as a reason for abusing substances. Many theorists talk about the extreme difficulty addicted individuals have with tolerating affective material in early recovery (S. Brown, 1985). Through these concepts, Khantzian (1997) enhanced our understanding of the addicted individual's experience from an internal, intrapsychic position. By implication, the therapist is to assist the patient in becoming more comfortable with affective states and in developing healthy alternatives to cope with them.

Khantzian (1981, 1982, 1985, 1997) and Flores (2004) viewed their theories as complements to sociocultural and biogenetic theories of the etiology of AOD disorders. Flores provided a theory of what actually motivates someone to initiate and continue alcohol and drug use and why certain individuals are particularly vulnerable to the rewarding properties of such substances. These two questions attempt to address the variability in how one person acquires the disease of addiction while others do not.

FAMILY MODELS

There are three family theory models that are commonly used within the AOD abuse field: family systems models, behavioral models, and family disease models. Although these three models are each distinct and have their own unique characteristics, most treatment centers use an amalgamation of the three, borrowing elements from each (McCrady & Epstein, 1996, p. 123).

Family Systems Model

The *family systems model* views the family as the major unit of analysis. Families are viewed as units governed by rules. In many cases these rules are implicit or unspoken but serve to maintain a balance or homeostasis within the family unit. The principle of homeostasis is central to family systems theory and refers to the family's attempts to maintain stability and balance within the system. Any action or behavior on the part of one family member affects the entire system. To the extent that this behavior becomes a destabilizing force within the family, the family system adjusts to restore this homeostasis.

In alcoholic families, even introducing sobriety can become a disruptive force after years of living with and adapting to a drinking lifestyle. In fact, alcohol may serve an adaptive function within the family (McCrady & Epstein, 1996). For example, a teenager may begin to drink in response to marital conflict between the parents. The drinking then serves the function of distracting the parents from their own marital discord and focusing their attention on the teenager's drinking. In fact, the teenager's acting out behavior may unify the parents in an effort to deal with the child's emerging crisis. Other possible adaptive functions of drinking would include dealing with anxiety about intimacy, avoidance of conflict, and so forth.

As alcoholism or addiction progresses within the family system, family rules often become increasingly rigid and inflexible. Once again, these rules serve the function of maintaining homeostasis. These rules might include things such as "Don't talk about Dad's drinking" or "Don't confront Mother about her drinking because she is fragile and this may push her over the edge." Gradually, family members learn that certain topics are taboo and must not be discussed. Often children growing up in these environments have difficulty identifying their feelings or trusting their perceptions. Living within this type of rigid family structure encourages them to deny the validity of their own perceptions and feelings. Steinglass (1979, 1981) did research that supports the notion of rigid functioning within families of drinking alcoholics. Steinglass found that families with a drinking alcoholic were most rigid in their functioning, followed by families who were in a transitional phase from drinking to sobriety, followed by families with a recovering alcoholic. Families in the latter group were the most flexible and open in their functioning.

Family systems theorists also focus on family boundaries (Thombs, 1994, p. 140). In alcoholic families, traditional boundaries or patterns of relationships (husband–wife or parent–child) often become disrupted. An example would be a mother whose son begins to abuse drugs. In an attempt to rescue her son, the mother becomes overinvolved and exhibits both smothering and enabling behavior. She becomes overprotective and makes excuses for him. The father, however, may go to the other extreme, becoming overly punitive or completely disengaging. As time progresses, the mother becomes more aligned with her son, and the father feels more like an outsider. In this way, traditional family boundaries and alliances become disrupted.

Family systems theorists talk about roles that individuals play within the family. These roles describe functions that individuals play to maintain the homeostasis. Within alcoholic families, a classification of different roles might include the chemically dependent person, the chief enabler, the family hero, the scapegoat, the lost child, and the mascot (Thombs, 1994, p. 174). The substance-dependent person, of course, is the addicted individual who is prone to acting irresponsibly. As stated previously, this behavior may serve a variety of different functions, including avoidance of marital conflict, intimacy, and so forth.

The *chief enabler* is usually the nondependent spouse. This is the one who makes excuses for the addicted person and tries to cover up or conceal his or her drug- and alcohol-using behavior. Usually, enablers are completely unaware of the fact that their behavior is shielding users from the consequences of their actions and thus contributing to the problem.

The *family hero* may sometimes be the oldest child who takes on responsibilities at a level that is developmentally higher than would be expected. This child often overperforms in athletics and scholastic activities. He or she helps to ease the tension in the family by overperforming and overfunctioning. Often these individuals tend to burn out later in life (Thombs, 1994).

The *scapegoat* is frequently another child who is blamed for all the family's problems. This child may act out the emotional turmoil that is just under the surface in alcoholic families. Often he or she identifies with an alcoholic parent. Scapegoats serve to direct blame and focus away from the alcoholic parent and onto themselves (Thombs, 1994).

The *lost child* is often difficult to recognize because he or she is so quiet. He or she seeks to avoid conflict and to smooth over tension at all costs. Later in life these individuals may become depressed or exhibit a variety of other emotional symptoms (Thombs, 1994). Their goal is to reduce tension by disappearing and not causing any conflict.

The *mascot* is known as the family clown and is useful in helping the family dissipate tense or conflicting situations. Mascots often do silly, immature things and make jokes even at their own expense (Thombs, 1994).

Family systems theorists view this model as useful in explaining both the initiation and maintenance of addictive behavior. As mentioned previously, the use of alcohol can serve an adaptive function, and systems theorists believe that explains why certain individuals engage initially in AOD abuse and continue with this abusive behavior in spite of a variety of negative consequences. They stress the power of family systems to influence individual behavior such as drug abuse. Furthermore, they suggest that the family roles, the rigid set of rules, and the boundary problems contribute to the maintenance of AOD abuse problems as the disorder progresses.

Bennett and Wolin (1990) conducted research to support this position. In a study of 25 alcoholic families they found that families that were able to maintain the integrity of rituals such as dinnertime and holidays evidenced less intergenerational transmission of alcoholism than families that allowed rituals to become disrupted or subsumed by the alcoholism. Therapeutic efforts generally focus on making explicit the implicit family rules, changing the family structure to reinforce traditional boundaries, and educating the family about the ways in which family roles have helped to perpetuate the problem. A review of the literature reveals a robust database of studies indicating that family therapy is an important component of treatment for patients with AOD-abuse problems (McCrady & Epstein, 1996, p. 130).

Family Behavioral Model

The second family therapy approach is the *family behavioral model.* The family behavioral model relies heavily on observations of interactions between family members with specific foci on significant behavioral interactions and patterns. This approach also involves using behavioral change techniques, such as contracting, to encourage new interactional and problem-solving modalities within the family. In 1973, Hersen, Miller, and Eisler observed interactions between alcoholic husbands and their wives (McCrady & Epstein, 1996, p. 121). They discovered that the wives looked at their spouses more closely when they were discussing alcohol than when they were discussing a neutral topic. In addition, in a similar study of alcoholic men and their wives, Becker and Miller found that the alcoholic spoke more when the topic being discussed was related to alcohol and the wives spoke more when the topic was a different issue (McCrady & Epstein, 1996, p. 121). These researchers concluded that the marital interactions were inadvertently reinforcing the alcoholic behavior by increased attention from the spouse and/or by the dominance of the conversation by the alcoholic husband.

McCrady and Epstein (1996) also reported on several other interactional studies. They concluded that "interactions of alcoholic couples change when alcohol is present or discussed, and that these changes have a variety of positive features that may reinforce and maintain the drinking" (McCrady

& Epstein, 1996, p. 122). As stated previously, the behavioral models rely on specific structured interventions to help couples change their interactional patterns. O'Farrell and Cowles (1989) developed a *behavioral management therapy* (BMT) that has specific change goals incorporated into the process. This is a structured program involving a set number of sessions. Both the alcoholic and the spouse must commit to specific goals, including abstinence, self-help, meeting attendance, and so forth. The program also has the spouse specify what he or she will do in the event of a relapse. In this way, O'Farrell and Cowles attempt to alter behaviors that may have been enabling or dysfunctional and to provide a structure from which the family can move toward a healthy state of recovery.

McCrady, Epstein, and Sell (2003) examined factors related to the maintenance of substance abuse, adopting a "cognitive–behavioral–systemic framework" (p. 123) to describe factors related to the maintenance of substance abuse. They focused on antecedents to drinking, cognitive and affective events that mediate these antecedents, consequences of drinking, and interactions between the drinker and his environment as contributing to the maintenance of substance abuse. They cited research to support their model. In regard to antecedents, research has shown that wives who remain engaged with their alcoholic husbands led to more positive outcomes than wives who were disengaged. Orford et al. (1975) and Moos, Finney, and Cronkite (1990) found that when wives were assertive and engaged, better treatment outcomes tended to occur than did with wives who disengaged in an effort to get their husbands to stop drinking. Negative family interactions are also antecedents, which are related to drinking. Rotunda and O'Farrell (1997) found that alcoholic families are more negative and conflicted and estranged than controlled families. In further research, Shoham, Rohrbaugh, Stickle, and Jacob (1998) found that alcoholic families tended to exhibit a specific type of negative communication pattern wherein the nondrinking spouse engaged in criticism of and request for change from the alcoholic spouse, which then led to the alcoholic spouse withdrawing from the interaction. This cycle led to increased stress and increased marital dissatisfaction for both partners and possibly further drinking. They labeled this a *demand–withdraw interaction* (Shoham, Rohrbaugh, Stickle, & Jacob, 1998, p. 125).

Furthermore, O'Farrell, Hooley, Fals-Stewart, and Cutter (1998) described what they labeled as *expressed emotion* (p. 125) in alcoholic families. This expressed emotion consists of criticism, hostility, and emotional overinvolvement by the nonalcoholic spouse directed at the alcoholic spouse. High expressed emotion was related to lower marital satisfaction as well as to increased rates of relapse and shorter times to relapse following behavioral marital therapy for alcoholism treatment; high expressed emotion was also related to a higher percentage of drinking days in the year following treatment. O'Farrell, Choquette, Cutter, and Birchler (1997) also found that sexual difficulties were another source of stress that led to maintenance of alcoholic behavior. In conclusion, this line of research indicates that a variety of spousal and marital interactions seem to be related to maintenance of alcoholic behavior and contribute to the cycle of addiction and alcoholism.

Family Disease Model

The third major model of addiction-related family therapy is the *family disease model*. This model arises from the traditional disease model concept and incorporates many of the traditions and techniques of the AA program. It is also the model that is most commonly used within traditional treatment centers. However, most programs incorporate elements of all three models.

The family disease model describes AOD addiction as a family disease, not of alcoholism but of codependence. Codependence is characterized by a preoccupation that the family member has with the addicted person, especially an investment in trying to change the behavior of this person. Codependents most often become enmeshed and obsessed with the behavior of the alcoholic or addicted spouse. They gradually lose their sense of self-esteem, self-worth, and even their sense of personal identity as they continue to lead a crisis-filled life centered on the behavior of the drinking or drug-using partner. The codependent spouse is driven by a need to change the behavior of the addicted spouse.

Family disease theory holds that a return to normalcy is possible only when that individual gives up this attempt to control the situation and is able to "detach with love." Thus, the focus of therapy centers on helping the codependent spouse achieve this sense of detachment. Typically this involves a personal program of recovery for the family member involving Al-Anon, Nar-Anon, Alateen, or other self-help groups. Although family disease theory strongly encourages continued family therapy attendance, it is believed that only through a personal program of recovery using the 12-step process (see Chapter 8, this volume) can the codependent become truly healthy and fully functioning.

Conclusion on Family Therapy Models

Family therapy models and techniques have contributed a great deal to our understanding of addictive disorders. There is now substantial data (McCrady & Epstein, 1996, p. 130) suggesting that the inclusion of family therapy into the mix of treatments for AOD abusers is significant in enhancing outcomes with this population. Family systems theory has added to our understanding of factors that might initiate and maintain AOD abuse within an individual. It is unlikely, however, that individuals would continue to experience the major life-threatening negative consequences associated with addictive disorders simply as a result of secondary gains to the family system. Addictive disorders are extremely complex and involve familial, intrapsychic, biogenetic, and learned behavior patterns, which all contribute to the initiation and maintenance of this disorder. The family therapy theorists have made a major contribution to our understanding of this disorder by emphasizing the need to include family members and by stressing the need to address family dynamics so that the family member with addiction can return to a more healthy, stable, flexible, and open family environment after treatment.

THE BIOPSYCHOSOCIAL MODEL:
AN INTEGRATED APPROACH

This section represents our attempt to combine the four major theoretical models and their supporting data into an integrated model called the *biopsychosocial model*. This biopsychosocial model accounts for multiple pathways to addiction, with specific factors playing a greater or lesser role for any given individual.

Biochemical Factors

In this model, biochemical factors play a significant role in the initiation and maintenance of AOD problems for a large number of addicted individuals. The strongest evidence for a genetic transmission of addictive disorders exists for alcohol, and a growing body of research data also suggests a biochemical, if not a genetic, basis for addiction to other drugs as well.

Neurotransmitter systems play an important role in modulating affective states, attention, and so forth. The introduction of mood-altering chemicals into the lives of some individuals can create powerful biochemical reinforcers that act like primary drive states (e.g., hunger, sex) precisely because they mimic and even stimulate the action of these neurotransmitter chemicals in the brain. The more a person abuses psychoactive chemicals, the more this neurotransmitter system may become depleted and perhaps even permanently compromised, resulting in cravings for psychoactive chemicals in greater quantities and with increasing frequency. For individuals who were born with a compromised neurochemical balance, the introduction of psychoactive drugs might provide a powerful positive reinforcer by allowing them some relief and control over affective states that previously seemed to dominate their lives. Thus, individuals may develop a biochemical susceptibility to alcohol and drugs as a result of years of abuse. This abuse may have started as a result of psychosocial factors such as painful affective experiences, family problems, or peer pressure, but over time the abuse of chemicals damages the neurotransmitter system.

For these individuals, the neurochemical imbalance creates a biochemical craving that acts like a primary drive state and powerfully reinforces the continued abuse of psychoactive chemicals despite a variety of negative consequences. The individual may experience the cravings as powerful enough to overwhelm cognitive factors such as judgment, insight, and impulse control as they propel the individual toward an AOD-dependent lifestyle. This is what Leshner (2001) meant when he said that drug dependence is the result of neuroadaptive changes that hijack the brain's primary reward and motivational circuits, resulting in the consumption of psychoactive drugs becoming the brain's top priority (p. 75). Consequently, the majority of the medical community now refers to addiction as a brain disease. Although there are individuals who are more genetically predisposed to this disease, anyone can develop the disease of addiction provided they consume enough drugs or alcohol over a long enough period of time.

Once the individual develops a dependency on alcohol and drugs, the disorder becomes a primary entity in and of itself. This entity has its own set of symptoms and natural progression toward increasingly destructive consequences. The individual will progress toward a lifestyle characterized by greater degrees of unmanageability and loss of control. The biochemical imbalances may help to explain why AOD-dependent individuals are no longer able to return to moderate levels of use.

Expectancies

Although the biochemical factors may be important, a number of other factors also contribute to the initiation, maintenance, and progression of AOD disorders. Not only the pharmacological properties of the drug itself but also the individual's expectations of the drug's effects contribute to the desire to use drugs (Marlatt & Gordon, 1985; Marlatt & Rohsenow, 1980; Monti, Rohsenow, Abrams, & Binkoff, 1988). Expectancy studies have shown that individuals who expect greater effects from alcohol and drugs in regard to tension reduction, euphoria, avoidance of negative affect states, and so forth are more likely to use and abuse these drugs. Expectancies may play a significant role in the initiation of AOD disorders, especially for adolescents. Peer group influences are extremely important in explaining the initiation of adolescent substance abuse (Bukstein, 1995; Rotgers, 1996, p. 182). In today's society, adolescents receive many messages that may reinforce positive expectancies of AOD use. These messages come from their peer group, adult role models, and the media. In many adolescent peer groups there is widespread AOD use, which normalizes this behavior for others. The peer group influence may glamorize it and provide respect for the ability to consume large amounts. The peer group attitude may lead to the expectation that AOD use will provide special status or increased popularity. Media and mass marketing through television, radio, movies, and magazines also may create positive expectancies.

As adolescents progress into a substance abusing lifestyle, they associate less and less with nondrug-using peers. They are less likely to receive negative information that might alter their expectancies. They also may discount negative messages about AOD use because the messages would challenge their increasingly rigid defense and denial structure. Thus, positive AOD expectancies remain intact even as the AOD use progresses and negative consequences accumulate. In this way, expectancies play a powerful role in the initiation, maintenance, and progression of AOD disorders.

Cue Reactivity

Cue reactivity studies have also contributed to an understanding of the maintenance and progression of AOD disorders. These studies have shown that addicted individuals develop a conditioned response to the set and setting of their drug use (Childress et al., 1992, 1999; Childress, McLellan, O'Brien, 1988; Kalivas & Volkow, 2005). Users who are exposed to drug paraphernalia or video presentations of drug-using situations develop powerful physiologic reactions as well as powerful craving responses. Studies show that exposure to drug stimuli, even after prolonged periods of abstinence, results in the release of dopamine in the brain. This dopamine release causes uncontrollable craving and drug-seeking behavior (Phillips et al., 2003; Schultz, 1998; Sutton & Beninger, 1999, as cited in Kalivas & Volkow, 2005). These studies help to explain how individuals maintain addictive disorders in spite of the negative consequences. As they become enmeshed in a drinking and drug-using lifestyle, they may become aware of the need for change, and they may achieve periods of abstinence on their own. However, the exposure to an environmental cue can pull them back into their old lifestyle. The alcoholic who passes by the bar or liquor store on the way home from work or the cocaine addict who sees a movie featuring cocaine use experiences powerful cues and stimuli to resume use of their drug. Without effective training in how to handle these cues, a substance-dependent person may relapse.

Self-Efficacy

Self-efficacy is the ability and confidence to cope with the environment and emotions in successful ways. Individuals who lack self-efficacy may also be more likely to abuse alcohol and/or drugs. Many substance-dependent individuals indicate that when they began to use, the substances seemed to help or medicate various psychological or functional deficits. They speak of alcohol making them more relaxed in social situations or relieving stress during traumatic events, such as a divorce, loss of a job, or death of a loved one. Adolescents talk about marijuana helping them to forget poor academic performance. For example, "After I began smoking pot I was still getting bad grades and my parents were still yelling at me, but it just didn't bother me anymore." As the AOD problem progresses, the psychological and functional impairments worsen rather than improve other problems, but the individual does not see the AOD use as a complicating factor. Instead, they frequently increase their use to further medicate, and the disorder progresses into more negative consequences and increased loss of control.

Attempts to enhance their functioning through social skills training, assertiveness training, anger-management skills, and so forth are all valuable interventions for addressing these impairments in self-efficacy (McCrady & Epstein, 1996; Steinglass, 1979, 1981). Therapists and self-help groups recognize the need to develop nonchemical coping skills for these problem areas. If AOD-dependent individuals have effective nonchemical coping skills and believe in their own ability to manage stress, they will be more likely to give up the AOD behavior (Hester, 1994; Miller et al., 1994; Rotgers, 1996).

Conclusion on the Biopsychosocial Model

In the biopsychosocial model, addictive disorders begin and continue because of biochemical factors, disorders of self, learned or conditioned factors, and family and social factors. There are multiple pathways to addiction, and the differential effect of these factors may vary from individual to individual. Once the individual progresses to the point of substance dependence, however, the addictive disorder becomes primary, with its own set of symptoms and a somewhat definable progression.

The evidence from neuroimaging studies is now sufficient to conclude that it is neuroadaptation or, more specifically, neurotransmitter dysregulation that is the predominant factor in the development of addictive disorders.

> Dysregulation means that the cause could be a disruption of chemical production or release, or it could be that the receptors for the chemicals are not working correctly. The dysregulation may be present before the person takes a drug or it may be caused by constant (chronic) drug taking or induced by a psychosocial stressor, such as trauma. Or it could be all three. (Erickson, 2007, p. 50)

Even though the explanation for compulsive, addictive drug seeking lies within the neurobiological adaptations, research also tells us that the environment can have a profound impact on neurochemical imbalances. For example, factors such as social dominance (Thanos et al., 2001) and stress (Papp et al., 1994) can affect neurochemistry.

A key characteristic of this disorder is loss of control. As the *Diagnostic and Statistical Manual of Mental Disorders* (4th ed., text revision; American Psychiatric Association, 2000) emphasizes, individuals consume more than intended, and their consumption leads to increasingly negative consequences such as ignoring social and work responsibilities, increased involvement with the legal system, loss of job, negative health consequences, and so forth. But why do addicted individuals behave this way? Our current understanding of neurobiology helps to explain the behavior. Neuroadaptation, as a result of prolonged chemical use, results in individuals responding to drug use in much the same way as they would respond to a primary drive state. This response is sufficient to overcome judgment, insight, and reasoning for the addicted individual. This response explains why addicted individuals are unlikely to return to a state of moderate or controlled use. For the addicted individual, the notion of existing without alcohol and drugs seems overwhelming and impossible. They feel their very existence depends on AOD. They use increasingly desperate (i.e., out of control) measures to ensure that their use continues. As the disorder progresses, these individuals become more self-centered, more grandiose, and less able to process information appropriately from the environment. They develop alternative explanations for their use that tend to rationalize or minimize the significance of the problem. Families become increasingly dysfunctional as they attempt to respond to the increasingly disrupted and out-of-control life of the addicted individual. Their efforts to control the situation result in rigid and fixed interactional patterns, such as enabling, distracting, and scapegoating, which unwittingly perpetuate the substance abuse. Successful treatment of addiction requires participation by family members to alter these dysfunctional patterns.

CONCLUSION

In this chapter, we have reviewed five theories of addiction that have much to offer to the treatment of AOD disorders. A theory or model is of value to a clinician only if it informs clinical practice in some meaningful way. Understanding the complex factors that account for the addicted person's attachment to and craving for psychoactive chemicals can help the therapist to devise behavioral strategies for coping with cravings. It might also help the therapist to react to relapses with empathy and hope instead of frustration. Fortunately, it is not necessary to fully understand all of the etiological factors to compassionately and effectively intervene in the lives of addicted individuals to help them cope with this most overwhelming and destructive disorder.

3

Assessment of Substance Abuse and Dependence

Assessment of substance abuse problems is a challenging task but one that is vital for the well-being of patients in any clinical setting. Studies indicate that substance abuse disorders are frequently undetected or misdiagnosed and that professionals are "even less likely to detect these problems when the patient is employed, married, white, insured, or female (Clark, 1981; Cleary et al., 1988; Moore et al., 1989; Wolfe et al., 1965)" (Schottenfeld & Pantalon, 1999, p. 109).

Clinicians in private practice can encounter substance abuse problems at the assessment and diagnosis stage or in the course of ongoing treatment when consequences begin to emerge. It is preferable for private practitioners to learn to address mild to moderate substance abuse problems in the course of their ongoing work. The generalist clinician may also need to refer substance-abusing patients to either a specialty treatment center or a private practitioner with greater expertise. The ability to make an appropriate referral depends on the ability to screen patients for substance abuse problems, conduct an intensive substance abuse evaluation, and match the patient with the appropriate treatment provider. In this chapter, we focus on accomplishing these tasks using the *Diagnostic and Statistical Manual of Mental Disorders* (4th ed., text revision; *DSM–IV–TR;* American Psychiatric Association, 2000) criteria for abuse and dependence, the diagnostic interview, screening and assessment measures, patient feedback, and treatment goals.

There are a number of elements in the assessment process. Assessment includes determining the degree of substance abuse or dependence, the need for medical detoxification, the existence of comorbid psychiatric disorders, and the current and past role of the family. Because physical and sexual abuse is so common in substance-using populations, it is important to include this as part of general screening and explore its link with substance abuse if appropriate. The final stage of the process involves assessing motivation for change, establishing treatment goals with the patient, determining the appropriate level of care needed, and linking the patient with the appropriate provider. Keeping these elements of the assessment process in mind facilitates the overall success of the process.

These elements suggest the complexity and length of time required for this process. The assessment often involves more than one session and a variety of different measures, including clinical interviews, screening or assessment instruments, patient feedback, and treatment planning. There may be times when this complexity is not possible. In a crisis situation, the clinician may do an initial triage and refer the person to an inpatient treatment setting. Nevertheless, in most cases substance abuse evaluation should be done as an ongoing process with care and thoroughness. An extended assessment may require 3 to 4 weeks and may be done in an inpatient, partial hospitalization, or outpatient treatment setting.

CLINICAL DIAGNOSTIC INTERVIEW

The centerpiece of any addiction assessment is the diagnostic interview. This interview requires the same set of interviewing skills that clinicians use with other disorders. A nonjudgmental attitude and empathy bring more effective results than a confrontational approach. In the beginning the therapist needs to develop a sense of rapport with the patient by listening to the patient's concerns and joining in a mutual exploration of the problems. Some therapists who are uncomfortable working with these clients believe that they should adopt a confrontational therapeutic style and convince the patient to do something that the patient does not want to do (e.g., stop drinking). In fact, research suggests a different approach. Those therapists who give feedback within an empathic, open, and nonjudgmental atmosphere generally produce more positive outcomes for their clients (W. R. Miller & Baca, 1983).

Substance abuse patients often suffer within a shame-based system and receive many messages from society and family members that they are failures and bad people. Premature confrontation or labeling only serves to reinforce these messages, often resulting in premature termination of treatment. Washton (1995) pointed out that "the intense shame, guilt, and self-loathing commonly associated with substance abuse place additional demands on the clinician to convey an empathetic, nonjudgmental, and accepting attitude towards these patients" (pp. 24–25).

Loss of Control

The diagnostic interview should help the clinician to determine the nature of the individual's relationship to psychoactive substances. The clinician needs to investigate the degree of loss of control and functional impairment, the chemical use profile, developmental and family history, comorbid psychiatric disorders, physical and sexual abuse, and the current role of the family.

The individual with alcohol and other drug (AOD) problems reveals an increasing loss of control and continued use of the substance despite negative consequences. The term *loss of control* has frequently been misunderstood as implying a complete or total loss of control every time the person drinks or uses drugs. In fact, the loss may be intermittent. In the early stages of abuse individuals may lose control infrequently. The individual may drink three times with no significant consequences. On the fourth episode, however, the individual may drink uncontrollably, experience a blackout, and drive the car into a tree.

The defining characteristic of loss of control is the inability to predict or guarantee that the individual will maintain control when he or she drinks. As AOD abuse increases, the individual often experiences a progressive loss of control and more frequent hardships and crises. During this increasing loss of control, the individual denies that the drinking or using is out of control in order to maintain the behavior. The individual sustains the behavior by minimizing or rationalizing consequences and by failing to connect the drinking or using with the increasingly negative consequences.

This denial system is the only way in which the addicted individual can manage the cognitive dissonance as increasingly destructive incidents mar his or her life:

> The individual's life gradually becomes dominated and organized by alcohol. The person's behavioral, cognitive, and emotional world— outer and inner—begins to shrink so that all incoming information and the individual's perceptions and interpretation of it will be shaped and colored by the need for alcohol and denial of that need. (S. Brown, 1995a, p. 31)

In many cases, substance abusing clients are most likely to appear for treatment in the midst of a crisis. Whether the crisis is marital, job-related, or legal, the individual fails to see the connection between the drinking or drug use and this particular crisis as well as a whole history of past negative consequences. The clinician's job in the diagnostic interview is to listen for examples of loss of control. The degree of loss of control ultimately determines the client's relationship with AOD use. It is the degree to which the individual now views his or her alcohol and drug use as a part of life that must be sustained at all costs.

The clinician may find the job of identifying and labeling loss of control and negative consequences more difficult than it might appear. Patients who have been denying the role of alcohol and drugs in their lives for many years become adept at devising alternative explanations for the difficulties in their lives. Therapists who are understandably invested in forming a bond with their patients may be susceptible to believing these explanations, thereby endorsing the patients' distorted rationalizations and minimizations. A clear-sighted and unswerving focus on loss of control is the clinician's ally in arriving at an appropriate diagnosis. "We listen for the organizing role of alcohol and label its central function and presence in the individual's life and the life of the family. We help bring this secret partner out of hiding" (S. Brown, 1995a, p. 32).

DSM–IV–TR

Determining the "organizing role" (S. Brown, 1995a, p. 32) of AOD abuse for the patient is exactly what the DSM–IV–TR criteria are designed to accomplish. Placing the patient on the continuum from abuse to dependence requires familiarity with these criteria. Older classification systems relied on tolerance and withdrawal as the hallmarks of the substance dependence syndrome. This emphasis sometimes fostered confusing situations in which a patient who abused a substance that did not create physical dependence (e.g., cocaine) could not receive a substance dependence diagnosis despite a highly malignant pattern of abuse.

The DSM–IV–TR includes five behavioral indicators in addition to tolerance and withdrawal in arriving at a definition of *dependence*. The five behavioral criteria are as follows: (a) the substance is taken in larger amounts over a longer period than was intended; (b) there is a persistent desire or unsuccessful effort to cut down or control substance use; (c) a great deal of time is spent in activities necessary to obtain the substance; (d) important social, occupational, or recreational activities are given up or reduced because of the substance; and (e) the substance use is continued despite knowledge of persistent or recurrent physical or psychological problems. In combination with physical tolerance and withdrawal symptoms, there are now seven criteria for substance dependence. A diagnosis of substance dependence requires that the patient exhibit three or more of these symptoms in the same 12-month period. Patients can be dependent without manifesting tolerance or withdrawal.

In the DSM–IV–TR, substance abuse is less severe than substance dependence. The DSM–IV–TR lists four criteria for substance abuse, with the patient needing to exhibit only one of the symptoms within a 12-month period: (a) recurrent substance abuse resulting in a failure to fulfill major role obligations such as those at home or at work, (b) recurrent substance use in situations in which it is physically hazardous, (c) recurrent substance use–related legal problems, or (d) continued substance use despite having persistent or recurrent social or interpersonal problems created or exacerbated by the effects of the substance. The definitions of both abuse and dependence focus on impairments in behavioral functioning. To the extent that we can make this abuse/dependence determination in a nonjudgmental and nonthreatening tone, we can successfully conduct a diagnostic interview without alienating the patient from the treatment process. Washton (1995) suggested phrasing the *DSM–IV* criteria as questions during the clinical interview, for example, "Have you often ended up consuming much more than you expected or intended to?" Asking questions such as these in a straightforward, nonjudgmental manner can help determine the diagnosis. Many patients have difficulty giving objective answers to these questions. The degree of their difficulty can often indicate their unawareness of the connections between their substance use and loss of control. A clinical example may help to illustrate this point.

> John is 25 years old and has smoked marijuana for 10 years. During the past 5 years he has smoked marijuana on a daily basis. Despite having a high school degree and vocational training in computers, John has never really developed a career. He lives at home with his mother and delivers pizza in the evenings. Both John and his mother are dissatisfied with this situation. John has a variety of explanations as to why his life is not progressing: "Good jobs are hard to come by," "I'm not in a good field," "My mother's nagging really brings me down." At no point does John acknowledge a connection between the drug use and the life problems. When asked specifically about this, he responds, "No, the drugs are not the problem. Besides, pot's not addicting. You should know that."

Clinicians sometimes mistake the individual's denial for an indication that he or she does not wish to get better. Rather, the individual is wary that acknowledging the true connection between AOD use and negative consequences will threaten the AOD use that may seem central to his or her existence. Therefore, the perception that life without AODs would be intolerable must be overcome in the early stages of treatment. Once the therapist addresses and lessens this perception, a strong desire for health and recovery often emerges. Frequently this desire has existed all along but has been suppressed by the fear of perceived consequences, physical and psychological, of stopping of AOD use. As we discuss in Chapter 5 of this volume, clinicians should not confuse denial with lack of information. Spending some time initially providing information and focusing on consequences of use may help to overcome resistance later.

Functional Impairment

Along with loss of control, the clinician should listen for impaired functioning during the diagnostic interview. Although he or she should not reach conclusions prematurely, the therapist must assess the degree to which the individual's functioning is impaired across many domains of functioning, such as work, family, peers, social and recreational activities, education, legal issues, physical health, and psychological issues. Frequently the clinician may see these areas of impairment before recognizing the extent of substance abuse. When the clinician does note impairment, he or she should not rule out possible substance abuse and/or dependence even when the patient denies significant levels of abuse. By focusing on functional impairment the clinician can avoid arguments about whether the patient actually is an alcoholic or addict. The clinician can simply note the areas of impairment and relate them to substance abuse as appropriate. The patient can form his or her own conclusions.

Substance Use Profile

To determine the present danger to the patient and the need for medical detoxification, the clinician needs to ask specific questions regarding the types and amounts of drugs used and the frequency of their use. The questions should detail the use for the past week. The need for medical detoxification is based not only on the types of drugs used but also on the amount and frequency of use.

Some knowledge of psychopharmacology is helpful. Withdrawal from drugs such as alcohol, barbiturates, and benzodiazepines can be life threatening. For the benzodiazepine-dependent patient, medical detoxification is almost always indicated because these are slow-acting drugs and the withdrawal can be protracted. Seizures can occur as late as 2 weeks after stopping use. Drugs that can be stopped abruptly without potentially dangerous medical consequences include opiates (except when there are medical conditions exacerbated by stress) and cocaine, including crack cocaine. However, cessation of these drugs creates such intense craving and physical discomfort that many opiate and cocaine users do require structured, medically supervised residential care for successful withdrawal. Even in the case of opiates and cocaine, patients who are older, frail, or psychologically impaired may be at high risk when they stop use abruptly without medical supervision. For example, an individual with a heart condition may experience medical complications from the stress of withdrawal. An individual with depression may become suicidal during the "cocaine crash" phase of withdrawal. In fact, for patients who have not had a recent routine physical examination, a referral to an internist is appropriate as part of the assessment process.

In the diagnostic interview the clinician should also cover past history and the progression from earliest use of psychoactive chemicals to the present day. This history shows the clinician how the individual's disorder has evolved over time and helps the individual see the increase in loss of control. The clinician may hear the patients make statements such as, "As a teenager I smoked pot, but told myself I would never go on to harder drugs. It was only 6 months later that I was doing LSD and cocaine." Another relevant statement might be, "I told myself that I couldn't be an alcoholic because I would never drink in the mornings. Just a few months later I realized I could become someone who needed a drink to get going." The clinician can hear these statements as examples of violating internal limits and illustrating the loss of control.

Developmental and Family History

Another part of the diagnostic interview is obtaining a developmental history. In addition to inquiring about the usual developmental milestones, the therapist should also inquire about areas that are correlated with AOD problems, such as learning disabilities, attention-deficit disorder, and antisocial or aggressive behavior. The clinician can also ask about the peer group and how it has changed.

The therapist should also cover family history and family dynamics. Substance dependence tends to run in families. AOD problems in one or more family members suggest that an added degree of concern is appropriate. Thus, for the individual with a history of substance dependence in his or her family, even occasional or sporadic abuse should be viewed with more concern than if family substance dependence were not present. It is often difficult to obtain an accurate family history of substance dependence. Sometimes the therapist must ask questions in such a way that the person or family thinks about the issues in a new light. Frequently, addiction and psychiatric problems are "in the closet" and emerge only after repeated questioning. If the family history indicates substance dependence, the clinician should inquire about the outcome of the disorder for those family members. Did the individuals die at a young age? Did they eventually get sober and lead successful lives, or was the outcome somewhere in between? Did these individuals ever receive treatment and were they helped? This information will most likely color the individual's view of the treatment process in either a positive or negative way.

Finally, it is most important to know what degree of support the individual is going to receive from the immediate family. The therapist should try to ascertain not only whether family members will participate in the treatment process but also the role they may have played in perpetuating the overall using behavior of the individual. Without this information, the clinician runs the risk of having therapeutic efforts overtly or covertly sabotaged by family members for whom change in the person's behavior can be threatening or disruptive. Sometimes family members accompany the patient to the initial interview and/or attempt to contact the therapist to round out the clinical picture. When the patient is an adolescent, the family members should be included in the assessment as a matter of course. In other cases, how the clinician deals with these collateral contacts is extremely important. To not violate the patient's confidentiality and trust, any contact between the therapist and family members must take place with the full knowledge and consent of the patient. Information from other family members may provide valuable clinical information. These contacts may also help the family to realize that their involvement in the change process is essential and that changes in their own behavior patterns will help the patient deal with the addiction problem.

The interview with the family provides an opportunity to explore the attitudes and behaviors of each family member toward substance problems and how these attitudes are likely to affect the patient's recovery. For example, family members may operate from a shame-based perspective that can make recovery more difficult, saying such things as, "You've never cared about anything, and now you've wrecked your life with drugs." A spouse may signal that he or she has had enough and is ready to end the marriage. Parents of a young person may have substance abuse problems of their own.

Coexisting Psychiatric Disorders

Part of the diagnostic interview is assessing coexisting psychiatric disorders. Coexisting disorders are now considered the norm rather than the exception in AOD disorders. Patients with substance use disorders are more likely to also have a co-occurring psychiatric disorder, and patients with psychiatric disorders are more likely to abuse substances (Greenfield & Hennessy, 2008, p. 63). The clinician should try to distinguish between psychiatric disorders that predate the substance use and those that are related to substance use or withdrawal. Treatment outcomes improve when both disorders are treated together (Greenfield & Hennessy, 2008, p. 63).

Common comorbid psychiatric disorders that are statistically associated with addiction problems include (a) conduct disorder, especially aggressive type in adolescents and antisocial personality disorder in adults; (b) attention-deficit/hyperactivity disorder; (c) mood disorders, especially major depression; (d) dysthymia, bipolar disorder, and cyclothymia; (e) anxiety disorders such as social phobia, posttraumatic stress disorder, and generalized anxiety disorder; (f) bulimia nervosa; (g) schizophrenia; and (h) borderline personality disorder (Bukstein, 1995). The clinician should be able to recognize psychiatric symptoms and, if they persist, to integrate the comorbid psychopathology into the treatment plan. For example, Kadden, Getter, Cooney, and Litt (1989) and Litt, Babor, DelBoca, Kadden, and Cooney (1992) demonstrated that patients who are antisocial and alcoholic do better in structured group settings that provide coping skills training rather than in more traditional psychodynamic groups. These patients also benefit from longer term therapeutic community interventions. Knowledge of these disorders and how they interact with substance abuse problems is central in designing an effective treatment plan.

Substance-induced disorders can and do mimic virtually every other form of psychopathology. The clinician should be aware of how individual drugs may affect the patient's mental status, especially in the early days of withdrawal. Cocaine withdrawal may produce an agitated depression (Kosten & Kleber, 1988). The risk of suicide is quite high and must be assessed carefully. In addition, prolonged cocaine or other stimulant abuse can lead to paranoid reactions that may be difficult to differentiate from paranoid schizophrenia or other paranoid delusional states. Patients under the influence of hallucinogenic drugs may appear to be psychotic. Even after cessation of use, flashbacks may occur some weeks or months later. Differentiating schizophrenia from hallucinogenic flashback experiences challenges many clinicians. Chronic abusers of marijuana may appear listless and lack motivation for weeks or months following cessation of use. In most cases, motivational levels return to normal after discontinuing use, but in the early weeks of abstinence this amotivational syndrome may mimic depression. Opiate addicts have a higher rate of depression than the general population (Kosten, Rounsaville, & Kleber, 1982). Individuals withdrawing from opiates may not only appear depressed but also exhibit signs of anxiety. Adolescents who have been chronic inhalers of solvents may appear to have organic brain syndrome and/or exhibit schizophrenic symptoms. It is difficult to differentiate substance-induced behavior from true psychiatric disorders. Premature labeling before a period of sustained abstinence can lead the therapist in the wrong direction.

Physical and Sexual Abuse

Many patients endure physical and sexual abuse secondary to their substance abuse. Still other patients were the victims of physical or sexual abuse prior to getting involved in alcohol and drug abuse. Because a high number of patients who appear in treatment centers grew up in alcoholic homes, many of these individuals have experienced neglect, abuse, and trauma at an early age. Substance abusers are also sometimes perpetrators of physical and sexual abuse. They may have medicated these traumas with alcohol and drugs and may experience painful affect bubbling to the surface while they achieve sobriety. For this reason, the clinician should be aware of the level of trauma and should anticipate the needs of these patients because painful affect gets uncovered during the therapeutic process. The clinician should ask specific questions about physical and sexual abuse during the diagnostic interview. In addition to the clinical interview, the clinician also can use a number of screening and assessment measures that can provide valuable information.

SCREENING AND ASSESSMENT MEASURES

Since the publication of the first edition of this book in 1998, a large number of formal screening and assessment measures have been developed. These measures not only assist in diagnosis and assessment of the severity of AOD problems but also give insight into issues such as motivation for change, relapse potential, and alcohol and drug expectancies. These issues are vital to effective treatment planning and matching patients to particular levels of care. Despite the increase in number and quality of screening and assessment measures, many clinicians fail to use them (Allen, 2003). "Researchers seem to place a much higher premium on formal assessment than do many practicing clinicians who appear to rely more heavily on interviews, review of past records (Nirenberg & Maisto, 1990), or clinical impression" (Allen, 2003, pp. 1–2).

Formal assessment procedures have several advantages over less structured clinical data. They can be used to develop standardized guidelines to triage clients to different levels of care. They can help staff in treatment programs to formulate diagnoses and communicate more effectively. Formal data often have more credibility not only with outside agencies but also with clients during feedback. Finally, the data from these instruments can be used to improve treatment program quality.

Assessment instruments can be divided into self-report screening tools, instruments for diagnosis of substance use disorders, and instruments that measure ancillary issues needed for treatment planning. For a listing and descriptive information about these instruments, the reader is referred to a publication available on the National Institute on Alcohol Abuse and Alcoholism's website (Allen & Wilson, 2003).

Screening Instruments

Screening instruments refer to brief questionnaires designed to detect individuals with substance use problems. They are aimed at those who have not acknowledged or are not aware of their problems, but they are not designed to actually diagnose either abuse or dependence. A good screening instrument should raise suspicions about the presence of a problem if the screen is positive. A negative screen, however, should indicate a low probability that a problem exists (Connors & Volk, 2003). Connors and Volk (2003) identified 14 screening instruments that have empirical support. Some of the more commonly used instruments are Alcohol Use Disorders Identification Test (AUDIT; Saunders, Aasland, Babor, de la Fuente, & Grant, 1993), Michigan Alcoholism Screening Test (Selzer, 1971), CAGE (Ewing, 1984), and TWEAK (Russell, 1994). Connors and Volk pointed out that the AUDIT in particular has shown a number of advantages in a variety of settings. The AUDIT is a 10-question measure that has been validated on alcoholic and heavy-drinking adults. It has been found to be superior in primary multiethnic health care settings (Steinbauer, Cantor, Holzer, & Volk, 1998).

In addition, the Substance Abuse and Mental Health Services Administration has developed a program that includes screening, brief intervention, and referral to treatment (SBIRT), when indicated. The program, designed primarily for use in medical settings, has collected data on almost 460,000 patients to date. The results are encouraging and indicate significant reductions in drug use as well as improvements in life functioning (Madras et al., 2009).

Diagnostic Instruments

Although the utility of diagnosis has been questioned, Maisto, McKay, and Tiffany (2003) made the case that there are "compelling reasons for continuing to assign diagnoses as part of clinical and research practice" (p. 5). First of all, assigning a diagnosis improves the ability of clinicians and researchers to communicate effectively with each other. Specifically, a diagnosis is a description, and to the degree to which that description is accurate, it improves the ability of clinicians and researchers to be able to talk effectively about a common problem. In addition, they pointed out that diagnoses can be valuable in terms of planning treatments specifically. If a diagnostic category consists of a variety of symptoms, knowing one symptom can often predict the existence of others. Although this alone may not lead to specific avenues of treatment, it can point the way to anticipating problems and dealing with specific issues that might arise during the course of treatment. Taken together, these issues provide a solid rationale for instruments that are designed to diagnose the presence or absence of alcohol and drug abuse and/or dependence.

Instruments for Treatment Planning

This area of assessment focuses on a range of personal variables that affect the AOD abuse problem. Some of these variables may be closely related to the substance abuse problem, such as motivation to change, whereas others may be less directly related, such as comorbid psychiatric problems (Donovan, 2003). All of these variables, however, are related to the treatment planning process and may be used to facilitate client/treatment matching as well as goal attainment (Allen & Mattson, 1993).

Some of the major areas that are covered in this area of assessment are things such as problem recognition and readiness to change. This would largely include measures based on Prochaska and DiClemente's (1986) stages of change model. Also included would be measures of alcohol and drug expectancies based primarily on Sandra Brown's work in this area (S. A. Brown, Christiansen, & Goldman, 1987; S. A. Brown et al., 1980). In addition, numerous measures to assess self-efficacy and relapse risk are also part of this area. There are also a variety of multidimensional instruments that attempt to assess domains of functioning in an effort to measure the impact of addiction on an individual's life in a broad sense. The most widely used instrument is the Addiction Severity Index (McLellan, Kushner, et al., 1992; McLellan, Luborsky, O'Brien, & Woody, 1980). Finally, the American Society of Addiction Medicine has developed measures to assist in patient placement (Hoffman, Halikas, & Mee-Lee, 1987; Hoffman, Halikas, Mee-Lee, & Weedman, 1991; Mee-Lee, Shulman, Fishman, Gastfriend, & Grifith, 2001).

Urine Drug Screens

Urine drug screens should be done as part of the diagnostic screening and assessment. Some clinical judgment is appropriate in determining when to use the screens. We have found the following guidelines helpful in our practices. We recommend drug screens as part of the initial workup for all patients for whom AOD use is an identified problem and as part of an ongoing monitoring program agreed to by the therapist and patient. We also use them when working with patients with legal charges, impaired professionals, or in any situation in which the therapist may want to document treatment adherence for the benefit of the patient. It is also helpful to use drug screens whenever there is reason to doubt the accuracy of the patient's self-report. In addition, we use drug screens more frequently with adolescents than with adults.

Although some clinicians hesitate to use drug screening for fear of the patient's reaction, our experience shows that the therapist's attitude heavily influences the patient's response. When clinicians present drug screening as a normal part of the assessment process rather than as a confrontation about the patient's veracity or commitment to change, patients usually accept the test. Becoming overly apologetic or appearing distrustful of the patient may sabotage the therapist's efforts. The therapist who approaches the situation in a matter-of-fact manner and stresses that urine drug screening is a matter of course for all substance abuse patients often can enlist compliance in even the most difficult patients. To be effective, urine drug screens must occur on a truly random and regular basis during the assessment and treatment period. In addition, these tests should be either observed or monitored (e.g., temperature-tested) to ensure their validity.

The quality of urine drug screens varies with the type of the test. The Emit Process test is commonly used for an initial screen. Positive results should then be confirmed through gas chromatography/mass spectroscopy, a more sensitive but costlier process.

Clinicians should be aware that drugs such as cocaine leave the body rapidly. Except in cases of heavy use, they can only be detected 48 to 72 hours after use. However, marijuana can remain in the system for an extended period of time and may be detected from a few days to a month after cessation of use. Other drugs, such as LSD and inhalants, are extremely difficult to detect and require specialized and costly procedures. For this reason they are not often included in the regular panel of drugs in a typical urine drug screen. Breathalyzers or Alco strips can be used to detect alcohol use. Alco strips react with any alcohol present in the body when they are placed on the patient's tongue.

ASSESSING ADOLESCENTS

There are several differences between assessing adolescents and adults. Adolescents may exhibit symptoms of abuse but only be temporarily experimenting with gateway drugs (Harrison, Fulkerson, & Beebe, 1998; Martin, Kaczynski, Maisto, Bukstein, & Moss, 1995). A variety of studies have suggested that unlike adults, it is the norm for adolescents to experiment with illegal drugs (Kandel, 1975; Yamaguchi & Kandel, 1984). Adolescents will go through a period of experimentation with so-called gateway drugs, such as alcohol and marijuana. They typically outgrow the need for experimentation and abandon use of illegal substances (Shedler & Block, 1990). Few adolescents advance from experimentation to more serious levels of abuse and dependence (Yamaguchi & Kandel, 1984).

Although it may be true that few adolescents who experiment with gateway drugs in the general population go on to develop abuse or dependence problems, this point is almost certainly less valid for those adolescents who are being evaluated in a clinical setting. First, these adolescents have exhibited enough symptoms or gotten into enough trouble with their AOD use that their parents have decided to consult a professional. In many cases this pattern suggests a progression of use beyond normal experimentation. Second, many of these clients may have come to the attention of school or legal authorities who have initiated the referral, once again suggesting AOD use beyond experimentation. Especially when these behaviors are part of a larger picture that might include other high-risk factors, such as a strong family history of addiction and/or early conduct problems, it is wise to assume that this is not just normal experimentation.

Another difference in assessing adolescents is that the *DSM–IV–TR* criteria may not be appropriate for that age group. Adolescents rarely exhibit tolerance, withdrawal symptoms, or related medical problems that come after years of continued drinking or drug use (Winters, 2003).

A third difference is that adolescents may be developmentally delayed with impaired social and emotional functioning resulting from prolonged drug use (Noam & Houlihan, 1990). As a result, they may not be able or willing to report accurately their AOD experiences. This is not to say that they overtly lie about their AOD use but rather they may not have the insight into their problems. Clinicians also must be careful to choose paper and pencil instruments that are written at an appropriate grade level for young people (Winters, 2003).

Finally, despite the previous statement, studies do show that self-reports of AOD use by adolescents are valid (Maisto, Connors, & Allen, 1995;

Winters, Stinchfield, Henly, & Schwartz, 1991), except in settings such as the juvenile justice system, in which it is not in the best interest of the patient to disclose drug use (Harrison, 1995; Magura & Kang, 1997). This last finding is somewhat problematic for treatment specialists who have many years of clinical experience with adolescents. One explanation may be that determining the accuracy of self-report data is a daunting task. The two most common methods are through the use of collateral contacts, such as parents, teachers, or probation officers, or through toxicology screens. As Harris, Griffin, McCaffrey, and Morral (2008) pointed out, both methods have problems. "Drug users often succeed in misleading collateral informants. . . . Biological tests can only confirm recent use, often very recent use, such as within the past 4–48 hours" (p. 348).

Marijuana does not typically remain in the system as long as is generally believed. For an individual who tests negative for marijuana and has a one-time slip, the tetrahydrocannabinol will clear the system in 2 to 5 days. As Knight, Hiller, Simpson, and Broome (1998) pointed out, "Understating use at baseline may result in assignment to less restrictive treatment programs" (as cited in Harris et al., 2008, p. 348). Thus, there is certainly a logical incentive for adolescents to underreport drug use in clinical settings.

FEEDBACK AND TREATMENT GOALS

The assessment process includes providing feedback to the patient and formulating treatment goals. This delicate process requires communicating the nature of the problem in a clear, but not overwhelming, way and enlisting the patient in forming an initial treatment plan. The therapist should be nonjudgmental and avoid direct confrontations. The clinician can make connections between the AOD use and the negative consequences that have been experienced. Simply restating the data gathered during the assessment often makes the connections clear. We offer a clinical example concerning Michael, a 29-year-old man who was referred by the court for evaluation after his second DWI.

> Michael, you told me that you were referred by the court after your second DWI. This DWI occurred 6 weeks ago, and your blood alcohol

level was just over the legal limit. You also told me that your first DWI occurred when you were 19 years old, and you stated that you used to drink a lot more at that time. During your teenage years and up until about the age of 22 you would frequently abuse alcohol and occasionally have blackouts. After you graduated from college and began your first job you made a decision to cut down on your use of alcohol and were able to successfully do so for a number of years. Your alcohol use increased at about age 27, when your marriage broke up. At that time, your wife indicated her concern about your drinking; however, you believe that this was simply her excuse for wanting to get out of a marriage that she really did not want to be involved in. For the past 2 years you have occasionally overdone it but have tried very hard to keep your drinking in moderation. Despite these efforts there have been times, especially when you were under stress at work, when you were prone to drink more than you should and this causes some concern for you.

We also talked some about your family background. As I understand it, your father was an alcoholic and he was verbally abusive to you as a child. He died at age 55 of alcohol-related causes. You grew up in a small town, and your father was not well regarded. He was looked down on by others in your community, and this caused you great embarrassment. One of the statements that you made when we discussed whether or not you might be an alcoholic was that you were determined never to be like your father.

As I see things now, you are in a state of some confusion. On the one hand, you are beginning to get concerned. Your second DWI is a serious situation. You have only been partially successful at moderating your drinking, and others around you, in addition to your ex-wife, have registered some concern about your drinking. However, it is your sincere determination not to grow up like your father. I think that this is an issue that we need to explore further. I would be interested in your thoughts. What do you think or how do you feel about what I have just said?

The goal of this feedback is not to hammer Michael over the head but to reveal the connections between his drinking and the negative consequences in his life. Over time, as the relationship with the therapist progresses, it will become easier for Michael to acknowledge the consequences. Once he is secure that therapy is not a shame-based environment, he will see the connections and begin to honestly explore the possibility of his alcoholism. The clinician can count on the progressive nature of the disorder to make the consequences more apparent.

> The client's alcoholism is our ally; we can count on it to create pain and suffering, losses and failures that our clients will reveal to us in different ways. Making the connection between these difficulties and drinking is our task. (Liftik, 1995, p. 88)

Treatment Recommendations

Once the connections become apparent, the therapist can begin to discuss treatment recommendations. As we discuss in Chapter 5 and Chapter 6, a time-limited abstinence contract may work well at this point. The clinician can also suggest attending a self-help meeting such as Alcoholics Anonymous or Narcotics Anonymous just to learn about the dynamics of addiction. The therapist can emphasize that they are working together to solve the perplexing and confusing problem. As the patient learns more about addiction, he or she will be better able to participate in this ongoing assessment process.

Readiness for Change

As stated earlier, patients come for assessment for a variety of reasons and under differing circumstances. Some come under coercion from the courts. Many come because of a marital or family crisis. Patients also come in different stages of readiness for change. Prochaska and DiClemente (1986) developed a model consisting of five stages of change. Their model can be used to assess the patient's willingness to change. The stages are (a) precontemplation, (b) contemplation, (c) preparation, (d) action, and (e) maintenance.

Patients in the *precontemplation* stage have no awareness that a problem exists. They rarely enter treatment centers unless they are coerced. Patients in the *contemplation* stage are ambivalent about seeking change. They consider the possibility that a problem exists, but they are not yet prepared to take specific action. Although they may express an awareness of the consequences of their substance use, they are still attached to the feelings that they experience while using alcohol and drugs. They are reluctant to consider positive steps toward change. Patients in the *preparation* stage are beginning to recognize that the negative effects outweigh the positive benefits of their alcohol and drug use. They may indicate a sincere desire to learn more about how they can stop using or correct the problem and they may have already experimented with attempts to control the situation on their own. Patients in the *action* stage are actively engaged in efforts to reduce or stop their substance abuse. They are good candidates for entering treatment. Patients in the *maintenance* stage have already initiated and put into place effective change strategies. The therapist can focus on sustaining the gains that have already been made and on developing specific skills such as relapse prevention.

Patients in the precontemplation stage will have different treatment goals than patients in the action stage. The therapist needs to assess both the readiness for change and the patient's personal goals for treatment. A man in the precontemplation stage who arrives under coercion from the courts may desire a letter stating that he does not have a problem and does not need treatment. The therapist will treat this patient differently from another patient who has serious concerns about drinking and strongly desires sobriety. Assessing the patient's readiness and the patient's goals can help to establish realistic treatment interventions without imposing the therapist's agenda.

Enhancement of Motivation

The therapist will also wish to enhance the patient's motivation to change and the desire to move to the next stage of readiness. W. R. Miller (1999) developed specific techniques to enhance motivation for treatment, discussed in greater detail in Chapter 5. Although enhancing motivation is most frequently used in the treatment phase, it is also important in assessment. Anything that the clinician can do in the early stages to help the patient "see the light at the end of tunnel" will enhance motivation for change and energize the patient toward investing in recovery.

Treatment Matching

After determining the degree of abuse or dependence, the coexisting psychiatric conditions, the level of readiness for change, and the patient's own treatment goals, the clinician can match the patient to an appropriate level of care and treatment setting. This is discussed in Chapter 4. The clinician should state in specific terms the recommended treatment, the appropriate setting, the frequency, and who is responsible. The level of care should match the needs of the patient. For example, a crack-cocaine addict desiring to achieve abstinence may experience such intense cravings that an inpatient or residential setting is necessary to allow the initial cravings to subside before the individual enters a partial hospitalization or intensive outpatient program.

PROFESSIONAL CAUTION

One professional caution is in order. Therapists risk colluding with the patient when they continue to work with patients and fail to maintain a focus on the substance-using behavior as a top priority. The therapist need not discontinue therapy with the majority of patients, even those who are drinking and abusing drugs. The therapist must assess, however, when he or she is becoming a part of the dysfunctional system surrounding the substance user. For example, an employer refers a man for assessment; the individual reports to his boss that he sees the professional in ongoing treatment but continues to abuse drugs. Over time it becomes apparent that the patient has no intention of stopping drug use. The most difficult part of an addiction assessment may be knowing when to step back and set a limit. Continuing psychotherapy in the absence of a commitment to sobriety may not be helpful to the AOD-abusing patient.

CONCLUSION

Assessment is something much more than putting together pieces of a puzzle such that a diagnosis emerges and the patient is told the nature and the severity of his or her disorder. An effective assessment pinpoints severity and risk factors through diagnostic interviews and structured instruments, makes connections between drug-using and drinking behavior and negative consequences, determines the patient's readiness for change, enhances motivation for further change, and engages the patient in a process of mutual exploration.

At the end of the assessment process the clinician wishes to leave the patient with a sense of hope. The resistance that individuals experience on diagnosis of alcoholism or addiction comes from an overwhelming hopelessness about the outcome. When this despair arises, the therapist must counter with an attitude and words of hope. Often, contact with other recovering individuals helps the patient to see the continuum from withdrawal to ongoing recovery, from the most difficult and frightening of times to a most rewarding and self-enhancing process.

4

Determining Appropriate Treatment

This chapter reviews the treatment options in the continuum of care and offers guidelines for selecting appropriate services. There is a remarkably wide range of activities and interventions in the substance abuse treatment field, and it is likely that psychologists will use only a few, depending on their own base of activity. However, it is important to appreciate the range of possibilities if for no other reason than to give a perspective for referral. This chapter examines how major models and modalities arose, their assumptions about how people change, key interventions or activities, sources of information and data evaluating the effectiveness of the model, and the strengths and limits of each model.

Some of the treatment settings are more accessible to working people with insurance, whereas others are funded by federal or state governments for the indigent population. Ironically, the latter may offer highly innovative programs (e.g., long-term residential programs for mothers and their children) not usually available to the middle class or even the very wealthy. In general, long-term programs are more common where the target population is indigent, because the clients have fewer interpersonal, social, and vocational skills to reclaim. Thus, they are more likely to need "habilitation" rather than rehabilitation. However, these distinctions may blur in practice. Many clients in public sector programs were originally working class or middle-class professionals but downwardly mobile because of their alcohol and drug use, and they return to a working- or middle-class lifestyle once in recovery.

TREATMENT SETTINGS AND MODALITIES

Substance abuse treatment occurs in both inpatient/residential and out-patient settings but has a unique variety of modalities. These range from specialty clinics that use medications as an integral part of addiction treatment to social model programs that rely heavily on recovering peers. It is important for clinicians outside the addiction treatment system to understand these modalities in order to make effective referrals.

Residential/Inpatient Treatment

Live-in programs include a range of treatment environments in which there is 24-hour supervision, thereby offering a protected setting in which the client or patient is insulated to some extent from the triggers and stressors of drug use. These may be hospital based, such as inpatient programs offering medical interventions (e.g., medically managed withdrawal) as well as programming aimed at psychosocial issues. The term *residential* is applied to a wide range of programs that exist outside medical settings as free-standing programs of variable duration, using a variety of approaches. These include therapeutic communities, inpatient programs, and social model recovery homes.

Therapeutic Communities

Therapeutic communities (TCs) are long-term residential programs that emerged in the 1960s as an alternative treatment for heroin addiction. They are based on a self-help model developed by Synanon founder Charles Dederich and a group of recovering alcohol- and drug-addicted members, with major influences from Alcoholics Anonymous (AA) and religious healing communities dating back a considerable period of time (Deitch, 1973; de Leon, 1994a). Over time, the resident population diversified and professionals were integrated. Currently, there are a wide range of settings, a variety of lengths of stay, and numerous adaptations that may or may not conform to the therapeutic community model. Two of the best-known programs are Daytop and Phoenix House.

The traditional, long-term residential programs have been studied continuously since their inception. Although it does not appear possible to conduct randomized, blind clinical trials, the empirical data support the conclusion that TCs result in the positive outcomes of reduction of illicit drug use and other criminal activity and an increase in economically productive behavior and other measures of positive outcome (Gerstein, 1994; Gerstein & Harwood, 1990). Newer adaptations, such as programs serving the severely mentally ill or adaptations of the model for outpatient settings, have been demonstrated to be effective for these challenging populations (Sacks & Ries, 2005).

In the TC model, drug abuse is viewed as a disorder of the whole person, which can affect some or all of the person's functioning (de Leon, 1994a). Thus, the intervention must be comprehensive, addressing in particular those psychological difficulties or social deficits that undermine the ability to maintain a drug-free lifestyle. Indeed, TCs are often said to promote habilitation rather than rehabilitation because residents frequently had never acquired prosocial attitudes and skills. Therefore, the program must develop qualities in its members that were never there, instead of reclaiming those that were temporarily lost. Recovery entails a shift in personal identity as well as lifestyle. The essential ingredient in change is affiliation, with the community as the primary agent.

George de Leon (1994b) elaborated in detail the essential concepts in using community as a method. Individuals contribute directly to all activities of daily life in the TC, which provides learning opportunities through engaging in a variety of social roles (e.g., peer, friend, coordinator, tutor). The primary sources of instruction and support for individual change are the observations and authentic reactions by peers. In addition, each member of the community has the responsibility of serving as a role model to peers. Collective formats guide individual change. Individual sessions, though they may be available, are viewed as adjuncts to the group activities. Education, training, and therapeutic activities occur in groups, meetings, seminars, job functions, and recreation. Beliefs and values stressing "right living" are explicit guidelines and are expressed in the vernacular and culture of each TC. "Act as if you are a responsible person and you can grow into it."

Open communication of private thoughts and feelings is an essential feature of the TC. Relationships with particular individuals, peers, and staff are essential to encourage the individual to engage and remain in the change process. These relationships are also the basis for the social network needed to sustain recovery beyond treatment. The organization of the work (e.g., the varied job functions, chores, and management roles) needed to maintain the daily operations of the facility is a primary vehicle for teaching self-development. Learning occurs not only through specific skills training but also through adhering to the orderliness of procedures and systems, through accepting and respecting supervision, and through behaving as a responsible member of the community on whom others are dependent.

TCs typically define stages of treatment: orientation–induction, primary treatment, and reentry. In contrast to the assumption that treatment readiness can be quickly assessed, TCs assume the initial period will clarify such issues as the resident becomes a participant in the activities of the community. Ambivalence is a given, and the orientation period (0–60 days) is designed to assimilate the individual and promote understanding and acceptance of the TC's norms. The isolation of the individual from the wider community, often a source of misunderstanding by professionals and significant others, is designed to bond the resident to the community by eliminating outside influences as much as possible. Dropout is greatest during this early period. Primary treatment (2–12 months) consists of educational and therapeutic meetings, groups, job functions, and peer and staff feedback. As residents display an understanding and acceptance of both the TC perspective and the daily regimen, they ascend in status and privileges in the leadership structure of the community, including job hierarchies. In this way, at the end of their stay in primary treatment, they set an example for others. Additional privileges include things such as greater privacy and desirable job responsibilities. The therapeutic process takes place in all facets of community life, from groups specially designed to focus on psychological issues (e.g., traumatic experiences, sex-role identity and conflicts) to job performance in which the feedback process is ongoing.

The reentry process prepares the individual for more autonomous functioning at a future time when he or she will no longer be in direct contact with the TC. Typically there is a reduction in structure, and the resident progresses to a looser form of affiliation. Many TCs offer gradations such as satellite apartments, in which residents who shared the common program experience live together without program supervision. In this way, the culture of the TC is transplanted into the wider community setting so that gradual transitions can promote stable progress.

Common stereotypes of the TC assume harsh confrontation, a feature of the original Synanon model that has evolved in productive directions in the more mature TC systems. In the 1970s, more participation by professionals led to the introduction of gestalt techniques, cognitive–behavioral strategies, and other approaches intended to broaden the repertoire of tools. Most TCs also endorse a family model in which the community is seen as a substitute family, often an improved version of what residents may have experienced in childhood. The TC family participates in holiday rituals and graduation for those who complete the program and offers support and caring as the context for exploration of difficult issues. Certainly TCs vary in the extent to which they establish a healthy and positive climate, but there are many examples in which the family spirit is vigorous, and the TC provides a culture for all involved that is more cohesive and inspiring than many available in the fragmented world of the typical addicted individual.

The Minnesota Model

The dominant paradigm for short-term inpatient treatment was developed in Minnesota during the 1950s at the fledgling facilities of Hazelden and Willmar (McElrath, 1997). Prior to that time, the prevailing belief that alcoholism was a psychological vulnerability to be treated in mental health units had failed to produce effective treatment. Guided by their successful experiences in AA, the founders of Hazelden and Willmar adapted these principles to create a new treatment model and brought it into hospital-based treatment. Over time, proponents of the model refined their treatment practices and restructured institutional relationships to emphasize the collaboration between professionals and noncredentialed recovering persons. By 1954, nondegreed counselors on alcoholism, usually recovering alcoholics, shared the responsibility and decision making for the treatment. Subsequently, national and state certification programs established training standards and document completion by counselors without graduate or undergraduate degrees. There are also an increasing number of licensed professionals in recovery in clinical and administrative roles.

The essential features of the model are its goals of complete abstinence and behavior change, its intimate link with the 12-step process of AA (discussed in more detail in Chapter 8) and program participation, and its multidisciplinary approach (McElrath, 1997). The Minnesota model became the prototype for hospital-based inpatient programs. McElrath (1997) described the key elements as follows:

- the grace of a beautiful environment that promotes respect, under-standing, and acceptance of the dignity of each patient;
- a treatment based essentially on the program and process of AA;
- the belief that a respite from the familiar environment and association with other alcoholics is central to recovery;
- simple behavioral expectations, including making your bed, comporting yourself "as a gentleman [sic]," attending the daily lectures on the 12 steps, and talking with one another;
- a multidisciplinary team approach;
- a systematic approach to the treatment of an illness defined as a primary disorder distinct from mental illness; and
- the need for and value of an aftercare program.

With many contributions from others, a model was developed and dis-seminated that viewed recovery as a physical, psychosocial, and spiritual process with recovering personnel as the primary element in delivering the service.

The term *chemical dependency* emerged during the cocaine epidemic and was extended to apply to all mood-altering drugs. Although this term is still used, it is not necessarily accepted by providers in other treatment modalities. Differences in historical origin and in populations served (e.g., heroin users on methadone maintenance) make the term alien to some providers; hence, it should not be assumed to be generic to addiction treatment.

A practical decision based on seasoned clinical opinion, but no data, shaped the modality for decades to come. McElrath (1997) reported that in the mid-1970s, when the state of Minnesota asked how much time was necessary to treat alcoholics, the response was "at least a month." With the subsequent mandate of 28 days of insurance coverage in the 1970s, the Minnesota model became more defined and proliferated. In McElrath's (1997) opinion, the huge expansion of inpatient programs in the 1980s also fostered a certain rigidity as incidental elements (e.g., the 28-day duration of treatment) diminished treatment innovation and creativity.

Much controversy existed about the necessity for 28-day rehabilitation programs even before the period of their rapid demise as a result of changing insurance reimbursement policies. Several decades of studies yielded equivocal results, partly because of inadequate methodological strategies. Within the private sector, the Chemical Abuse/Addiction Treatment Outcome Registry (CATOR) was developed to document positive outcomes. This private Minnesota corporation contracted with treatment programs to track individual patients. Data were collected during treatment and transmitted to CATOR, which conducted and reported on the follow-ups (Institute of Medicine, 1990). Although these data are useful in exploring treatment issues, the information is often used in marketing efforts without adequate cautions that it is unwarranted to assume that a positive outcome reflects treatment efficacy. For example, studies following a matched sample concluded that given certain patient characteristics, improvement will follow minimal or no intervention as well as intensive intervention. A well-known review of outcome data comparing inpatients and outpatients concluded that, in general, the data did not justify costly inpatient treatment (W. R. Miller & Hester, 1986). However, intensive treatment may be differentially beneficial for those who are more severely deteriorated and less socially stable; these are not the individuals who have ready access to such programs. Randomized controlled trials provide the most rigorous means of evaluating outcome, but they are expensive, time consuming to conduct, and may be precluded by ethical concerns.

Meanwhile, managed care companies established in the 1980s to contain rapidly escalating costs dramatically reduced access to inpatient treatment and shifted the emphasis to outpatient modalities (Rawson, 1990–91). Researchers are in the process of clarifying questions of how to match people to programs or treatments, such as criteria for intensive services, and guidelines are rapidly evolving and being refined. In the 1990s and beyond, growing acknowledgement of the prevalence of co-occurring psychiatric disorders led to the integration of services at the clinical level, despite difficulties with funding mechanisms. In addition, the growing emphasis on implementing evidence-based practices brought a questioning of rigid ideological positions in favor of utilization of data to improve outcomes (W. R. Miller, Zweben, & Johnson, 2005). Studies do support the efficacy of AA-based treatment (Project MATCH Research Group, 1997), but many of these programs in the community incorporate a variety of approaches, although they may emphasize their allegiance to the 12-step model.

The Social Model and Other Environmental Approaches

Social and community model approaches represent an important influence on a variety of treatment and prevention activities. They can form the basis of complete programs, or they can be components or elements in other types of programs. The goals of social model programs are to provide recovering people with alternative social environments that support recovery and to promote changes in larger communities to prevent alcohol problems and support abstinence-based recovery (Dodd, 1997). Emphasis is on the micro and macro community rather than on the individual, who is generally the focus of clinical model programs.

The characteristics of social model programs are summarized as follows (Wright, Clay, & Weir, 1990):

- Experiential knowledge about recovery is the basis of authority.
- The primary therapeutic relationship is between the person and the program rather than between the person and a staff member, therapist, or other professional.
- The program is peer oriented, and hierarchy is minimized.
- The fundamental framework is derived from AA principles and emphasizes the values of honesty, tolerance, willingness to try, and emphasis on helping others. In addition, social model programs endeavor to make good use of community resources such as public health clinics, social services, therapists, and any other activities that benefit participants.
- A positive sober environment is crucial, with clean, homelike, comfortable surroundings setting the tone.
- Alcohol problems are not only individual problems but are also defined in terms of families, communities, and the larger society.

The range of social model programs includes social setting detoxification, alcohol recovery homes (short- and long-term; also referred to as *halfway houses*), and community recovery centers. Social model detoxification programs were developed initially at the Addiction Research Foundation in Canada in 1970, and shortly thereafter a model was opened as a demonstration in Stockton, California. The goal was to create a system to provide services to intoxicated people in crisis or emergency situations when there was no medical indication for costly hospitalization or outpatient medical management. This system was also designed to foster appropriate use of alcoholism programs and other community agencies, organizing the referral process and creating a continuum of care in a network of community services. Consistent with the larger social model perspective, the physical setting and environment were designed to protect the alcoholic from the stigma frequently encountered in other settings and to promote constructive behavior changes. "Sobering centers" provide a comfortable and supportive environment for those withdrawing from alcohol. Medication is not used in most of these settings, but staff members are trained to observe warning signs of potential problems. Linkages with hospitals permit immediate transfer in the case of medical complications (O'Bryant & Peterson, 1990).

Alcohol recovery homes surround the alcoholic with a community that supports the lifestyle changes needed to promote recovery. Like therapeutic communities, residents participate fully in the operation of the home, but the atmosphere of recovery homes tends to be less structured and less confrontational. The presence of role models and community reinforcement are key change factors. Peer influence, rather than control by the social service, health care, or criminal justice systems, is the dominant force.

Community recovery centers are another form of social model program that may include the sobering services and residential services described earlier and also a wide range of other activities identified as useful to support recovery. Typically center staff are knowledgeable about community resources and also willing to devise strategies to create resources that are needed but do not currently exist. They view themselves as "guides" rather than case managers, coaching participants in the appropriate use of resources outside the program itself. Other activities include discussion groups on specific topics such as parenting skills, stress reduction, women's issues, and recreational activities designed to promote clean and sober fun, especially during weekends, holidays, and other times when recreation was previously organized around drinking. Centers also create a comfortable environment to provide unstructured opportunities to relax and meet people in a friendly, undemanding, alcohol-free setting (Wright et al., 1990). These centers provide important safe havens in drug-infested inner cities.

The great contribution of social model programs is to emphasize, by example, the importance of the support system outside the boundaries of professional treatment. In many cases, this may be entirely adequate to promote the transition to an alcohol- and drug-free lifestyle. Clinicians may forget that we see a subgroup of people in distress; there are many who find the path to healing outside professional treatment. For those who use professional assistance, social model programs provide a context for that effort with the potential to greatly amplify the impact of the treatment effort. It is also a model with applicability to mental health and other social problems.

Outpatient Treatment

Outpatient treatment programs can be brief or long term and can stand alone or be integrated into larger medical systems or attached to residential programs. Their labels do not have consistent meanings, and it is important for clinicians making referrals to inquire about the availability of specific services, for example, medications for psychiatric conditions. Because of the focus on cost savings in the private sector and the lack of resources in the public sector, appropriate services may not always be available.

Outpatient/Intensive, Outpatient/Partial Hospitalization

Throughout the 1980s, 28-day programs dominated the landscape for insured populations, and outpatient treatment was viewed as "second best." Under pressure to offer a service that was less disruptive to employed patients, short-term outpatient models were developed, often by scaling down the inpatient version and offering programming for 3 to 4 hours on weekday evenings. These programs typically lasted 5 to 8 weeks, following which the patient participated in aftercare of considerably reduced intensity. In the sector serving the indigent population, outpatient programs were of longer duration and increased their range of services as the Center for Substance Abuse Treatment appeared in 1990 and began to encourage the provision of comprehensive services. Current outpatient programs vary considerably in content, intensity, and duration. The lack of standardization in program design (e.g., the same program may be called *intensive outpatient* or *partial hospitalization* by different providers) and evaluation methodology makes it difficult to identify effective ingredients. However, with the development of patient placement criteria (PPC) by the American Society of Addiction Medicine (ASAM; 2001), greater consistency in definitions can promote research efforts. For example, a matching study using a computerized version of the PPC indicated that mismatching patients to a lower level of care may be associated with excessive hospital use (Sharon et al., 2003).

Despite the variety of programs available, ASAM offers general guidelines. *Level I outpatient treatment* is described as a professionally directed alcohol and other drug (AOD) treatment occurring in regularly scheduled sessions usually totaling fewer than 9 hours a week. It consists of a combination of individual and group sessions in conjunction with self-help group participation. *Level II intensive outpatient treatment* (also referred to as *partial hospitalization* or *day treatment*) is a more structured program with a minimum of 9 hours of treatment a week. Patients can live at home or in special residences supervised to ensure they remain clean and sober (ASAM, 2001). Program sites include hospital-based facilities, homeless shelters, and community-based organizations. PPC are discussed in more detail later.

Opioid Maintenance Treatment

Methadone maintenance is a major treatment modality for opioid users who have tried abstinence but not succeeded. Initially it was offered to heroin users, but the rise of prescription opiate abuse in the past decade has brought a new group of patients to methadone maintenance. It is considered the last resort for "intractable" heroin addicts. In the mid-1960s, the upsurge of heroin addiction and its higher visibility in young (15–35 years old) and middle-class populations led to increased federal efforts to develop effective treatment modalities. This era produced the resources to establish, proliferate, and study both methadone maintenance and therapeutic communities, which have been the subject of continuous study since that time. As of 2007, there were approximately 262,684 patients in methadone maintenance treatment in 1,200 programs across the country (Substance Abuse and Mental Health Services Administration, 2008), more than twice as many as reported in the first edition of this book.

Methadone maintenance treatment (MMT) was developed in the mid-1960s by two physicians, Vincent Dole and Marie Nyswander, who postulated that a metabolic defect accounted for the inability of heroin addicts to remain abstinent for more than brief periods of time and intended for methadone to be used indefinitely as a corrective medication. As methadone was being formally approved for clinical use, professional and public opinion shifted to a new goal: to use it to transition heroin users to a drug-free lifestyle. Once this was accomplished, methadone was to be discontinued. Research in the following decades indicated that fewer than 20% of those who are on methadone will be able to discontinue methadone and remain drug free (Zweben & Payte, 1990).

In work for which he won the Lasker Award, Dole (1988) postulated that a receptor system dysfunction resulting from chronic heroin use leads to permanent alterations, which the clinical community does not now have the means to reverse. Thus, indefinite maintenance is corrective but not curative, in much the same way that thyroid or insulin replacement normalizes body functioning. Studies have indicated that methadone is a relatively benign medication that shows stability of receptor occupation and thus permits interacting systems to function normally (Martin, Zweben, & Payte, 2009). It is this stability that results in evenness in functioning. This distinguishes it from heroin, a short-acting narcotic producing rapid changes that make a stable state of adaptation impossible. A user maintained on heroin would go through 4-hour cycles of intoxication and withdrawal; even if supplied with a clean and legal source, the short duration of action makes heroin undesirable as a maintenance drug. Even with long-term use (20 years or more), methadone continues to have a withdrawal prevention effect in which patients do not experience craving or other withdrawal phenomena and are able to function normally without somnolence (Martin et al., 2009).

MMT in combination with educational, medical, and counseling services has been thoroughly documented to assist patients in reducing or discontinuing illicit drug use and associated criminal activity, improving physical and emotional well-being, becoming responsible family members, furthering their education, obtaining and maintaining stable employment, and resuming or establishing a productive lifestyle (Gerstein & Harwood, 1990; Hubbard et al., 1989). Despite 3 decades of research confirming its value and safety, MMT remains perhaps the most stigmatized of all drug treatment modalities and the one that is least understood (Murphy & Irwin, 1992). It remains a source of contention among treatment providers, the general public, and health care policymakers. After a long period of isolation from other forms of treatment and recovery interventions, the AIDS epidemic stimulated a reexamination and renewed interest in this modality. MMT has been demonstrated through education, reduced needle use, and increased safer sex practices to slow the spread of HIV disease and to slow the progression of the disease in those who have contracted it (Batki & Selwin, 2000). On closer examination, the "controversies" about MMT usually reflect several common misunderstandings rather than a difference of opinion between informed parties.

One primary source of opposition is the notion that use of methadone is "just substituting one addicting drug for another." This notion is often shared by the patients themselves, who may lack information and have usually internalized the stigma. Technically, this is correct; MMT is drug replacement therapy in which a long-acting, orally administered medication is substituted for a short-acting illicit opioid that is used intravenously. These differences have significant consequences. The long duration of methadone's action (24–36 hours) allows most patients to receive a daily dose and function in a stable manner because their blood level remains relatively constant. This stands in contrast to the 4-hour cycles of euphoria and withdrawal that are characteristic of heroin use. It is this feature that promotes lifestyle changes by permitting normal functioning.

In addition, there is widespread misconception among both the public and professionals about what constitutes addiction. Addiction treatment professionals increasingly distinguish between physical dependence and addiction (see Chapter 2, this volume). Physical dependence itself is a factor to be considered but one that in and of itself does not constitute addiction, which is characterized by behavior that is compulsive, out of control, and persists despite adverse consequences. The key question is whether functioning is improved or impaired by use. Benzodiazepines are an example of a medication that is dependence-producing at therapeutic doses but that can be used beneficially for long periods for people with anxiety disorders. Patients with chronic pain are another example in which assessment focuses on whether the patient's functioning is improved or impaired rather than on physical dependence itself as the deciding factor.

Another common misconception is that "methadone keeps you high," which reflects misunderstanding of a properly adjusted dose. While a patient's dose is being stabilized, he or she may experience some subjective effects, but these usually diminish or disappear once stabilized. This is precisely why methadone is a good tool: Once stabilization is achieved, the patient should be able to function normally.

Extensive research on safety has indicated that long-term use of methadone results in no physical or psychological impairment of any kind that can be perceived by the patient, observed by a physician, or detected by a scientist (Zweben & Payte, 1990). There is no impairment of balance, coordination, mental abilities, eye–hand coordination, depth perception, or psychomotor functioning. Patients on methadone who are identified through workplace drug testing and threatened with negative consequences have succeeded, through advocacy efforts, in maintaining their jobs; the Americans with Disabilities Act of 1990 contributes to their protection.

Because of historical disputes and political controversies, the current treatment system is overburdened by regulations and inappropriate expectations (Rettig & Yarmolinsky, 1995), producing a delivery system so dehumanizing that programs usually make efforts to assist the patient wishing to taper off methadone. However, it is important to remember that studies have indicated that although it is common for patients to remain opiate-free for a short time, relapse is the norm for 80% or more (Ball & Ross, 1991; McLellan, 1983). Because a history of treatment failures is required, only a subset of opiate users qualify for methadone maintenance, and it is likely that neurobiological factors significantly raise the vulnerability to becoming addicted to opiates (Dole, 1988). High motivation is necessary, but not sufficient, for successfully tapering off methadone. It is unfortunately common for uninformed professionals, family members, and others to encourage or coerce patients on methadone to discontinue their medication (Zweben & Payte, 1990). The decision to taper should be made by the patient in collaboration with professionals experienced in methadone treatment and should not be based on bias against this medication. The relapse rates of methadone users are so extraordinarily high that the risks are considerable. Therapists should be cautious about encouraging a patient to discontinue methadone maintenance because pressure is often applied by the family or by other treatment providers on the basis of stigma instead of careful review of the case. The results of misguided interventions such as these can be lethal. Therapists dealing with patients on methadone who continue to use opiates should first rule out the possibility of an inadequate dose of methadone, because this can occur for a variety of reasons. The usual dose range is between 60 and 100 mg daily, with more being required for some patients. Once the medication dose is adequate, the yield is much greater for psychosocial intervention.

The majority of patients in the MMT system are indigent or working class; of these, many are downwardly mobile from the middle class as a result of their drug and alcohol use. However, depending on clinic location, there may be surprising numbers of successful and high-functioning individuals who conceal their participation in MMT from colleagues and even family members. Prescription drug abusers are increasingly represented in this group. It is possible that under better circumstances, MMT would be the treatment of choice for multiple relapsing opioid users with more middle-class characteristics.

Clinicians have observed such patients who flounder for long periods, unable to maintain abstinence, or who substitute alcohol and deteriorate. The addiction treatment programs in which they were likely to seek treatment often claimed an expertise they did not possess in treating opiate users, particularly heroin users, and they lacked long-term follow-up studies to assess the efficacy of their efforts. Such patients report being highly stigmatized by the more populous cocaine users because their drug preference was heroin, and they report being labeled "more disturbed" by treatment staff. An Empire Blue Cross and Blue Shield (EBCBS) study concluded there is a large population of opiate users who may be excluded from the estimates of overall number of opiate users because they are less likely to be counted by contact with government agencies (Eisenhandler & Drucker, 1993). They estimated that between 1982 and 1992, EBCBS (New York metropolitan area) insured approximately 141,000 opiate users,

85,000 of whom were insured with them at the time of the study. They recommended that the social characteristics of opiate users should be reconsidered because many middle-class heroin users may be overlooked and undertreated.

Despite progress in removing regulatory barriers and addressing stigma, the use of methadone remains highly charged. Illicit use of oxycodone (OxyContin) has led to high death rates in some states, resulting in physicians shifting to methadone as a way to manage pain. This in turn led to increased quantities available for street sale, with a predictable increase in deaths, especially when it is used with other substances (Cone et al., 2003; Cone et al., 2004). In addition, a rapid increase in nonmedical use of opiate medications beginning about 1995 has brought new populations into treatment (Wunsch, Boyd, & McMasters, 2009). Many of these would not consider, or do not have access to, methadone treatment. In this context, buprenorphine was a welcome new addition to the tools available to practitioners.

Buprenorphine is a partial opioid agonist that became available through the Drug Addiction Treatment Act of 2000. It binds to the receptor but has less strength than a full agonist such as methadone. However, buprenorphine binds tightly to the receptor (high affinity), blocking the action of heroin or other opiates if they are used. This has given it a significant advantage of a high margin of safety with little chance of a lethal overdose. The ceiling on agonist activity reduces the danger of overdose as well as the abuse liability (Fudala & O'Brien, 2005; Stine, Greenwald, & Kosten, 2003). For example, there is much less chance of severe drug-induced respiratory depression with buprenorphine. Because of this, the U.S. Food and Drug Administration permitted its administration in office settings (rather than specially licensed clinics) by qualified physicians who have completed the educational requirements to be granted a waiver. This opened the door to widespread use by patients who find methadone, or the settings in which it can be obtained to treat addiction, to be unacceptable.

It is important for clinicians providing psychosocial treatment to recognize that patients with a high opiate tolerance may find buprenorphine inadequate to control their symptoms because of the inherent dose ceiling.

They may experience significantly better results with methadone, though they may be resistant to trying it. It is difficult for some patients and therapists alike to accept that motivation is important, but brain chemistry has a profound influence on outcomes, including the influence on the efficacy of psychosocial interventions. It is easy to criticize opiate users for being inconsistent in their motivation or unwilling to make full use of therapy or the self-help system. However, many have been given poor advice by professionals, including those in the addiction field, and have lost years or decades in repeated struggles with relapse. High-prestige treatment settings may be the least conducive to raising the possibility of using an opioid agonist or may fasten on buprenorphine as the only acceptable medication and for short term use only. Ultimately, it is important to acknowledge that long-term maintenance on buprenorphine may be necessary for many patients who hope that detoxification will be enough.

Smoking Cessation

Smoking cessation was initially offered mainly in primary health care settings or by smoking cessation specialists and remained relatively unintegrated with the rest of the addiction field. Attention began to focus on it in the mid-1980s, as reflected in Wallace's (1986) editorial "Smoke Gets in Our Eyes: Professional Denial of Smoking." He challenged the minimization of health consequences and the complacency about addressing it, especially given the high percentage of smokers among patients in treatment for addiction. He also noted that the prevalence of smokers among recovering staff members presented a troublesome role model and constituted a source of resistance to no-smoking policies. Since that time, research has documented the significantly higher frequency of smoking among alcoholics and polydrug users, established that smoking cessation does not in itself increase relapse as previously feared, and refined intervention techniques to promote success (Jarvik & Schneider, 1992). Smoking cessation has become much more integrated into addiction treatment and also continues to be provided by health care organizations and private practitioners. As insurers and the government focus on the many costs associated with smoking-related illnesses, one can expect increasing support for identification and treatment outside addiction treatment settings as well. In addition, recent magnetic resonance imaging studies suggest that neurobiological recovery in abstinent alcoholics is adversely affected by chronic smoking (Durazzo, Gazdzinski, & Meyerhoff, 2007), thus providing added incentives for clinicians to promote smoking cessation as a part of addiction treatment.

Short-term behavioral therapies have long been prominent in smoking cessation. Many are able to achieve high initial cessation rates, but success rates at 1 year averaged 15% to 30%, unrelated to the initial quit rates (Jarvik & Schneider, 1992). This may be related to a lack of emphasis on relapse prevention. The behavioral strategies that are effective in initiating abstinence are different from those needed to maintain it, and reliance on short-term treatment makes it less likely that long-term maintenance strategies will be provided at the time they actually become relevant.

The recent development of effective pharmacological withdrawal agents has been shown to greatly augment the success of behavioral strategies (Fiore et al., 2008). Nicotine dependence and craving varies among smokers, and these agents significantly decrease discomfort. Nicotine replacement in the forms of transdermal patches, sublingual nicotine tablets and lozenges, nasal spray, and inhalers are available. Bupropion (Zyban) is a nonnicotine product that is effective in promoting abstinence and reducing relapse (Hurt, Ebbert, Hays, & Dale, 2003). Varenicline (Chantix) is a partial agonist that reduces cravings and decreases the pleasurable effects of smoking. Clinicians are enthusiastic about the results of its use. The Smoking Cessation Guidelines from the federal Agency for Health Care Research and Quality (Fiore et al., 2008) summarize the issues pertaining to selection and application of both pharmacological and psychosocial treatments. Studies have supported the view that combination therapies show greater effectiveness than pharmacotherapy or behavioral interventions alone. Social support is a key element in smoking cessation, as with other drugs; thus, the proliferation of antismoking regulations at the work site and in other public settings will likely improve treatment success rates.

Psychiatric comorbidity has emerged as a key element in successful smoking cessation; therefore, treatment planning should take this into account. Strong relationships have been reported between depression and smoking. In the early 1990s, Glassman (1993) reported that both major depression and depressive symptoms are associated with a high rate of cigarette smoking, and lifetime history of major depression has an adverse impact on smoking cessation. In this vulnerable group, there is also a significantly higher likelihood of the patient developing a depressed mood during the first week of withdrawal, and the entire withdrawal syndrome was more severe. Emergence of depressive symptoms predicts failure of the attempt to quit. Therefore, it is important that the clinician assess depression and include appropriate interventions in the treatment plan. For example, it may be advisable to wait until the patient has been stabilized on antidepressant medication before encouraging action on quitting. A variety of behavioral strategies designed to enhance affect regulation have also been demonstrated to be effective for this group (Kahler, Leventhal, & Brown, 2009).

Clinicians working with patients with schizophrenia have a more complex dilemma. Although the serious health risks are indisputable, it appears that nicotine confers some benefits that must be considered in smoking cessation efforts. Reviews have noted the high rates of smoking among people with schizophrenia: between 74% and 92%, compared with 35% to 54% for all psychiatric patients and 30% to 35% for the general population (Goff, Henderson, & Amico, 1992). Current smokers with schizophrenia received significantly higher neuroleptic doses and displayed less parkinsonism and more akathisia (i.e., restless movements induced by neuroleptics). Patients reported that it produces relaxation, reduces anxiety, reduces medication side effects, and ameliorates psychiatric symptoms (Goff et al., 1992). It has been postulated that nicotine provides transient symptomatic relief through stimulation of cholinergic nicotinic receptors, enhancing the gating mechanism that permits patients to filter out irrelevant stimuli (Freedman et al., 1994). Thus, efforts to promote smoking cessation in people with schizophrenia, especially abruptly when they enter smoke-free hospital environments, must take into account these complex considerations. Success will likely depend on a better understanding of the mechanisms of the positive benefits of smoking and development of alternatives (e.g., transdermal patches for nicotine maintenance).

In summary, the wide recognition of health consequences for smokers and those around them, along with stricter laws targeting smoking, will likely result in increasing demand for assistance, in which both clinicians and researchers will play an active role.

Psychotherapy in the Treatment of Addiction

Although psychotherapy alone is not usually considered an appropriate treatment for addiction, in reality many therapists in the community diagnose and attempt to address addictive behaviors ranging from mild to severe. Increasingly, they combine their efforts with a referral or insistence on AA or Narcotics Anonymous attendance. For many, the issue of drinking and using is given priority and the combination of psychotherapy with self-help group participation is considered adequate, although there is no referral to formal addiction treatment. There are no empirical data on how often this process occurs and how effective it is. Many addiction specialists view the community therapist as being in a prime position to do effective early intervention, arresting problems before serious deterioration occurs. However, it is also apparent that some therapists in the community are not sufficiently concerned about lack of progress in changing behavior. They do not inquire regularly about AOD use unless there has been a recent crisis. It would be valuable to study this therapeutic process in more detail, defining parameters for effective intervention in this context, looking at outcome, and formulating guidelines for when referral to the specialty system is advisable.

TREATMENT IN THE CRIMINAL JUSTICE SYSTEM

The greatest expansion of addiction treatment services is occurring in the criminal justice sector, which is rapidly becoming a major employer of professionals. Treatment monies are diminishing steadily in the health care system and increasing in the criminal justice system. As managed care creates discouraging work conditions, increasing numbers of professionals are migrating into the criminal justice sector, where they face new challenges to provide appropriate care.

The majority of those incarcerated have an alcohol and/or drug problem to which their offenses are directly or indirectly related (Office of National Drug Control Policy, 2010). It is estimated that 70% of inmates in state prisons and 80% in federal institutions are serving time on charges related to drug trafficking and possession (Robert Wood Johnson Foundation, 2001). Criminal justice system interventions take place both in the community and inside the institutions. Various forms of intervention have been developed for different targets in the criminal justice system. These include pretrial and diversion efforts after arrest and before trial, treatment inside jails and prisons, and community treatment for probationers and parolees (Peters & Wexler, 2005).

It has been known for some time that treatment is effective in reducing recidivism. A rigorous review by the Institute of Medicine in 1990 suggested that despite disappointing findings in the overall research literature on prison-based treatment, addiction treatment programs that are sufficiently comprehensive and well-integrated into the criminal justice system do achieve a significant reduction in recidivism (Anglin & Hser, 1991; Gerstein & Harwood, 1990; Vigdal, 1995). The therapeutic community movement has been particularly influential in prison treatment, partly because of outcome data supporting effectiveness and partly because its tight structure makes it more acceptable to corrections personnel than more loosely structured models. Appropriate treatment in prison leads to reduced drug use on release and fewer arrests and episodes of reincarceration (Field, 1989; Wexler, Falkin, & Lipton, 1992). Best results are obtained when there is a relatively seamless transition into community treatment (Field, 1998; Hubbard et al., 1989; Wexler, de Leon, Thomas, Kressel, & Peters, 1999).

A growing number of states have enacted legislation and provided funding for treatment in lieu of incarceration. Drug courts and other diversion initiatives represent ways to use the criminal justice system to promote initiation, engagement, and retention in a treatment effort. Studies have supported the benefit of mandated treatment in improving outcomes (Kelly, Finney, & Moos, 2005).

Efforts to use the leverage of the criminal justice system to promote outpatient treatment efforts began in the 1960s with the Civil Addict Program, which committed addicted people to compulsory drug treatment (Anglin & Hser, 1991; Vigdal, 1995). More recently, there has been a rapid expansion of special problem-solving courts requiring participating in treatment, monitoring it closely, and applying sanctions for noncompliance and rewards for progress. Drug courts began in Miami, Florida, in 1989 and have spread throughout the United States and abroad. Outcome data have supported their effectiveness (Huddleston, Marlowe, & Casebolt, 2008). The drug court model has been expanded to include other types of problem-solving courts, such as those centered on mental health, domestic violence, truancy, veterans, and many other problems (see http://www.ncsconline.org/D_Research/ProblemSolvingCourts/Resources.html). In these models, the courts collaborate with community treatment providers to integrate the treatment with legal case processing. Other community corrections programs include contracts with the criminal justice system to purchase residential beds or outpatient capacity outside the institutions.

Findings about the success of coerced treatment are particularly important in the light of a belief on the part of many professionals that such treatment does not work. In fact, in addiction treatment, retention is the variable most highly correlated with a positive outcome. Those who remain in treatment longer than 6 months look similar, independent of whether the treatment attempt was initiated voluntarily or through legal coercion. Clinicians have noted the positive effects of pressure from social services or Supplemental Security Income, which brought many individuals into treatment who had never sought it before and influenced them to remain long enough to begin to see benefits for themselves.

From the clinical perspective of the addiction specialist, this is not surprising. People who are actively using alcohol and drugs do not make good decisions. Once this cycle is interrupted and they get some distance from alcohol and drug use, they are more likely to take a different view of their circumstances, particularly if offered an opportunity for self-examination in a supportive treatment setting. Many current drug users come from families in which there may have been multiple generations of alcohol and drug users. They have no model for an alternative lifestyle and no conviction that a better life is possible for them. Coercion may provide the opportunity and impetus to enter a recovery process, the motivation for which gradually becomes internal. The AA motto "Bring the body; the mind will follow" is wisdom that is repeatedly confirmed in the area of coerced treatment. It is important for the clinician to focus on the development of a new identity and life goals as recovery progresses.

Currently, the criminal justice system severely limits the clinician's ability to determine appropriate treatment because many options are simply not available. However, there are several reasons to believe that the wider application of existing approaches has great potential for improving treatment outcome in criminal justice populations. Outcome studies of therapeutic communities and methadone maintenance have consistently shown reductions in criminal behavior (Gerstein & Harwood, 1990; Hubbard et al., 1989). Making quality treatment more available to those with criminal justice system involvement can be expected to produce meaningful gains, reducing the cost of long-term incarceration for some in this system.

A second promising avenue of investigation is the value of consistently integrating treatment for psychiatric disorders within treatment efforts focused on criminal justice populations. A large-scale epidemiological study reported that in institutional settings comorbidity of addictive and severe mental disorders was highest in the prison population (Regier et al., 1990). Schizophrenia, antisocial personality disorder (APD), bipolar disorder, and dysthymia were the most common, with a 90% concurrence of an addictive disorder among this group. Jails may contain disproportionate numbers of severely mentally ill persons with alcohol and drug abuse disorders; Abram and Teplin (1991) noted that police often arrest the mentally ill when treatment alternatives would have been preferable but are unavailable. McFarland, Faulkner, Bloom, Hallaux, and Bray (1989) interviewed family members about their chronically mentally ill male relatives and documented that substance abuse significantly predicted arrest. More than half were arrested after unsuccessful attempts by the family to commit the patients during a crisis. In Abram and Teplin's (1991) analysis, the narrow parameters of the caregiving systems serve as a formidable barrier to treatment. The mentally ill, particularly those with comorbid disorders, engage in disruptive behaviors and become criminalized. Abram and Teplin noted that "jails, unlike many treatment facilities, have no requirements or restrictions for entry" (p. 1042).

Despite the fact that comorbidity is especially high in the criminal justice client, treatment programs still may not provide adequate services to address the needs of both the addictive and the comorbid disorders. This is an area in which investigation is likely to be of increasingly great importance. Though skeptics may object that many of those in the criminal justice system are diagnosed with APD and thus have a poor prognosis, there are reasons to be cautious about such a conclusion. Overdiagnosis of APD is likely to lead the clinician to assume a poor prognosis and discourage efforts to secure quality treatment. It is crucial to assess APD independent of substance abuse (Gerstley, Alterman, McLellan, & Woody, 1990). When this is done rigorously, the percentage of those with a primary antisocial disorder declines dramatically. Gerstley et al. (1990) speculated that those whose antisocial activity is directly related to their drug use might show a better treatment response, a view shared by other clinicians. Gerstley and colleagues also discussed the possibility that antisocial behavior can be an expression of an affective disorder. Another important factor is the extent to which the context (i.e., court-related referral) biases the clinician to see the patient's pathology in antisocial terms (Travin & Protter, 1982). More recently, it has become clear that those who are high on the numbing cluster of posttraumatic stress disorder symptoms (e.g., avoidance, detachment, restricted range of affect) can also be misdiagnosed with APD. Thus, childhood histories of abuse may be associated with violent behavior in adulthood. The clinical complexities of adjudicated populations are becoming better understood as professionals have increasing access to these populations.

GUIDELINES FOR SELECTING APPROPRIATE TREATMENT

Before reviewing treatment options for individual patients, it is useful to elaborate on collaboration, a skill as important as therapeutic skills in addressing addiction. It is rare to find an addicted patient whose treatment does not warrant collaboration with other professionals and systems. Precisely because addiction is a biopsychosocial disorder, the clinician must be prepared to interact with physicians, social workers, psychologists, lawyers, probation officers, and other addiction treatment professionals with specialty credentials. It is useful to think of the other disciplines as "subcultures" with their own language and assumptions about what people need in order to change. Mental health providers often underestimate the need for integrated addiction treatment, assuming that if the mental health disorder were addressed, the addictive behavior would correct itself. Physicians may underestimate the importance of sustained participation in psychosocial interventions. In working with the criminal justice system, divergent interests (e.g., promoting public safety vs. individual welfare) may overshadow the common interest of achieving stable recovery. The more the practitioner understands the perspectives of those with whom he or she is collaborating, the greater the likelihood of the kind of teamwork that leads to success. The individual therapist may need to be the patient's advocate, educate other professionals, and assist in problem solving to formulate and implement a treatment plan.

The existing system is fraught with obstacles that multiply with the number of problem areas in the individual patient. The separate systems in which various disorders (e.g., psychiatric disorders, medical problems) normally are treated have different assumptions about what goals are desirable and how people can achieve them, a different language, and to some extent, different values. For example, goals are formulated differently when one focuses on a terminal illness such as AIDS than when one has a relatively normal life expectancy. Abstinence goals, the usual organizing principle of addiction treatment, may result in harsh treatment when inflexibly applied to a deteriorating AIDS patient. The right of the individual to make certain value judgments about drug use must be weighed against the social cost of permissiveness about alcohol and drug use.

There is an abundance of other evidence that alcohol and drug use increases medical costs in an otherwise healthy population. Indeed, a key priority of the 2010 National Drug Control Strategy is to identify, assess, do brief interventions, or refer to specialty treatment the approximately 68,000,000 Americans who present in the health care system with varying levels of "harmful use" (Office of National Drug Control Policy, 2010). With the exception of those recently trained, most mental health practitioners are not skilled in motivating their patients to address their AOD use; this issue was seldom addressed in their basic training. They attempt to address the AOD use by referral to the addiction treatment system, which is not well equipped to deal with those who are highly ambivalent in their motivation and not prepared to make a wholehearted commitment. Thus, a large group in need of attention and amenable to appropriate intervention does not usually get their needs met in either system. Private practitioners or therapists in other settings are in an excellent position to develop "treatment readiness" in the patients through the application of the motivational enhancement strategies described in Chapter 5.

SEQUENTIAL, PARALLEL, AND INTEGRATED TREATMENT MODELS

Although it is widely acknowledged that the social services, mental health, addiction, and criminal justice systems are seeing many of the same people, in many communities it is still necessary to deal with multiple systems to get an appropriate treatment plan implemented. Many obstacles are inherent in this process. At best, it is time consuming, and it frequently overwhelms the patient with the task of meeting contradictory expectations. HIV adds the dimension of fatigue and susceptibility to other people's diseases, as well as the inability to drive or use public transportation. By contrast, integrated treatment models permit addressing multiple client needs within one system. Ries (1993, 1994) discussed the strengths and limits of sequential, parallel, and integrated models for different patient profiles and described treatment approach similarities and differences. Private practitioners doing psychotherapy may need to match the patient with mental health or addiction treatment services in the community to provide missing elements. It is important to consider which model best meets the goals that need to be achieved.

In *sequential treatment,* the patient is treated by one system (addiction or mental health) and then by the other. Many clinicians believe that the addiction treatment must always be initiated first, and the patient must be abstinent before psychiatric treatment can be effective. Some psychotherapists, impressed by the futility of ignoring alcohol and drug use, insist that the patient address the addictive behavior first before work on other issues can proceed. Indeed, there are times that this is the preferred approach, although the rigidity of some clinicians is cause for concern. It is more likely that the therapist will need to make the case over a period of time for an abstinence commitment and focus on exploring the patient's resistance to doing so. Patients with severe psychiatric disorders may need to have those addressed first. First, it is important to rule out the possibility that the symptoms are substance induced. Once this is done, it is important to stabilize the patient who has symptoms of a mental health disorder. Addiction treatment may be ineffective until antipsychotics take effect or antidepressant blood levels are higher.

In *parallel treatment,* the patient is simultaneously involved in addiction and mental health treatment. For example, a woman with depression may be placed on antidepressants, participate in psychotherapy, and attend classes on coping with depression at a mental health center while participating in 12-step meetings, recovery group, and alcohol- or drug-refusal classes in an addiction treatment program. These forms of treatment are provided by clinicians within different systems or who are peripheral to them and who may rarely if ever communicate with each other. If the patient becomes caught between conflicting expectations and philosophies, there may be no obvious mechanism for resolving issues. This situation is likely to interfere with good treatment outcome.

In *integrated treatment,* mental health and addiction treatment are combined into a unified and comprehensive treatment program involving clinicians who have been cross-trained in both approaches. This includes a unified case management approach that makes it possible to monitor and treat patients through both psychiatric and AOD crises. The burden of treatment consistency and continuity is placed on staff in a setting designed for simultaneous treatment of both disorders.

Models for the treatment of coexisting disorders are rapidly evolving and under extensive study, but it is not currently possible to make data-based comparisons between models. Many clinicians working in this area are convinced that the integration of psychiatric treatment within the treatment and recovery setting has the greatest chance of success with most patients. Even with aggressive case management, follow-through on referrals may be difficult, especially because multiple diagnoses magnify stigma, and patients are keenly sensitive to the negative attitudes they encounter. Bouncing between two or three systems usually results in the patient being given conflicting messages with inadequate opportunity for resolution and diminishes the chance of compliance with any treatment plan. However, sequential or parallel treatment may work well when patients have a severe problem in one area but a mild problem in the other. The therapist in private practice should be prepared to play a coordinating and advocacy role to assist the patient who becomes caught in conflicting expectations or practices.

Therapists searching for a good program should make a careful inquiry when a program markets itself as "dual diagnosis" or "co-occurring disorders." Some programs have done nothing more than add a consulting psychologist or psychiatrist who comes in several hours a week for patients with obvious symptoms. The ASAM PPC, discussed later in this chapter, describe the kinds of staffing patterns and activities appropriate to differing levels of psychiatric severity.

The impetus to shorten the length of stay and reduce the intensity of treatment runs counter to the needs of patients with not one but several chronic relapsing disorders. In the addiction field, treatment outcome research done on public sector populations over the past 3 decades has been consistent in its findings about the relationship between retention and outcome (Gerstein & Harwood, 1990; Hubbard et al., 1989). The longer people stay in treatment, the better they do. Gains begin to be enduring after about 6 months' participation. Such findings suggest that in a managed care environment, many with multiple disorders will not receive care that is effective by objective measures. The "positive outcomes" described by some managed care organizations appear to be based on an absence of immediate casualties or protest by members. They do not use the same treatment outcome criteria as the addiction or mental health provider. The National Institute on Drug Abuse (NIDA) offers a good summary of effective principles and practices in its *Principles of Drug Addiction Treatment: A Research-Based Guide* (http://www.nida.nih.gov/PODAT/PODATIndex.html).

Individual psychotherapy can fit into the following models and situations in a variety of ways. Often the patient arrives at the door of the addiction treatment system referred by his or her therapist, who may continue to see the patient during and after specialty treatment is completed. Others seek psychotherapy after a period of sobriety, to address many painful issues once obscured by alcohol and drug use. Limited psychotherapy is even becoming available to adjudicated populations, as recognition grows that inadequate resources have brought many with psychiatric disorders into the criminal justice system as their untreated symptoms escalated and appropriate help was unavailable. It is imperative that the individual therapist familiarize himself or herself with the expectations and constraints of the relevant systems and be flexible enough to tailor treatment to accommodate the extensive and sometimes conflicting demands of the patient. Providing education, support, and therapy for family members while a patient is away at residential treatment is an important function, especially if treatment is out of state and family members have a hard time accessing the treatment center's family program.

FORMULATING A TREATMENT PLAN

We now look briefly at attempts to standardize principles for deciding level of care and a range of services that should be included and how they can be matched with patient needs. Although these principles are under continuous revision, they provide sensible guidelines for current practice. It should be noted that most of the vast literature on matching in both alcohol and drug treatment modalities has failed to yield dependable, practical methods for assigning patients to programs or particular treatments. For example, a national study found that three commonly used approaches were effective but for most of the hypotheses did not obtain evidence about which matching variables indicated which treatment. Only psychiatric severity demonstrated relevance as a matching variable (Project MATCH Research Group, 1997). Most studies in the literature used a patient–program matching strategy in which efforts are made to match particular types of patients to particular types of programs. Attempts to apply these matching principles encountered access barriers in the programs selected. Long waiting lists made admission difficult, and geographical obstacles limited participation. Programs rapidly emerged and disappeared in the unstable funding climate. Patient–program matching has increasingly come to be viewed as impractical.

PROBLEM–SERVICE MATCHING

A well-known group of researchers in Philadelphia reviewed conceptual and methodological issues in an effort to chart a more productive course for this complex endeavor (McLellan & Alterman, 1991). Research by this group has focused on problem–service matching, a promising strategy that can be used by individual private providers as well as by agencies. Despite the commitment to individualizing treatment, research has shown that many programs do comprehensive assessment but assign patients to the same treatment activities. In problem–service matching, specific problem areas are identified with the Addiction Severity Index (McLellan, Alterman, Cacciola, Metzger, & O'Brien, 1992), and a brief patient interview (Treatment Services Review; McLellan, Kushner, et al., 1992) is used between short intervals to make sure the patient is receiving needed services. The programs that provided the most services that were focused on a specific treatment problem generally showed the best outcome. Thus, the specificity and relevance of the treatment services actually delivered to each individual appears to have a major influence on differential effectiveness. A subsequent study demonstrated that even well-trained clinicians in accredited programs did not necessarily match their level of attention to the patient's most severe problem areas in the absence of a disciplined quality assurance process (McLellan et al., 1997).

CENTER FOR SUBSTANCE ABUSE TREATMENT
COMPREHENSIVE CARE MODEL

The Center for Substance Abuse Treatment (CSAT) offers a detailed framework for matching patient needs with services in public sector programs. These patients typically have far more complex practical problems (e.g., housing, medical, educational, vocational) and often require more comprehensive services to stabilize their psychosocial functioning. In 1990, CSAT began (as the Office for Treatment Improvement) with the task of expanding the availability of effective services for addiction treatment. A key element in CSAT's mission is to facilitate the application of the vast body of knowledge generated by the research institutes, NIDA, and the National Institute on Alcohol Abuse and Alcoholism. This necessitated engaging the system of state and local government agencies and public and private treatment providers responsible for the delivery of addiction treatment services (Primm, 1990). In an effort to upgrade the standard of care, CSAT articulated in detail the ingredients in effective treatment for the population it serves.

Guidelines for model treatment programs were disseminated widely by CSAT through vehicles such as its request for applications for funds, treatment improvement protocols, and various other publications carrying a range of economic and other incentives. These guidelines may prove useful for those trying to select either a public or private sector program for a particular patient. The guidelines include comprehensive assessment, rapid intake, provision of medical care and health education, random drug testing, pharmacotherapeutic interventions, a variety of types of counseling, peer support groups, liaison services, social and recreational activities, housing, clinical supervision, and evaluation of outcomes. A "one-stop shop" is considered the most desirable, but services are often obtained through collaboration with other community organizations. Thus, AOD use is the ticket through the door, but the goal is to attend to the needs of the whole person. Implementation of these guidelines was imperfect, but the impact was to enlarge the vision of treatment providers and map out a process for upgrading quality. Although not all of these services are necessary for higher functioning patients, this is a useful framework to help evaluate the strengths and limits of particular programs.

AMERICAN SOCIETY OF ADDICTION MEDICINE PATIENT PLACEMENT CRITERIA

Clinicians in the private sector rely on a variety of guidelines in selecting appropriate settings. Decision making takes into account various barriers to access, particularly financial limitations. Those with health insurance coverage have access to different types of programs than those who do not, though the relationship among quality, cost, and outcome is often elusive. Programs with fine reputations and impressive staffing do not necessarily produce outcomes that are superior to those that occur in populations with good prognostic factors at the outset. Though assessments are conducted, placement often has more to do with ideology and availability of reimbursement rather than on empirically derived matching criteria. Outcome data have often emanated from the marketing department and have not stood up to rigorous scrutiny. Communities vary in the options available for the indigent population; federal funding provides more opportunities in some locations than others. Recent efforts are intended to systematize this process and strengthen its empirical database.

ASAM has refined a biopsychosocial model to specify the treatment which that matches the patient's clinical severity. This necessitates accurate assessment of the nature and severity of the patient's medical, psychological, and social problems and the availability of services to respond to the needs identified. ASAM's goal is to arrive at uniform PPC to determine appropriate levels of care. The latest revision addresses the needs of patients with co-occurring disorders (recognized as the norm, not the exception) and strengthens the criteria for adolescents (ASAM, 2001). The following dimensional criteria are used to select levels of care (Mee-Lee & Schuman, 2009):

- acute intoxication and/or withdrawal potential,
- coexistence of biomedical conditions or complications,

- emotional/behavioral conditions and complications (e.g., psychiatric conditions, psychological or emotional/behavioral complications of known or unknown origins, poor impulse control, changes in mental status, transient neuropsychiatric complications),
- readiness to change,
- recovery environment, and
- recovery/living environment.

These criteria are used to determine an appropriate level of early intervention, outpatient, intensive outpatient, inpatient, or residential care. Staffing patterns and available services are described in detail for each level of care.

The PPC represent a basic framework that encourages the use of multidimensional assessments to make placement decisions and provides criteria sufficiently objective to facilitate research. The PPC are expected to be elaborated more fully and to be continuously validated through empirical research.

CONCLUSION

There are a variety of conceptual frameworks used in the addiction field to determine appropriate treatment. The problem–service matching strategy permits assessment, quality assurance, and outcome evaluation to be accomplished in a relatively straightforward manner. The CSAT comprehensive care model offers a way of identifying basic elements of treatment that can be found in a wide variety of settings. ASAM's PPC are widely used as a means of determining what level of care is appropriate for the patient. All these frameworks are used, more or less explicitly, by practitioners in the addiction field. In the arena of coerced treatment, state-of-the-art practices combined with adequate evaluation will be important to justify allocating resources to treatment rather than to a purely punitive approach. Clinicians will increasingly find themselves interacting with these systems and will hopefully be able to meet the collaborative challenge.

5

Individual Psychotherapy

This chapter focuses primarily on the role of the private practitioner in addressing addiction issues. Our goal is to help therapists address alcohol and drug use in situations in which the patient has sought help for other problems. Clinicians, especially those in private practice, have a long history of underestimating the role of alcohol and other drug (AOD) use in producing or exacerbating the presenting symptoms and in negatively influencing the response to treatment (see Chapter 3, this volume). AOD use has been documented in almost all clinical populations, and it is important that therapists and clinical supervisors are trained to address it. Mild to moderate abuse problems can often be handled by therapists in private practice or in agencies outside addiction treatment settings. Such early intervention can have a powerful impact on both the success of the treatment and the quality of the patient's life.

If treatment in a specialty setting is needed, therapists have an important role in helping patients become "treatment ready." To accomplish this, it is important for therapists to build collaborative networks. This includes a variety of professional resources: a physician familiar with addiction medicine and options for residential or outpatient addiction treatment and addiction specialists available for assessment and consultation. Networks may also include community resources, such as self-help groups and halfway houses. The therapist's collaborative task may be complex at particular points in the treatment. For example, many individual therapists do not manage the acute treatment alone but tap other resources in the early stages of treatment and at other times, such as during a relapse episode or period of heightened relapse vulnerability. Issues such as eating disorders, gambling, and compulsive sexual behavior or spending also frequently require collaboration. Therapists who develop strong networks can maximize the effectiveness of their own work.

Having established a context, this chapter focuses on the activities of the individual psychotherapist. We begin by considering several concepts that have served as barriers to good communication between psychotherapists and addiction treatment professionals. We then discuss strategies for enhancing motivation and present a model for intervention that is recovery oriented. The material represents a blend of empirical studies and clinical experience. The literature in this area includes not only systematic investigations but also clinically based discussions from a variety of perspectives. The goal of the chapter is to provide a synthesis, a framework for prioritizing and integrating AOD interventions with those needed to address coexisting disorders.

IDEOLOGICAL HOT BUTTONS

Most therapeutic systems contain concepts and language that lend themselves to professional squabbles and disparagement or rejection of patients (e.g., "acting out," "narcissistic"), and the addiction field is no exception. *Enabling, codependency,* and *denial* are examples of three concepts that capture important phenomena but have also been greatly misused. It is important to understand the essential meaning of these concepts, their utility, and their perils.

Enabling refers to behavior by other people that protects the AOD user from the consequences of his or her behavior and thereby colludes in perpetuating it. Six styles of enabling derived from the literature are avoiding and shielding, attempting to control, taking over responsibilities, rationalizing and accepting, cooperating and collaborating, and rescuing and subserving (Nelson, 1985). These behaviors, although understandable attempts to cope with the situation and protect family members and others (e.g., employers), can postpone the alcoholic's or addict's full recognition of consequences for long periods of time.

In the past, therapists acquired a reputation for being professional enablers by allowing patients to talk about their problems without acknowledging the detrimental effects of AOD use and without emphasizing the need for a change in behavior. Indeed, one has only to attend 12-step meetings to hear painful stories of people who had been given poor guidance or had been actively discouraged from focusing on their AOD use by their therapist (e.g., "Deal with your underlying problems and it will take care of itself"; "You don't have an alcoholic personality"). Some therapists allowed patients to preserve the illusion of working on problems without translating insights into meaningful action. Many recovering people felt they had lost years of their productive lives in this manner and formed a vocal subgroup in Alcoholics Anonymous (AA) that cautioned against involvement with therapists. Some of these people formed grassroots groups that succeeded in getting legislation mandating education in substance abuse for licensed therapists.

Over the years, the situation has improved. By 1996, the AA membership survey indicated that 60% of the members received some kind of treatment or counseling, and 77% of that group felt it played an important role directing them to AA (Alcoholics Anonymous World Services, 2007a). The 2007 membership survey reported almost exactly the same percentages (AA World Services, 2007b): After attending AA, 62% received treatment or counseling, and 85% of those said it played an important part in their recovery. Thus, the antipathy toward professionals appears to be lessening, but it is important for the therapist who encounters it to be mindful that its basis is understandable.

Codependency is another concept that refers to a similar phenomenon, in this case, the distorted adaptations made by others in an effort to cope with the behavior of the alcoholic or drug user. Several authors have critiqued the concept, in particular as a "symbol of stigmatization" that exacerbates guilt by labeling significant others as pathological and blameworthy, and they have also noted that the majority of those to whom this label is applied are women (Haaken, 1990; Harper & Capdevila, 1990). In clinical settings, such labels often substitute for distinguishing between individual and interpersonal problems and between what is healthy and what is emotionally destructive in the complex relationships between active users and their significant others.

Unfortunately, both concepts have also been repeatedly used to discourage appropriate forms of helping. An intact family or support structure is a key element in promoting positive treatment outcome, so the therapist needs to help significant others distinguish between constructive and undermining efforts (see Chapter 6 for a further discussion of these issues). Some therapists have been known to ban the use of the terms *enabler, codependent,* or *co,* asking patients to specify the behaviors they find objectionable or problematic rather than use labels. This discourages the use of jargon in the service of expressing anger, clarifies problem areas, and promotes constructive efforts at conflict resolution.

Denial is another concept so brutalized by misuse that it is wise to use it selectively and with caution. It refers to the "refusal to admit the reality of, disavowal of the truth of, refusal to acknowledge the presence or existence of" (Campbell, 1989, p. 190). Before invoking the label of denial, it is useful to hypothesize lack of information. For example, the elderly man who disputes that alcohol could be a problem because he drinks the same two glasses of wine with dinner as he has for 30 years needs first to be informed that aging changes the body's response to a wide range of drugs and medications, and indeed what was once not problematic may have become so. Before interpreting behavior as resistance, it is important to build a foundation of information. Even among highly educated persons, the absence of information or the presence of misinformation can be quite striking. For example, many (men in particular) view a high tolerance for alcohol as evidence of a "better physical system," particularly because it is culturally valued in many subgroups. They are often surprised to hear it is a marker for alcoholism. Education provides the foundation to interpret resistance and also allows for charged issues to be introduced in a more neutral framework. The clinician can note areas of defensiveness while demonstrating empathy and support as he or she provides the information.

S. Brown (1985) described denial as a cognitive phenomenon, which she referred to as a *thinking disorder*. As negative consequences begin to accumulate, the drinking individual must construct a reality that externalizes the problem, often assigning another source. Marital conflict and work stress become common explanations for drinking, and the role of drinking in exacerbating problems is minimized or ignored. Addressing denial involves connecting the drinking with its consequences and aiding the patient in accepting the reality of loss of control. The patient must begin to see drinking as the problem, not the solution. Brown noted that the question "Why do you drink?" often elicits excuses. Better focus is achieved by asking about the function or purpose of the drinking. This facilitates recognition of the importance of drinking, and once one has acknowledged that it serves a purpose, its merits can be called into question. Thus, the therapist helps the patient examine the possibility that the solution or coping mechanism has now become a problem.

S. Brown (1985) stressed the importance of the cognitive factors in this phase because these are what maintain and explain drinking behavior. The therapist repeatedly brings the patient back to a focus on alcohol, challenging the patient's illusion of free choice and the "accounting system" by which drinking is rationalized. Moving beyond denial requires a total revision of a belief system characteristic of the drinking phase, shifting two central beliefs. The conviction "I am not alcoholic—I can control my drinking" is gradually replaced by "I am alcoholic—I cannot control my drinking." This provides the basis for the transition to abstinence. It is evident from Brown's work that the time required for this process is quite variable from individual to individual. It is the therapist's consistent focus that dismantles the denial system, and there is no specified time frame or encouragement of harsh confrontation techniques. Therefore, a sophisticated understanding of denial, as exemplified in Brown's work, is enormously helpful to clinicians seeking to move the patient into a serious recovery process.

At its worst, the concept of denial is used to make practitioners feel better about their impotence and frustration. It allows them to disclaim responsibility for difficult clinical problems and shift responsibility to the patient. When used in confrontation (e.g., "You are in denial"), it can be a form of invalidation that leaves many patients feeling frustrated, criticized, and misunderstood.

> Sophie was in intensive outpatient treatment in a hospital affiliated with a prestigious university. She and her husband had had intense conflict over her marijuana smoking, which he deplored. He reported having several alcoholic relatives but insisted his own drinking was not a problem. Sophie had stopped smoking marijuana for 9 months, until they had a major fight. She left to stay with a friend for a few days, during which time she smoked marijuana twice. When she and her husband made peace, he insisted she enter drug treatment, which she did. The otherwise extensive intake process did not include a careful assessment of his drinking pattern or the role of marijuana in their relationship. In groups in the treatment program, she was repeatedly assailed about "being in denial" when she stated she no longer smoked marijuana and did not think it was her main problem. No attempt was made to address the marital conflicts or to examine her husband's drinking, despite his being at high risk of alcoholism. After 3 weeks of feeling her self-esteem was being battered and her concerns ignored, she dropped out of treatment.

This vignette illustrates a common dilemma: Denial is a frequent characteristic and a legitimate hypothesis, but the clinician needs to avoid coming to this conclusion prematurely. In this example, the treatment program was strong in some areas but lacked the family perspective that would have generated further query into the marital dynamics. In other cases, the patient's report of a mild to moderate problem may reflect the changing cultural threshold for recognition. In the past, alcoholics and addicts arrived at treatment after years of damaging consequences. With widespread media attention and a large popular literature, awareness has been heightened in both users and significant others, bringing people to seek help at earlier stages. In such cases, the therapist may not need to challenge the patient's perception of severity but can emphasize the desirability of taking the problem seriously in its early stages to avoid difficulties later on. If denial is in fact influential, this will become apparent, and the patient will likely be more cooperative than if challenged prematurely.

INTEGRATING INSIGHT-ORIENTED PSYCHOTHERAPY

In a recovery-oriented model, the tasks of the recovering person determine the nature of the therapist's intervention. These tasks can be summarized as follows: recognizing alcohol and drug use is a problem and becoming willing to address it, establishing abstinence, and consolidating abstinence and changing lifestyles to support a comfortable and satisfying sobriety (Washton & Zweben, 2006). Therapists with an eclectic intervention repertoire will find this work more congenial. Those who rely on a single approach, especially psychodynamic psychotherapy, will find some of the necessary shifts more difficult. A psychodynamic model is frequently useful in clarifying the issues presented by the patient. However, as an intervention strategy, it can be a trap, particularly in early recovery. Many people can and do stop drinking and using drugs with little understanding of why they initiated or continued their substance use. Conversely, many others avoid making behavior changes for years while engaged in an inner exploration they believed would "naturally" bring an end to the alcohol and drug use once they resolved the "underlying" issues.

In a recovery-oriented model, insight-oriented explorations are useful to help the patient understand and address his or her ambivalence about giving up alcohol and drugs. Once the commitment to become abstinent occurs, the most useful interventions are cognitive–behavioral strategies focused on how to become clean and sober. The AA motto "Bring the body; the mind will follow" illustrates an effective approach at this stage. Psychodynamic understanding remains useful but only if applied in a focused way and combined with an emphasis on learning the behaviors of abstinence (S. Brown, 1985). These issues are elaborated in the section of this chapter on establishing abstinence. As the period of abstinence lengthens and lifestyle changes occur, insight-oriented therapy becomes increasingly useful, improving the quality of sobriety substantially. However, probing anxiety-provoking issues prematurely often results in a resumption of alcohol and drug use, stalling the therapy and perhaps resulting in dropout. Thus, the therapist who is able to make the appropriate shifts, drawing on both cognitive–behavioral and insight-oriented techniques, has the best prospects of facilitating a successful outcome.

We begin by focusing extensively on the condition in which many therapists find themselves: The patient is drinking and/or using, the effects of this behavior are unclear, and the patient is at best ambivalent about making changes in this area.

> Marsha, a single parent, came to treatment struggling with depression and loneliness and coping with raising her two children who exhibited behavior problems since her marriage broke up. She reported smoking marijuana nightly to relax and expressed reluctance to give it up because it was her most reliable friend.

The therapist considers the possibility that her marijuana smoking exacerbates her depression (which it appears to do in some people but not all), undermines her stamina and ability to be consistent in her dealings with her children, and promotes social withdrawal. How can the therapist present this to the patient in a manner that will be acceptable?

We review the motivational enhancement strategies, on which there is now an extensive published literature, and also discuss psychodynamic reasons for wanting to resist an abstinence commitment. Once an abstinence commitment has been secured, we describe some of the cognitive–behavioral strategies used to achieve abstinence and how to formulate goals with respect to coexisting disorders for patients at this stage. We then discuss the tasks of later stages of recovery, in particular that of consolidating abstinence and creating a satisfying alcohol- and drug-free lifestyle. This chapter describes some of those issues; Chapter 8 focuses more extensively on relapse.

DEVELOPING A COMMITMENT TO ABSTINENCE

AOD use can produce such a wide array of symptoms that there is no reliable way to quickly determine how great an influence it has (S. A. Brown, Irwin, & Schuckit, 1991; S. A. Brown & Schuckit, 1988; Schuckit, 2005). The therapist does not need to "prove" that alcohol and drugs are the source of the patient's distress, but he or she can suggest a period of abstinence to explore this issue productively. Ideally, this period will extend past the 2 to 4 weeks needed for the withdrawal symptoms to subside and expand into the longer period needed for the body to readjust to the absence of drugs. Usually, AOD use makes the patient appear more pathological than he or she will look after a period of abstinence (see Sacks & Ries, 2005). Although the patient will often continue to experience periods of depression, irritability, and other forms of distress, he or she will normally show signs of healthier functioning and better resources to bring to bear on the problems that inevitably emerge.

It is not necessary to convince the patient that he or she is an alcoholic or addict to justify abstinence from mood-altering drugs. These labels are highly stigmatizing and generate unnecessary resistance. The therapist can suggest that because AODs, even in moderation, can exacerbate distress, a moratorium allows both patient and therapist to examine the ways in which they are woven into the patient's life, and how they influence symptoms. There is no attempt to prove they are causing symptoms, only an effort to engage the patient in a time-limited "experiment with abstinence" (Zweben, 1989, p. 127), also called "sobriety sampling" (W. R. Miller & Page, 1991, p. 227), to observe what changes when intoxicants are eliminated. This approach helps the therapist avoid power struggles around issues such as how much wine with dinner is "too much," and it eliminates the pressure to probe frequently to determine whether the patient is minimizing use. The concept of attachment is also a useful, less stigmatizing way to discuss the issues. The therapist can take the stance that most people have attachments that are stronger than they realize until they try to give them up; hence the exercise is fruitful. The choice of time period for the experiment with abstinence is an opportunity for exploration. Patients are hard pressed to explain why a several month "holiday" from drinking and using drugs is objectionable if they are not addicted; hence this strategy often precipitates recognition of their own resistance. In practical terms, the therapist should aim for 1 to 3 months' abstinence, though this is often negotiated in shorter, more manageable time units.

STRATEGIES FOR ENHANCING MOTIVATION

Once the therapist has identified where the patient is located on the continuum of readiness to change described in Chapter 3, specific motivational techniques offered by William R. Miller (1999) can be used to move the patient forward and enhance readiness for treatment. This work was based on extensive empirical research and then translated into materials for practicing clinicians. Miller discussed five principles applicable to substance abuse issues.

The first principle is to express empathy. Through the use of accurate empathy, the patient develops a sense of acceptance that seems to free him or her to change, whereas nonacceptance often feeds resistance. The patient's ambivalence about maintaining sobriety is framed as a normal part of human experience rather than a lack of motivation for change or a lack or seriousness about the therapeutic process.

The second technique is to develop discrepancy. The therapist notes the gap between where the patient is and where he or she wants to be. In developing discrepancy, it is important for the therapist to realize that the patients must be able to give voice to their concerns. The therapist should be sensitive to those statements that reflect an awareness of a discrepancy between the patient's achievements and goals. For example, in adolescents an awareness of how substance abuse may have affected school performance, family relationships, and even peer interactions can often be a starting point for developing discrepancy. A goal of motivational interviewing is to develop discrepancy, and heighten it, to illustrate the contradiction between the patient's goals and what his or her behavior is likely to bring.

The third technique is to avoid arguments. When resistance is encountered, one must be prepared to shift strategies. Arguments over the label of *alcoholic* or *addict* are particularly fruitless. Fighting against patients distracts from the goal of motivating them for change.

The fourth technique involves rolling with the resistance. When the therapist encounters defensiveness or resistance, he or she is encouraged to retreat and then approach the problem from a slightly different perspective. Turning questions back to patients and allowing them to struggle with their own answers is particularly effective. As the therapist watches the patient struggle, he or she becomes a participant with the patient, to support but never directly oppose his or her view of the situation. It is assumed that the patient is capable of developing insight and moving in a healthy direction.

The fifth concept is to support *self-efficacy*, that is, the patient's confidence in his or her ability to cope with or manage a specific challenge. The patient who sees the possibility of achieving sobriety is more likely to achieve that goal than the patient who sees no hope for this outcome. Providing the patient with specific skills such as assertiveness training or stress reduction techniques can support self-efficacy. Also, linking the patient up with community support groups can enhance self-efficacy by helping the patient to identify individuals who are successfully recovering from alcohol and drug abuse problems.

Understanding the emotional elements in resistance is crucial to moving the patient toward a commitment to abstinence. So long as the therapist maintains focus on both dynamics and behavior, exploration can be highly productive. One of the most common reasons to resist an abstinence commitment is fear of failure. A thorough assessment includes a review of past efforts to stop using: how long they lasted, what worked, what did not work. Detailed inquiry usually reveals flaws in the patient's strategy (e.g., hanging out in the bar trying to "be strong," instead of staying out of the bar in the first place). The therapist can use such flaws to lift morale: "You made a good effort, but you didn't have very good coaching." The therapist can then offer to educate the patient about effective strategies for stopping.

Fear of withdrawal phenomena is a related problem. It is a mistake to assume that the most important force behind the resistance to abstinence is the patient's continuing desire to get high. Motives and reinforcers change as people move from being naive (new) to chronic users, and much continuing use is perpetuated by a fear of withdrawal discomfort. For the heroin user, this can be violent nausea; for the cocaine user, severe depression; for the alcoholic, unmanageable anxiety, delirium tremens, seizures, even death. Describing an appropriate psychosocial and medical detoxification structure can be reassuring and can help build motivation to tackle the task of becoming abstinent.

Although the patient's desire to get high may not be the most important force behind resistance to abstinence, another belief is similar and common. Often patients fear that giving up the drug will be like losing a best friend. They may fear there will be no more fun in their lives, that everything will be black and white and without color. The actual experience of the drug, "the rush," the high, and the accompanying rituals are all extremely powerful, and therapists should not underestimate them.

A second reason to resist an abstinence commitment has to do with AOD use in the family of origin and/or in the current household. Complex dynamics come into play here, and it is important to maintain focus on motivational goals while exploring these obstacles. If there was AOD use in the family of origin, it is common for family functioning to be organized around such use in a myriad of ways family members are unaware of and do not discuss (Brown, 1988). Often alcohol use is a way of "belonging," as is evident in family rituals organized around drinking. For many men, drinking with Daddy is both a pubertal initiation ritual and an ingredient in ongoing bonding experiences. Marijuana may also be a key element in socializing. Giving up alcohol and drugs can be felt as "being orphaned"; the patient may correctly realize that entering a recovery process puts him or her in uncharted territory. Usually, the fears are not clearly articulated, and it is worth the time needed to elicit a fuller picture of the nature of the apprehension and the patient's picture of what his or her life would be like without alcohol and drugs. A related reason may be survivor guilt—leaving significant others behind and possibly becoming more successful as a result.

A third common reason to resist a commitment to abstinence is the belief that alcohol and drugs constitute effective self-medication

(Khantzian, 1997; Khantzian, Halliday, & McAuliffe, 1990). Here again, people may have legitimate reasons to believe they are effectively medicating a disorder, without realizing that their attempts to cope are actually exacerbating their disorder and undermining them in other ways. For example, many stimulant users cite depression as an impetus without appreciating that chronic stimulant use exacerbates depression by depleting key neurotransmitters (Gold & Jacobs, 2005). Patients need to be reassured that their withdrawal discomforts will be appropriately attended to, but they also need to know that if sustained abstinence does not result in improvement, other effective approaches (including medication) can be tried.

People with a history of traumatic experiences pose difficult challenges in this regard because unlike many others, they often feel considerably worse when they attempt to abstain from alcohol and drugs. In such cases, a firm safety structure and patience in working toward abstinence goals are crucial. Therapists' refusal to work with patients who are actively drinking and using is particularly untenable at this point. Patients with histories of severe trauma will often never get to abstinence unless the therapist is able to move them in this direction while working to reduce the frequency and destructiveness of drinking and using episodes. Seeking Safety (Najavits, 2002) is a research-based intervention designed for early-stage stabilization. It has been well received by patients and therapists alike.

Early-stage abstinence is often difficult, and depending on the length and intensity of use, patients may get worse before they get better. They may become more irritable, moody, depressed, and so forth, and this can last for months. Not everyone gets better after achieving initial abstinence. The key variable seems to be whether they can acquire the necessary coping skills or recovery program to manage life without alcohol and drugs.

ESTABLISHING ABSTINENCE

Once the patient has expressed a commitment to changing behavior, the therapist can assume a broader role as "coach" to help achieve that. It is particularly useful for the therapist to discuss action strategies to achieve new goals, rather than assume insight will produce the appropriate behaviors.

Psychosocial Intervention Issues

It is widely agreed that for substance-dependent individuals, abstinence from alcohol and drugs is the foundation for therapeutic progress on other issues. When possible, it should be the primary goal. This does not mean that other issues are ignored but, instead, that the therapist maintains focus on the task, addressing content from the perspective of the tasks of the recovering person. For example, if a woman reports that conflict with her husband is her main trigger to drink, the therapist could ask how she might cope with this situation without drinking (e.g., call a friend, go to an AA/NA meeting, go out walking). Couples' work on conflict resolution is usually too emotion-laden to be successful if one member of the couple is struggling to establish abstinence. Psychodynamic and interpersonal issues should be explored for the purpose of understanding how to create a structure that will support abstinence, without the expectation that issues can be resolved at this stage. Insight-oriented therapists frequently neglect to make the bridge between understanding and action, assuming that insight will occur on its own. Persons in early recovery need simplicity and structure. They do not necessarily draw obvious implications, no matter how intelligent and educated they are. Therapists often underestimate the distress and vulnerability of patients struggling with establishing abstinence, particularly if the patient is highly articulate and high functioning.

Cognitive–behavioral strategies have long been a key ingredient in the effort to establish abstinence. Assisting the patient to formulate a sound action plan is one of the therapist's most important tasks. The patient is helped to focus on behaviors that sustain the addiction or break the cycle. A *recovery checklist* helps the patient identify specific behaviors that will promote a successful outcome and, in the process, identify obvious gaps. Generating a checklist for triggers helps the patient to gain a conceptual understanding of how conditioning operates to produce craving and to identify his or her specific triggers to allow coping strategies to be generated. *Thought-stopping techniques* are tools for breaking the cycle that leads from trigger to thought to continued thoughts, followed by cravings and use. Specific materials for this purpose can be found in the various manuals listed near the end of this chapter.

In the early stages of recovery, emphasis is on avoiding hazardous situations when possible, devising ways to reduce the risk when it is not, and engaging in activities that promote recovery. The therapist can work with the patient to identify internal and external triggers and make a plan. He or she can challenge assumptions that keep the patient in high-risk situations. Patients at this stage often attempt to stop drinking and using without changing much else (e.g., continuing the fishing trips with their hard-drinking buddies). They may need support for the idea that avoidance is honorable and necessary in the early stages and perhaps for longer periods as well:

> Brian came to treatment when his wife made it clear she would leave him if he did not stop his heavy drinking. He had begun to threaten her with harm during drinking episodes. He was troubled by his own behavior, agreed that it always took place when he was intoxicated, and reluctantly agreed to a trial period of abstinence. He agreed to stay out of bars but refused to attend AA. He was adamant that he could socialize with his old drinking buddies and withstand temptation.
>
> He continued to participate in one of their favorite rituals, deep-sea fishing trips. He proposed that he would be "safe" if he brought non-alcoholic drinks for himself. On the first such trip, he did not drink, though he was shaken by how difficult it was. Emboldened, he planned another and did not drink then. By this time he had been abstinent for 10 weeks, the longest he could remember since age 17. On the third such expedition, he persuaded himself that one beer was okay to celebrate their splendid catch. Two days later, he drank to intoxication and had another ugly scene with his wife.

Brian had prematurely assumed he had mastered an important trigger when he participated in two fishing expeditions without drinking.

His unwillingness to participate in recovery-related activities (other than his individual sessions) and to change most of his social habits (at least temporarily) made him vulnerable. He also failed to understand that a conditioned trigger, such as years of fishing and drinking with his buddies, could have a delayed effect; he was misled by his ability to confine himself to one beer after the third fishing trip. These events provided an opportunity to deepen his understanding of his addiction as well as to reconsider which behavioral tools he was willing to use.

Specialized knowledge about addiction and recovery and information about the intoxication and withdrawal effects of various drugs are invaluable at this point. A fund of practical information that can be used to support and motivate is acquired gradually, through reading, discussion, and experience. Through the psychoeducational stance, the therapist provides support, reassurance, and information that help the patient understand and endure what he or she is experiencing. Detailed knowledge of the distinctive characteristics of various drugs of abuse helps guide the patient through the immediate difficulties and anticipate and plan for likely ones. Education also provides the foundation from which resistance can be interpreted; if the patient is uninformed, one must start there.

As described earlier, the therapist should first consider the possibility of lack of information before concluding that denial is operating. A common example is the need to abstain from all intoxicants, not just the drug of choice. Patients and their significant others often assume that the use of another drug is less serious or even acceptable. In fact, abstinence needs to be applied to all intoxicants. Long clinical observation and some empirical data (Rawson, 1994) indicate that those who retain or resume use of other drugs relapse at much higher rates than those who do not. Most assume that if a drug—for example, alcohol—was not a problem prior to cocaine use, one may return to drinking once abstinence from cocaine is well established. In fact, cocaine users are often engaged in more serious alcohol abuse than they recognize. They have high vulnerability to substitute alcohol, or to relapse to cocaine, independent of whether they were demonstrably alcoholic before or during the period of their cocaine use.

This topic remains a challenging clinical issue throughout treatment. In the early stage, it is important to introduce the concept and make sure all parties involved in the treatment understand it.

Psychoeducational sessions should always allow enough time for discussion of material after information is presented. In addition to providing a forum for participants to apply the information to their own situation, it is common to find charged issues raised in a veiled form. Thus, these activities provide an opportunity for participants to "get their feet wet" in the less threatening "classroom" format.

Withdrawal and Detoxification

The educational process should include a review of the intoxication and withdrawal effects of the drugs the patient has been using (Schuckit, 2005). Defining an approximate time frame, particularly the length of time serious discomfort usually lasts, gives comfort and a framework within which to plan extra support activities. Many people assume that the greatest dangers manifest early in the withdrawal period and are caught off guard by hazards that typically occur later. For example, the greatest danger of withdrawal seizures from Valium (a benzodiazepine) occurs within 5 to 8 days following cessation of use (Wesson, 1995). Staff working in one of the many types of nonmedical settings may be completely unprepared for such an event. Those abstaining from cocaine often experience a period of anhedonia after acute withdrawal phenomena have subsided. They underestimate the danger of this anhedonia because it is less dramatic than the acute misery following recent cocaine cessation. However, the boredom and joylessness frequently trigger resumption of drug use.

It is useful to consider two main bodily processes while the patient or client is in recovery: the process of the drug clearing the body and the process by which a new equilibrium or homeostasis is established. The former is usually what is referred to as the *detoxification* or *withdrawal* stage and may be appropriate to manage with medication (N. S. Miller & Kipnis, 2006). The second takes place over a long time and can include specific upsurges of withdrawal symptoms referred to as a *protracted abstinence syndrome.* It is variable in individuals, influenced by genetics, medical condition, nutrition, exercise, living environment, strength of recovery program, and other factors. Because many assume that a relapse after a period of abstinence merely indicates weakening motivation, it is important to understand that complex biological processes as well as psychosocial factors may be influential.

Some drugs can be discontinued abruptly without health threat, though there may be great discomfort. Opiates (heroin, morphine, codeine) are an example of such drugs. However, the stress of withdrawal may precipitate a crisis due to other health conditions, such as heart problems. Cocaine and marijuana generally pose no problem to stop abruptly. However, alcohol, benzodiazepines, and barbiturates should always involve physician screening or a protocol to determine what level of care is needed. Alcohol withdrawal is often uncomplicated, but it can result in seizures or delirium tremens, both of which can be fatal. Seizures cannot be predicted, and the signals of ongoing delirium tremens can be missed if there is no monitoring of vital signs. Medical monitoring (e.g., temperature and blood pressure checks of someone withdrawing from alcohol) can identify indications of an impending medical crisis.

Detoxification can occur in a residential type setting where there is adequate medical backup in case of problems. This option is currently much less available to those who need it than would be the case in an appropriately designed treatment system. Medical screening and management (e.g., physician observation, medication) is needed for benzodiazepine and barbiturate withdrawal. Patients also combine drugs, both prescribed and illegally obtained, in ways that increase the need for physician collaboration. Major medical problems can pose a complicating factor. A fuller description of detoxification procedures and considerations can be found in *Detoxification and Substance Abuse Treatment* (N. S. Miller & Kipnis, 2006). It is advisable for outpatient clinics and private practitioners to have clear screening criteria and protocols for problems requiring medical attention.

Ultrarapid opiate detoxification has been heavily marketed in some communities to appeal to opiate users whose work or personal schedule is not compatible with longer term detoxification. Naltrexone, an opiate antagonist, is used while the patient is under general anesthesia to expel the opiate from the receptor sites, sparing him or her much of the discomfort of opiate withdrawal. Most reviews and the limited controlled trials have concluded that the increased risks of adverse events due to the anesthesia do not justify its use, particularly given the added expense (Stine & Kostem, 2009).

Routine toxicology screens on admission can prevent many problems. It is common for patients to focus on their primary drug of abuse and ignore or minimize other drug use. Drug screens reveal the presence of such drugs and thus indicate when physician consultation or intervention is necessary. They also identify issues that patients, with the best of intentions, may have overlooked. Given the prevalence of alcohol and drug use in all clinical populations, drug screens can be presented as a routine part of the intake process. By normalizing them, the stage is set for further toxicology screening if signs and symptoms warrant it.

Nonphysicians are wise to establish a relationship with a physician who is familiar with addiction medicine and collaborate whenever there are medical issues. The American Society of Addiction Medicine is a specialty society through which one can identify physicians with an interest or certification in addiction medicine. This provides some assurance that the physician is familiar with the specific needs of alcohol and drug users, particularly some of the prescribing hazards with this population. State chapters may also be a source of additional referrals and consultants.

Patients may prefer to see their own physician. If possible, it is good to assess the physician's familiarity with addiction medicine because there is wide variation in the training of physicians in addiction-related matters. A patient expressing a preference for his or her regular physician should be asked whether he or she is willing to be completely candid about alcohol and drug use; otherwise, a referral is in order to someone with whom the patient is willing to be honest.

There is no consistent relationship between managing withdrawal and long-term abstinence. However, doing so provides a window of intervention that allows for enhancing motivation and laying the ground-work to sustain a recovery process. Making a patient more comfortable certainly contributes to a positive attitude toward treatment. Unrealistic expectations for what medically managed withdrawal could accomplish led to disappointment and reductions in funding that made it less accessible than would be desirable. If medical management is combined with efforts to connect the person to an ongoing recovery process, it can play an important role because it contributes to the longer retention that is associated with positive treatment outcome.

Other Psychosocial Interventions

The specific elements previously discussed should be woven into a treatment plan that maximizes structure in the early months of recovery. Patients at this stage do not plan and manage their time well and can benefit from attention to mundane details, such as regular eating, sleeping, and exercise patterns. Many programs use a monthly calendar in which the patient can enter specific activities and also indicate days of abstinence. The therapist should be attentive to whether the patient has scheduled too little or too much. Unstructured time, particularly evenings, weekends, or other periods when drugs were regularly used, is a definite hazard. Overambitious plans are also risky. Solitude is often a problem. Outpatient AOD programs usually offer a menu of activities designed to address these problems. The private practitioner has the task of assembling a program from various elements available in the community.

Drug cravings and drug dreams are often a problem at this stage. Many patients do not experience cravings in the sense of a distinct drug hunger they can identify. Cocaine users are more likely to experience distinctive urges, but for users of other drugs, the experience can be more ambiguous. For some, craving emerges in fantasies of using or in related fantasies such as musings about how to access money without a spouse's knowledge. For others, it manifests as irritability, often a withdrawal symptom not recognized as a manifestation of craving. Patients need to be taught to identify and manage these states. They often interpret them to mean a failure of motivation or progress and need to be reassured they are often merely physiological states, signs that the brain is healing. Drug dreams can be highly distressing, particularly when patients awake unsure of whether they actually drank or used. In the early stages of treatment, dream interpretation should be kept simple and oriented to the present. For example, patients can be asked to explore a drug dream from the perspective of its message about how they need to augment their support system to reduce their vulnerability. A fuller discussion of the use of dreams can be found in Flowers and Zweben (1996, 1998).

Initiating 12-step program participation is invaluable at this point. Specific resistances and suggestions for handling them can be found in Chapter 8. In most urban communities, an extensive selection of meetings makes it possible to fill the vacuum left by eliminating AOD use with meetings and related activities. Thus, it is possible to quickly access a sub-culture that supports recovery and does not have financial barriers. The therapist's vigorous efforts to connect the patient with the 12-step system will greatly increase the chances of success at establishing and sustaining abstinence. Resistance to attending should not be met with ultimatums (e.g., "I won't see you unless you go") but rather with an insistence that the patient who feels strongly opposed to going needs to identify and commit to alternatives that will provide the support and learning structure offered within this system. Some therapists assume that regular participation in a self-help group constitutes addressing the addiction and that they need not become involved with the issue. However, self-help groups do not give the kind of systematic attention to issues central to the individual patient that the therapist can be expected to provide.

COGNITIVE–BEHAVIORAL THERAPY
TO TEACH COPING SKILLS

Much research has been done on cognitive–behavioral interventions (Rounsaville, Carroll, & Beck, 2009), often studied as individual therapies because conditions are easier to control. When compared with no treatment, about 29% had better substance use outcomes (Magill & Ray, 2009).

When compared with other well-structured therapies, however, the differences were more modest; only 8% would do better than a typical person in the comparison groups. The authors noted two other advantages. Some (but not all) studies have supported the view that the effects persist and may even amplify over time when the treatment is discontinued. It is also important that cognitive–behavioral therapy lends itself to manualization. This is a great advantage for widespread implementation. It allows therapists to have a "guidebook" for incorporating these tools, even if training is not readily available. These can be useful to the therapist who is not a substance abuse specialist. Many are available at no charge.

Commonly used manuals and guides include the following.

- Motivational enhancement:
  Enhancing Motivation for Change in Substance Abuse Treatment (W. R. Miller, 1999)
- Early recovery and relapse prevention skills:
  Cognitive Therapy of Substance Abuse (Beck, Wright, Newman, & Liese, 1993)
  A Cognitive–Behavioral Approach: Treating Cocaine Addiction (Carroll, 1998)
  Cognitive–Behavioral Coping Skills Therapy Manual (Kadden et al., 1995)
  Counselor's Family Education Manual: Matrix Intensive Outpatient Treatment for People with Stimulant Use Disorders (Center for Substance Abuse Treatment, 2006b)
  Counselor's Treatment Manual: Matrix Intensive Outpatient Treatment for People with Stimulant Use Disorders (Center for Substance Abuse Treatment, 2006c)
  *MAA*EZ: Making AA Easy* (Kaskutas & Oberste, 2002)
  Seeking Safety: A treatment manual for PTSD and substance abuse (Najavits, 2002)
  Twelve-Step Facilitation Therapy Manual (Nowinski, Baker, & Carroll, 1994)

Emerging research findings on effective treatment interventions can be found through the Dissemination Library of the Clinical Trials Network, National Institute on Drug Abuse (http://ctndisseminationlibrary.org).

EARLY AND ONGOING RECOVERY ISSUES

Once abstinence is well established, many changes must occur to sustain gains. Time frames are hard to specify because of the considerable variation in individuals, but in general, 3 months continuous abstinence from all intoxicants is a frequent marker for moving into a second (but still early) stage of recovery. During this period, coping strategies need to be devised or strengthened to replace alcohol and drugs as a way of managing life difficulties and challenges. The abstinent individual is in a better position to acknowledge existing problems and address them, but the magnitude of this task can be daunting. Relationships are often quite damaged. Work performance may have been affected. Old developmental issues, including traumatic experiences, become more visible. The therapist needs to help the patient prioritize these issues from the perspective of sustaining and building on the recovery achievements to date. The manner in which an issue can be addressed in someone with 4 months sobriety is different from what is possible after 2 years. Through all this, a deeper change is hopefully underway. S. Brown (1985) described in detail the identity transformation that takes place in recovery, emphasizing that behavior change is only the beginning of a process that will greatly affect self-concept, thinking, and behavior.

Accepting the identity of a recovering person is an important achievement at this point. It is unfortunate that the media has focused on some examples in which this identity is dominated by self-disparagement, and it is certainly appropriate to examine ways in which "person in recovery" is a negative identity. The desirable end point is to integrate "recovering person" as a central (but not sole) dimension, accepted comfortably and without shame, as an element that brings awareness of the need for ongoing self-care. This includes the recognition, "I am an addict/alcoholic; I cannot drink/use" (S. Brown, 1985). It also involves attention to stress management, health practices, and relationship issues that could constitute relapse hazards. A recovering person who has done the inner work often exemplifies a level of personal awareness and honesty comparable with what is considered a "good" patient for psychotherapy. Certainly, recovering people involved in their program make excellent psychotherapy participants because the processes are so complementary.

A patient who resists integrating the identity of recovering person may terminate treatment or recovery-related activities prematurely. Several months of complete abstinence leaves most patients feeling a great deal better, and it is tempting to view alcohol and drugs as "the problem I used to have" and withdraw energy from the recovery process. The desire to avoid the stigma associated with being an addict or alcoholic can also influence their desire to disconnect. Wishing to believe that so long as they do not drink or use, they do not have to remain attentive to this area of their lives, they reduce or eliminate recovery-related activities. This makes them vulnerable to being taken by surprise by the many risk factors that emerge.

Euphoric recall is common among stimulant users and occurs with others as well (Washton & Zweben, 2009). Painful negative consequences fade in memory, and a cloud of denial settles in as the person begins to have fantasies of the pleasures of using. "I feel better now; I'm together in a way I wasn't before. I can handle it," they muse. It is important that the therapist create a climate in which the patient can share these fantasies of drinking and using when they occur. Therapists need to be firm in their recommendations of abstinence while conveying a realistic acknowledgment that people have given up something they like very much and will have urges or even try to convince themselves they can drink or use again. The therapist must make these issues a part of the discussion without making them the focus of a power struggle. A common error at this point is to attempt to deal with the issue by elaborating at length on the disease model rather than by clinical exploration to clarify the nature of the current issues. Education provides the basis for interpreting resistance early in treatment, and basic tenets do need to be repeated, but if the clinician is not clear what the issues are, interventions can fall on deaf ears.

Instead, the therapist needs to determine what factors operate to increase the patient's interest in drinking or using drugs. These can range from growing anxiety over emerging psychological or interpersonal problems; social pressure or feelings about "not being normal, like people who drink"; unidentified triggers, such as approaching celebrations or vacations; and feelings of deserving a reward "for being so good." While exploring these issues, the therapist should encourage the patient to strengthen his or her behavioral supports for abstinence, such as good self-care, self-help meeting attendance, and so forth.

At this point in the process, the use of other intoxicants frequently becomes an issue. Patients will state that they are not in danger because "I never had a problem with alcohol before I used cocaine" or "I don't like benzos as much as I like drinking; the effect is not at all the same, so I don't see how it can become a problem." In fact, both clinical observation and empirical data indicate two major risks: substitution of another drug, which quickly or gradually becomes a problem, and use of another intoxicant as a precursor to relapse to the primary drug of abuse. In the case of the former, the substitution of a drug in the same or a related class as the primary choice (e.g., the patient with alcoholism on Antabuse who develops a need for antianxiety medication, such as alprazolam, known as Xanax) is an obvious danger, but it is also common for other substitutions to become problematic. For example, a former cocaine user who, after 2 years of abstinence, begins to drink wine with dinner may not appear to have an alcohol problem for some time. Problems with alcohol typically develop over a longer time frame, and it would not be unusual for such persons to appear to drink "normally" for several years and then gradually escalate their drinking.

In the case of the use of another intoxicant as a precursor to relapse, there are several possible scenarios. Most users will readily acknowledge that if they have consumed even a small amount of a psychoactive substance (e.g., alcohol), their chances of navigating successfully should their primary preference mysteriously appear (e.g., someone in the bar producing cocaine) are small. Thus, the idea that the use of another intoxicant is an immediate risk factor does not meet with much resistance. However, it is also common when one reconstructs an episode of relapse to the primary drug of abuse, to find that the use of another intoxicant occurred within a month or two prior to the relapse. One can speculate that this is part of the psychological setup for relapse (e.g., the desire to get high) or that the use of another intoxicant stimulates hunger in the brain for the primary drug of abuse; likely, it is a combination of factors. As in the first example of drug substitution, negative consequences removed in time are difficult for patients to connect. Thus, they downplay the role of the beer at the baseball game in the relapse 3 weeks later. However, this occurs so regularly that therapists should take the use of any intoxicant as an important warning sign. These issues are by no means easy to settle; the therapist should prepare for extended observation and discussion. It is also helpful to encourage the patient to bring these issues up in recovery groups, in self-help meetings, and with sponsors. This gives them the opportunity to discover how common they are and what can happen if they are not acknowledged or addressed.

Another major task in ongoing recovery is to reconfigure the social networks to support abstinence. Over time, people modify their social behavior to conform to their alcohol and drug use patterns. For example, they invest more in relationships with those who drink at the same level they do and often leave nondrinking friends behind. Once sustained abstinence is the goal, they find themselves uncomfortable in many familiar social situations. Some attempt to learn to fit in anyway, rather than face the intimidating task of starting anew. Ultimately, however, that is the more productive approach. Many can reconnect with friends who do not drink at all or do not drink heavily. Avoiding illicit drug use is usually easier, except for the indigent. Others need to regenerate their social network, not a welcome task in adulthood. For adolescents, this issue is especially important because peer influence is often the primary trigger for relapse. Therapist support and direction is important here, affirming that the task is crucial to consolidating gains.

Coping with feelings and ambiguity is another potential focus of work in ongoing recovery. Alcohol and drug users come to lean heavily on substances to manage unpleasant feeling states, and recovery often demands that one develop new capacities and learn new skills. As described in detail in Chapter 2, Khantzian (1981, 1985, 1997) has written at length about how those with long histories of chemical use are often underdeveloped in their ability to identify their feelings and express themselves appropriately. Khantzian described four types of self-regulatory impairments that must be addressed throughout the recovery process but are a particular focus of work in ongoing recovery: impairments in self-care, vulnerabilities in self-development and self-esteem, troubled self/object relations, and deficits in affect tolerance.

Impairments in self-care are particularly evident from early abstinence on as the patient looks for coping methods to fill the vacuum left by alcohol and drugs. Ongoing recovery permits more thorough examination of underlying issues. Vulnerabilities in self-development and self-esteem, as well as troubled object relations, certainly not unique to substance users, are also best examined in depth once abstinence is solid. Affect tolerance can be addressed in a variety of ways. Alcohol and drug use represents an attempt to prevent being overwhelmed by terrifying affect; particular drugs are chosen for their specific psychopharmacologic action. For example, stimulants are attractive to women with eating disorders because they enhance feelings of powerfulness and suppress appetite. Once abstinence is established, these other issues come sharply into focus. Here again, a firm basis in abstinence is especially important as a foundation for anxiety-provoking explorations.

Tools such as those used in Gestalt therapy can aid patients in learning to notice, track, and express their feelings appropriately. Focusing on learning to simply tolerate an experience, rather than forcibly changing it with a drug, can be valuable at this point. Ambiguity tolerance can also be a focus because the all-or-none thinking characteristic of alcohol and drug users can persist for long periods into recovery. These kinds of process variables can be more elusive than content areas, but they are important elements in the inner transformation that solidifies recovery. Patients with a strong 12-step connection will be exposed to a variety of people with long-term recovery who are active in working with these issues and who elaborate on them in meetings. This provides support, encouragement, and insight to enhance the therapeutic process.

Later recovery is also the period when developmental issues, trauma history, and similar problems can be addressed in more depth. In the process of doing this, it is important to maintain a focus on the alcohol/drug axis (S. Brown 1985). This means periodic inquiry, even of someone with long-term abstinence, and encouragement to revive behavioral strategies (e.g., more meetings, attention to sleep, diet and exercise) during periods of emotional upheaval. Although the therapeutic work at this point is primarily that of conventional psychotherapy, the therapist should never underestimate the relapse risk and should maintain awareness of relapse dynamics.

CONCLUSION

This chapter gave an overview of the recovery process, primarily from the perspective of the therapist in private practice settings. With specific stages of recovery as a framework, we described how to integrate insight-oriented work with other types of interventions to facilitate the patient's progress through the stages. We also reviewed safety issues that can emerge in withdrawal and identifies other points at which collaboration with physicians and other care providers is important. The chapter summarized clinical dilemmas typical at each stage of recovery, giving guidelines and recommending evidence-based interventions when available.

6

Family Therapy

The family is usually an enduring support system, and improving its ability to support the recovery process is important. The stereotype of alcoholics and addicts as loners, cut off from contact with their families and living an "alley cat existence" is, in fact, incorrect (Stanton & Heath, 2005, p. 680). In reality, substance abusers, especially drug addicts, have more contact with their families than age-comparable individuals in the general population. Systematic research also supports the view that the family should be included in the treatment process. These data are consistent with a pattern of addicted individuals who have failed to thrive and whose family members have become interconnected with them in unhealthy ways. For these reasons family therapy is essential for treatment to be successful. Family therapy can be viewed as an adjunctive or stand-alone treatment.

Chapter 5 focused on the therapist working with the individual patient to assist him or her with admitting the problem and becoming willing to address it, establishing and consolidating abstinence, and changing the lifestyle to support recovery. This chapter deals with how the therapist can support the family through that process. The tasks of the family therapist involve engaging, joining, stabilizing, educating, analyzing family systems, developing coping strategies, and developing relapse prevention strategies. Although these tasks are presented sequentially, in reality they are intertwined. The therapist may often go back and forth between education and stabilization interventions within the course of the single session. Likewise, the therapist will probably be educating the family members and the patient in the first session.

ENGAGING: GETTING THE PATIENT INTO TREATMENT

The first task of the therapist working with patients with alcohol or other drug (AOD) use disorders is engaging the patient or family members. *Engaging* refers to techniques or strategies that encourage either the identified patient or other family members to acknowledge that a problem exists and to participate in the therapeutic process. It is an attempt to help the client move through the stages of change from precontemplation to contemplation to action (see Chapter 3, this volume).

Interventions

With adults, the process of engagement often involves what has come to be known as an *intervention*. Although the oldest and best-known intervention method is the Johnson Institute method (Johnson Institute, 1987), it is by no means the only method. There also exist other methods that have greater or lesser degrees of empirical support. These methods include A Relational Intervention Sequence for Engagement (ARISE; Landau & Garrett, 2006), the Pressure to Change (PTC; Barber & Crisp, 1995), and Community Reinforcement and Family Training (CRAFT; Smith & Myers, 2004).

In two types of situations, the therapist in private practice may be asked to help in an intervention. The first is with individuals who are in the precontemplation stage and who are highly resistant to the suggestion that their drinking or drug use is a problem. They are refusing to discuss it and are certainly not going to talk to a therapist about it. The family members feel frustrated and as if they are at the end of their rope. Negative consequences have accumulated over the years to the point where family members have had enough and are ready to throw the individual out. Or they are scared and fear for this person's life. In this situation, it is probably best to refer the family to an interventionist who is trained in one of the formal intervention techniques mentioned earlier. The therapist can still be involved in the ongoing therapy afterward, if appropriate, but doing the formal intervention is a specialization that takes training. Interventionists must know how to prepare the family in advance, how to transport the patient, and how to prepare for violence or other untoward circumstances.

The second type of intervention is more common. The client may be in the precontemplation or contemplation stage of change but is less hostile and less resistant. The therapist may not need an interventionist and may be able to handle the situation in his or her office. The basic approach is invitational, not confrontational. First, the family meets the therapist without the patient in the office. They discuss their concerns and issues, and the therapist explains the agenda of the coming meeting with the patient as well as the tone of that meeting. The tone should be one of caring, not anger or blame.

The family members write statements to the patient about his or her specific behaviors that have caused them concern. They should let the patient know that they are committed to his or her getting better and prepared to set certain boundaries. The boundaries can include no longer making excuses for the patient or the patient not living at home anymore, depending on how serious the situation has become. These prepared statements should be brief and written. The therapist should review the written statements in advance to be sure they are appropriate. The family then tells the patient that they have met with the therapist and invites the patient to join the next session. The important point is to invite the patient to participate with the other family members in a process of becoming healthy.

With adolescents who refuse to go, a simple approach works well. The parents are instructed to tell the adolescent that there will be a meeting at a certain date, time, and place, and he or she is invited to attend. They tell the adolescent that decisions will be made about his or her future. If the adolescent refuses to go, the parents are not to argue, but they are to remind the person that he or she will then have no input into the decisions about his or her future. Usually, the adolescent will attend the meeting. If he or she does not, the therapist can meet with the parents, collect background information, and make recommendations. The recommendations can range from restrictions and loss of privileges to residential treatment.

Other Intervention Methods

ARISE is a three-step approach (Landau & Garrett, 2006). The first step involves telephone sessions plus an in-person meeting of family or network members with the therapist to mobilize them to support treatment for the substance abuser. The second step is an "invitational intervention" with the substance abuser (Landau & Garrett, 2006). This intervention is not a surprise and does not involve consequences if treatment is refused. The third step is a surprise intervention similar to the Johnson Institute method (Johnson Institute, 1987).

The *PTC* method was developed for heavy drinkers who refuse to change (Barber & Crisp, 1995). This approach uses learning theory to teach five increasing levels of pressure to encourage the drinker to change. These range from educating the family member about the seriousness of the drinking problem and about PTC, to directly confronting the drinker about the negative effects of his or her drinking and making a simple request to change or seek help.

The *CRAFT* method also uses learning theory in a six- to eight-session program that teaches family members to use positive reinforcement and negative consequences to discourage substance abuse. CRAFT also places emphasis on identifying situations that could lead to violence in the family, by focusing on cues before violence begins. Finally, CRAFT teaches effective ways to suggest treatment options to the substance abuser (Smith & Myers, 2004).

JOINING: AFFILIATING WITH FAMILY MEMBERS AND THE PATIENT

Joining, another task of the family therapist, refers to the therapist affiliating with each individual family member. The therapist carefully listens and conveys that he or she is interested in what the family members have to say. Also, the therapist attempts to understand each individual's point of view and to address each individual's concerns:

> The quality of the relationship between the counselor and the family is a strong predictor of whether families will come to, stay in, and improve in treatment (M. S. Robbins, [Szapocznik, Alexander, & Miller,] 1998). Studies have found that the therapeutic relationship is a strong predictor of success in many forms of therapy (Rector, [Zuroff, & Segal,] 1999; Stiles, [Agnew-Davies, Hardy, Barkham, & Shapiro,] 1998). (Szapocznik, Hervis, & Schwartz, 2003, p. 25)

Initially it is important for the therapist to respect rather than to challenge the defensiveness of the family. Often these families have led lives centered on the frequent crises created by the behavior of the identified patient (the alcoholic or addict). Sometimes it seems to the family as if the drinking or drug use is the source of the entire problem. Therapists often hear, "If only he or she would stop drinking, then our lives would be fine!" They should challenge this assumption and introduce the idea that once abstinence occurs, other problems will become visible. First, when the alcoholic or user stops drinking or using, family life is often initially more chaotic and more confrontational. Emotions and feelings that have been medicated through the use of alcohol or drugs rise to the surface after these substances been removed. Often family tensions and underlying conflicts that may have contributed to the disorder in the first place are revisited after the person achieves sobriety.

Initially the therapist can acknowledge that drinking has certainly taken its toll on the entire family, and the therapist can sympathize with the family's concern over the patient's continued drinking. The therapist needs to communicate that he or she intends to take this issue seriously by making it a major focus of the therapeutic endeavor. He or she can say,

"Given the involvement of the entire family, including the identified patient, we can jointly develop a plan to address this issue."

Another common misconception poses a greater challenge for the therapist: the notion that alcohol or drugs are not the problem. In this regard, the family therapist does not directly challenge the family rules early in therapy. Instead the therapist works within existing family structures and supports areas of family strength, especially for those family members who are most threatened (Kaufman, 1994). An example of this clinical presentation is the family in which the adolescent is presenting with all the signs of an emerging substance abuse problem.

> The boy's grades have been declining for the past several years. For the past 6 months he has been staying out late, either missing curfew or sneaking out late at night. He has become increasingly isolated, spending more time in his room. He has a new peer group of adolescents who have either had difficulties with juvenile authorities or have dropped out of school. The precipitating event that led to the therapy appointment was the boy's arrest at a party where alcohol and marijuana were being used. The police determined that he had been drinking. Rolling papers but no actual drugs were found in his possession. The young man's story is that he was drinking for the first time and the rolling papers belonged to a friend.
>
> The parents begin the session by assuring the therapist that it is not a substance abuse problem. Each parent has a somewhat different perspective on the problem. The mother believes that the father is a workaholic who pays no attention to the children and that this is the source of the problem. She says, "A teenage boy needs a father to keep him in line." She continues, "When he does come home, he is often too tired to bother with the children. He is moody and irritable and has only negative things to say. He puts the boy down all the time." The father, however, thinks that the mother is too soft with the kids. "She is always making excuses for them and never holds them accountable," he explains. "Of course I am irritable," he says. "When I try to intervene and discipline the kids she is always there to undermine what I am doing. She can't stop protecting them for one minute."

Both parents are united on only one point. They insist that the problem is not drugs, and they do not want alcohol or drugs to be the focus of the intervention. They begin by stating that they took their son to one of those treatment centers, where they were told that he might have an addiction problem. They immediately left and brought their son to see you, the clinician, who would understand that their son is struggling with issues of self-esteem.

Here the therapist is in a bind. The parents have presented a clinical picture that suggests substance abuse but at the same time have given a clear warning that this topic is off-limits and should not be the focus of the therapeutic efforts. In a somewhat controlling way, they have said or implied that the last therapist who tried to focus on the substance abuse issue was fired and in continuing to work with this family it would be unwise to head down that same road. The bind, then, is how to join with this family and acknowledge their concerns without totally accepting the directive to defocus from the teenager's abuse of substances. The underlying family rule is clear: "Don't talk about the substance abuse problem."

Perhaps the mother comes from an alcoholic family herself where there was tremendous family disruption (e.g., constant crisis, chaos, physical or verbal abuse) and where a negative outcome ensued (e.g., death, institutionalization). Perhaps the father has a moral or judgmental view of people with substance abuse problems and cannot tolerate the idea that this problem exists within his family. Perhaps both parents have an overwhelming fear that their son could turn out to be a "druggie," and this would be unthinkable. Whatever the underlying issues, the family is warning the therapist that this is a brittle, sensitive issue that should not be confronted right away and must be dealt with in a sensitive and caring manner only after a trusting bond has been established.

In this instance, the therapist must acknowledge the fears that both parents have. The therapist can say, "Sneaking out at night, declining school grades, and the other symptoms mentioned are all important. We must look at the underlying reasons and try to develop a plan to address the problem." The therapist would also be remiss, however, if he or she did not raise the issue of the importance of the teenager remaining free from alcohol and drugs as a prerequisite for addressing these other issues. Most parents are willing to support the concept of an alcohol- and drug-free life for their teenager as a positive goal. Helping parents to see the link between regular drug use and low self-esteem, as well as other psychological problems, can help to fortify their resolve on this issue. Requesting their assistance in monitoring this through alcohol and drug screens, and emphasizing that this is a routine part of the procedure in such cases, is often received as a positive, affirming step, even by families with such a rigid defense structure. In this way, the notion of substance abuse as a possible confounding variable in the overall symptom or problem pattern is introduced without identifying substance abuse as the source of the problem. Later, the family's particular sensitivities about substance abuse issues can be examined and perhaps addressed more directly. Also, depending on the outcome of the monitoring process through alcohol and drug screens, the true nature of the problem may become more apparent.

Kaufman (1994) suggested *mimesis,* or using the family's preferred adaptive mode and styles of communication, as a way to join with the family. In the example of the teenager, for instance, when speaking to the father, the therapist might state in a more authoritative voice, "Yes, I agree rules are important. One of the things we are going to try to do in here is to set up reasonable rules and make sure that they are consistently applied." In speaking to the mother, however, the therapist might say in a somewhat softer, comforting voice, "We must also look at self-esteem. It is important not only for your son to learn how to feel good about himself but also for the whole family to learn how to feel good about this family unit." In this way, the therapist has supported each parent without undermining the other.

STABILIZING: GETTING TO ABSTINENCE

The next task of the family therapist who works with patients with AOD disorders is stabilization. *Stabilization* refers to a set of intervention strategies that are designed to assist the patient in either abstaining from mood-altering drugs completely or, where appropriate, reducing AOD use to the point at which the patient's functioning is not impaired. Most family therapists, regardless of their theoretical orientation, stress the importance of establishing abstinence before meaningful therapeutic work can be undertaken (S. Brown & Lewis, 1995; Kaufman, 1994; O'Farrell, 1993; Sisson & Azrin, 1993).

> The therapist must structure treatment so that the control of the alcohol abuse is the first priority before attempting to help the couple with other problems . . . [because] the hope that reduction in marital distress will lead to improvement in the drinking is rarely fulfilled. (O'Farrell, 1993, p. 172)

Achieving abstinence often occurs over an extended period of time. During this time, the therapist can help family members to see how their dysfunctional interactions serve to support the patient's substance-using behavior. The therapist should consider discontinuing therapy only when the identified patient and family members continually resist moving toward abstinence, thereby undermining therapeutic progress.

In many cases, however, this focus is the opposite direction from the one in which the family wishes to proceed. The family members have often joined with the alcoholic or drug addict in rigidly maintaining the existence of alternative explanations for the identified patient's problems. Thus, the family member may believe the source of the problem is not the husband's drinking but the stress of his job or perhaps the death of his father 2 years ago. In the clinical example of the adolescent, the source of the problem from the mother's perspective is not the AOD use but the father's parenting; from the father's perspective it is the mother's enabling behavior that creates the difficulties. When these explanations are in danger of breaking down, other explanations can be added or substituted. Therapists frequently hear parents say, "He failed the algebra class because of the bad teacher" or "She drinks because she is under tremendous pressure from her peers."

Faced with these rigid defenses, the therapist's job is to gently but firmly shift the focus back to the drinking and drug use. Fortunately, cracks begin to appear in the defense structure over time. The therapist highlights these cracks, notes the discrepancies, and focuses the family on the meaning of these episodes. Thus, the adolescent skips school; drinks or uses drugs; and, as a result, misses a test and drops a full letter grade. This event shows the loss of control over AOD use. The therapist needs to highlight the loss of control and define it for what it is: an example of drinking and drug-use behavior that needs to be stabilized. Also, the therapist can suggest that if AOD use is not a problem, it should not be a problem to stop for a period of time. By keeping the focus on the drinking and drug use, by highlighting episodes that illustrate loss of control, and by interpreting the meaning of these episodes, the therapist accelerates the process by which the family's defense structure collapses. The reality of the AOD use becomes too blatant to ignore.

Behavioral contracting is a specific method in which the therapist can help maintain the focus on alcohol and drug use and help move the patient toward abstinence. If in the early stages of therapy an abstinence contract is not achievable, the therapist can use a behavioral contract that will help to move the patient closer to an abstinence contract. The therapist, the family members, and the identified patient jointly agree on certain behavioral goals. For the adolescent these goals might include going to school, passing courses, coming in on time, and so forth. For the adult they might include enhancing performance at work, accepting responsibility at home, increasing involvement with the children, and so forth. The goals might also include complying with a specific therapeutic regimen such as taking disulfiram for the heavy drinker, agreeing to attend group therapy, or going to a certain number of self-help meetings per week.

The therapist and family should create an abstinence contract as soon as they can, because achieving abstinence is a prerequisite for any meaningful therapeutic change. The abstinence contract needs to be long enough to allow the physical and psychological realities of not drinking and using drugs to impinge on the identified patient. These realities include not only the physical withdrawal phase that can often be endured through determination, coping skills, and a good plan but also the waves of psychological craving that are sure to follow. A contract should be for at least 30 days, but a 60- or 90-day contract is preferable.

During the contract period the therapist can see the impact of sobriety on the family members as well as on the patient. Family members may insist that the situation has worsened. In some cases, wives have suggested that the husband return to drinking because he was more likable the old way. Still other family members may find themselves feeling surprisingly empty and lost because the crisis-centered nature of their existence has slowed down. If their role has been that of the rescuer, family members may feel as if their main function in life has been usurped. Most important, during the abstinence contract period, the identified patient has the opportunity to examine feelings that arise that are secondary to sobriety. He or she can focus on dreams, feelings, and thoughts about alcohol and drug use that are indicators of how attached the individual was to the substance.

Establishing a contract allows for the imposition of structure on a previously chaotic existence. It allows the family members and the identified patient to set specific goals by which progress can be measured. Setting specific goals and measuring progress on a weekly basis can help the resistant individual to understand how out of control his or her life has become and the need to move in a different direction. Likewise, contracting for a specific therapeutic regimen also can help to reinforce the need for structure in the lives of the patient and family members. If the patient agrees to attend five self-help meetings a week, and the family members agree to do the same, it soon becomes clear when these goals are not being met. When the patient, for example, misses meetings on a regular basis, this becomes grist for the mill to explore resistance by discussing unpleasant feelings or reactions to the meeting environment.

At this point the family may enter a true crisis stage. The identified patient often finds him- or herself in the uncomfortable position of having stopped drinking but having absolutely no coping mechanisms. Physical violence, suicide attempts, and other forms of acting out are not uncommon. The patient is more in touch with issues such as loss of control and is more aware of the destabilizing role that AOD use has played in the overall family problems. As this awareness emerges and behaviors begin to change, the patient is left without access to his or her primary coping mechanism, AOD use. An underlying sense of panic often emerges. The therapist must be prepared to intervene with other strategies to support, reassure, and guide the patient and family members once the drinking and drug using has stopped.

EDUCATING: WHAT IS NORMAL AND WHAT COMES NEXT

Education can be extremely helpful in the therapeutic process at this stage. It is important to normalize for the family the behaviors that the identified patient is exhibiting. To be helpful, the education must be based on knowledge of the normal pattern that ensues as the patient moves from drinking or using drugs to a recovery lifestyle. Two books by Stephanie Brown are helpful here: *Treating the Alcoholic* (1985) and *Treating Alcoholism* (1995).

The patient's regression in behavior occurs as a normal part of recovery. In early abstinence people often experience intense craving for the drug or alcohol. Often, discussing addictive craving directly with patients and family members is beneficial, comparing it with a primary drive state (see Chapter 2).

Family members, especially parents of adolescents, often become concerned because the patient is not performing to their expectations. "Sure, he's sober, but he still doesn't bring home any books from school. He never studies, and he seems uninterested in playing sports like he used to," is a common refrain. The father of an adolescent patient exclaimed angrily, "He needs to get on with his life. It's his senior year in high school and he has football, he has academics, he has college applications. Why is he so uninterested in all of this?" At this point the therapist can encourage family members to scale back expectations and to keep focused on the target. In the early days of recovery, abstinence is a full-time job.

The therapist should encourage the patient to immerse him- or herself in a recovery program. The therapist should encourage the family members to step back and allow this process to happen, supporting it when they can but certainly not obstructing it. Family members, especially spouses, may become jealous of the time that the husband or wife spends going to self-help meetings. Therapists often hear the refrain, "He spends more time with them than he spends with me." Family members may feel that the identified patient has become addicted to the program itself.

The answer to the family's questions is that patients' reality in the early days of sobriety is one of hanging on for dear life, trying not to use but not possessing many recovery skills of their own. They are attracted to a support group precisely because they are so desperate. They see others at these meetings who seem happy but who also understand the craving that they are experiencing. These recovering people do not judge or analyze the situation; rather, they provide support and give the patient concrete tools for staying sober "one day at a time." Slowly, patients learn how to structure leisure hours that were previously devoted to drinking and using drugs. They learn to telephone their sponsor in times of crisis. They learn the soothing effects of daily meditation and reading related literature that speaks to their experience. A sponsor is someone who has been abstinent and sober in the 12-step program for a length of time and is now ready to help newcomers and others on their path to sobriety (see Chapter 7). Forming new relationships and new behavior patterns makes it easier to let go of the old. This process is the full-time job of recovery.

At this stage in the process the therapist's knowledge of addiction and recovery stages is vital to the family. They are desperate for information, especially knowledge about the sequencing of recovery-related behaviors and knowledge about what they can expect in the future. They want to know how long before the identified patient is his or her old self again. The patient wants to know how long before he or she will not wake up in the middle of the night dreaming about using. Parents want to know whether their child can return to the old school environment or can be transferred to another one. All family members want to know what is safe to talk about at home. Will they trigger a relapse if they say the wrong thing? The therapist must be prepared to respond to these questions with factual information based on experience.

Especially valuable at this point is referring family members to self-help meetings of their own, such as Al-Anon. This rapidly accelerates the learning curve because they are immediately exposed to other family members who have progressed further through the process and can provide knowledge and support for them. Soon family members' resentment of the patient's time at self-help meetings lessens because they are deriving nourishment and support from their own recovery programs.

The therapist must also be prepared to address the underlying emotion of fear, which is expressed by the questions "Will he ever get better?" or "Will he survive?" or "Will he ever be normal?" The family is seeking reassurance at this point, and some should be forthcoming. "Of course he can get better, and there is no reason why he should not. Millions of others have gone before him and have recovered, so he can too." By the same token, such questions also provide an opportunity for education. If the patient is truly AOD dependent, recovery is closely tied to remaining abstinent from all mood-altering drugs. Both the patient and family members need to know this principle early in the process.

Another series of questions often posed by family members involves the process of rebuilding trust. Parents wonder, "How can we ever believe anything our child says again?" Often parents will say, "He used drugs for years right under our noses. We are afraid of being burned again." Although their fear is real, the therapist can remind the parents that they are now more educated about this topic than they were in the past. Most appropriately, the therapist can review the warning signs that the family observed but perhaps ignored in the past.

The patient is afraid of relapsing, whereas the family is afraid of returning to the chaos and crisis that permeated their lives for so many years. A frank discussion of this issue is in order. The therapist should support the family members at this point by communicating something such as, "You should never have to return to that type of chaos. Let's develop a plan for dealing with it should it arise." A statement of this type can effectively lead into a discussion of a relapse prevention plan. It is often appropriate at this point for the patient to state what he or she plans to do in the event of a relapse and to discuss some ways of regaining sobriety.

Rather than a rigid plan such as going to long-term treatment, a more flexible plan is preferable, such as, "In the event of a relapse we (the patient and family members) agree to contact you (the therapist) immediately and jointly develop a set of strategies and recommendations." These recommendations might include increasing the frequency of meeting attendance, increasing the frequency of therapy sessions, or attending a special group for assertiveness training. Another recommendation, according to the nature of the relapse, might be long-term treatment.

The essential point is that the therapist and the family members as well as the patient are not locked into a predetermined plan that might not be appropriate to the nature of the regression. All relapses are not equal; therefore, it is impossible to specify in advance an appropriate intervention for a given relapse. Once again, these issues are educational points that need to be stressed to the patient and family members during the early stages of the recovery process.

Other questions that family members ask involve signs of knowing when the patient is not doing well. The answers revolve around three essential warning signs. The first warning sign of not doing well is the use of any psychoactive drug. The patient whose drug of choice is cocaine and whose abuse has progressed to the level of dependency cannot drink alcohol and expect to be successful. Therefore, the patient who attempts to use any psychoactive drug on a responsible basis should be considered in relapse. Although conceptually useful for the therapist, it is not helpful to distinguish between a slip, a lapse, or a relapse when talking with patients and their families. These labels inevitably lead to arguments about what this particular incident is. It is more effective to say that any use at all constitutes a relapse while at the same time acknowledging that not all relapses are equal.

The second sign that the patient is not doing well is a failure to comply with the therapeutic plan. The patient may stop attending recovery meetings, refuse to take medication as prescribed, or refuse to attend scheduled psychotherapy sessions. Of particular significance are situations in which a patient does not show for appointments and/or refuses to be monitored by drug and alcohol screens that had previously been agreed on.

The third major warning sign is a return to old habits and patterns. For adults the signs may be staying out late, becoming isolated from the family, experiencing increased irritability and moodiness, and/or failing to fulfill responsible duties in the family (e.g., parenting duties, chores around the house). For adolescents the signs may be declining school grades, running away, sneaking out at night, and a declining interest in extracurricular activities. For both adults and adolescents, returning to old friends who use AODs and frequenting old AOD places sends a strong signal of increased relapse potential.

Both the patient and the family members feel a sense of relief and satisfaction when these warning signs are discussed openly. Patients sometimes describe it as feeling that a safety net has been erected. Although they (especially adolescents) tend to protest, they know that those who love and care for them will never again be so easily manipulated. They know that their conning and deceiving is not likely to go unnoticed. As one alcoholic put it, "If I ever relapse again, I hope someone will stop me."

For family members, knowing the warning signs can sometimes free them from trying to control the patient so much. "If he is using, we are all going to know about it sooner rather than later" is a therapeutic statement that relieves some of the family's and patient's anxieties.

Although these interventions are described as educational in nature, they also serve a psychotherapeutic purpose. They address underlying insecurities, anxieties, trust issues, and fears that are common to family members and patients alike. They begin to help the family members and patients feel a sense of control over a previously unmanageable situation.

ANALYZING FAMILY SYSTEMS

Once abstinence has been achieved, the task of the family therapist becomes that of analyzing the family system and structures that may have contributed to the AOD problem. In some cases, the family dysfunction precedes the alcohol and drug abuse; in others, it comes in response to the substance abuse. In either case, the family therapist can help the family members see how their own dysfunctional behavior has contributed to or sustained the substance abuse problem.

Sometimes family behaviors serve to perpetuate the substance use (Stanton & Heath, 2005, p. 681). An example is when the addicted individual begins to improve, the parents begin to fight and develop a distance from each other. When the addicted person returns to using behavior, the parents become united in attempts to deal with the new crisis, thus shift-ing attention away from their problems.

The alcohol or drug use plays an increasingly dominant role in the lives of the patient and other family members. Daily routines of sleeping, wak-ing, mealtimes, and shopping are changed to get some semblance of normal family life (Steinglass, Bennett, Wolin, & Reiss, 1987, p. 63). Family rituals also change over time. The alcoholic who is drinking may disrupt family vacations. As a result, the family plans vacations that are less stressful to the alcoholic or stops vacations altogether. Thanksgiving dinner may be eaten at home rather than at a relative's house so that the alcoholic can be brought to the table at least for a few minutes (Steinglass et al., 1987, p. 73).

Family problem solving is affected. Reactions to problems are often dis-proportionate and overly aggressive in relation to the magnitude of the prob-lem (Steinglass et al., 1987, p. 69). Family rules and problem solving become rigid. In some families, the expression of certain behaviors (e.g., expression of affect) occurs only in the presence of intoxication. Other behaviors may occur only in the presence of sobriety. Over time, the patient's drinking or drug use becomes the central organizing principle of family functioning.

Individuals who are involved with alcoholics or drug users sometimes live a reactive lifestyle in which they are enmeshed in the day-to-day activ-ities of the addict. This is referred to as *codependence.*

> As a result of this emotional enmeshment, the codependent tends to lose all sense of "self" or identity and to become emotionally depen-dent upon the addict. The addict's mood dictates the codependent's mood. In a sense the codependent becomes an appendage to the addict and the substance abuse. (Thombs, 1994, p. 161)

The codependent and other family members are encouraged to develop a sense of detachment. To "detach with love" is the way out of the trap. Detachment comes by acknowledging one's powerlessness over the behav-ior of the addicted individual and by stopping the controlling and enabling behavior patterns.

S. Brown and Lewis (1995) explained that during the initial stages of therapeutic work it is often necessary for the alcoholic and the family to both hit bottom and thus allow the alcoholic system to collapse. As this process proceeds, the therapist must work with each family member to shift focus away from the identified patient and toward a personal program of recovery. The family members "must disengage from their unhealthy addictive attachment to the alcoholic and focus on themselves" (S. Brown & Lewis, 1995, p. 295). The therapist must work closely with the entire family to help them tolerate the separation of different recovery programs and to support their ongoing involvement in this process.

The task of the family therapist at this point is first to help the family members see how alcohol has invaded the routines and rituals and, second, to help the family restructure daily functioning so as to not reinforce drinking and drug-using behavior. This point is a difficult one in the therapeutic process because the therapist's suggestions are usually those that the family has already considered and rejected. For example, the therapist may suggest behaviors that allow the substance user to experience the consequences of his or her behavior. The therapist might suggest that a wife allow her husband to sleep on the floor after he has passed out drunk or not call his boss in the morning to make excuses when he is unable to appear for work on time. The therapist might suggest allowing the adolescent to experience the consequences of the juvenile court system when he has been arrested for possession of marijuana.

The family members might view these suggestions with astonishment, thinking that the therapist has taken leave of his or her senses. Sometimes it helps to start with small steps such as encouraging the family to plan a night out together. The therapist might reinforce the notion that this outing is to take place with or without the participation of the identified patient.

Once again, Al-Anon or Nar-Anon can be helpful. Contact with other families of recovering addicts allows family members to see their problems in a different light. Family members often note the remarkable similarity between their issues and those discussed at meetings. They begin to see the role that alcohol and drug abuse has played in organizing family life. They hear about concepts such as enabling, codependence, and detachment. They learn that by not allowing the alcoholic or drug addict to experience the consequences of his or her behavior, they are enabling the process to continue. They learn that allowing the substance-abusing individual to hit bottom provides the best hope for positive outcomes. They also learn that by allowing patients to experience consequences, the family members are constructing a "higher bottom" for the addict so that the patient will reach for help sooner.

Family members initially view this advice and new learning with skepticism because it runs so contrary to their thinking. Through support, sharing, and confrontation by other group members, the family members begin to see the value of this new behavior. They then become more amenable to the restructuring suggestions of the therapist. Because both the therapist and the support group are giving a consistent message, the strength of that message assumes greater power. The family slowly begins to change behavior patterns and with great fearfulness awaits the results.

Now the therapist must be willing to provide extra support. Telephone calls after hours are common as family members need to be reassured that they are doing the right thing. One particular situation occurred with the mother of a substance-abusing young adult who refused to stop using and was eventually asked to leave the home. Over the next 6 months this young man would periodically appear at the mother's doorstep and request readmission to the family. As the weather turned colder his requests were more urgent and forceful. The advice to the mother was always the same: Offer the young man treatment and tell him that he could return home after 1 month's sobriety in a halfway house. The mother called each time the young man appeared at the door, and she asked the same question: "Is it okay to do the same thing and stick with the plan?" The answer was always in the affirmative, and the mother would say, "Thanks. I just needed to hear that." After 6 months the young man entered treatment.

The therapist must be able to openly acknowledge the fears of the family members as they move toward new ways of dealing with the patient's drinking or drug using. At the same time, the therapist must stay firm in the resolve that the family "stay the course" even when it looks as if things might not work out. Frequently, family members object at this point because of the possible negative results of the person leaving home. Getting arrested, overdosing, or contracting HIV are possibilities. The therapist cannot minimize these concerns or even suggest that the family is resisting setting limits, even if that is partially correct. Rather, the therapist can acknowledge these concerns and point out that the risks are high either way. The choice may be whether the addicted person stays at home, continually sheltered from the consequences of drug use, or leaves to face the consequences of using AODs. It should be emphasized that the family should not make the decision to set limits until they are ready and that they should not threaten to set boundaries if they are not prepared to follow through. The therapist should stress that this is the family's decision; he or she can support them in the process but not make the decision for them.

Families nearly always experience this stage of recovery as a destabilizing time. Once enabling behaviors have been reduced or stopped and the alcoholic or addicted individual is allowed to hit bottom, the work of the family therapist is to help the family tolerate the stress. The introduction of sobriety into the lifestyle of the family is expected to be positive but rarely is. The therapist now begins the next task: helping the family to develop new coping mechanisms that will better serve them in their new lifestyle.

DEVELOPING COPING STRATEGIES

The next stage in the therapeutic process involves helping the patient and the family to tolerate the anxiety that inevitably goes with change. The next stage involves the development of new coping strategies, such as enhanced communication skills and dealing with conflict, so as to sustain the therapeutic gains that they have fought so hard to achieve.

One of the first coping skills that the family needs to learn is how to explore and talk about affective material. Although uncovering affective material is an important part of therapy with addicts, as with other psychiatric disorders, timing is of the essence with patients with AOD use disorders. S. Brown and Lewis (1995) explained the importance of timing in the use of psychodynamic concepts in the treatment of addicts and alcoholics. They observed that uncovering deep-seated affective material too early in the treatment of alcoholics can often lead to relapse. If too much painful affective material is uncovered, it can trigger overwhelming anxiety and depression for the alcoholic in the early stages of recovery. Because these individuals usually have no coping skills other than the use of alcohol and drugs, they are likely to drink or use drugs to blot out the painful affective experience.

Family members of patients who are addicted are also often threatened by the emergence of affective material too soon in the therapeutic process. In many instances, alcoholic families have developed rigid boundaries with inflexible rules. These rules typically include prohibitions against speaking about affectively laden material. The family often believes that talking about conflicts could trigger more drinking or drug using on the part of the addicted patient. As the family accommodates itself to the invasion of alcohol (Steinglass et al., 1987), they attempt to completely dampen or suppress affective material. Thus, painful feelings fester beneath the surface for years.

For these reasons the therapist should uncover affective material gingerly at first. Inevitably, painful feelings and discussions of traumatic events emerge as the patient and the family move toward greater recovery. In the early stages of family therapy, however, the focus is not an in-depth discussion of traumatic events or a deep exploration of affective material but rather on how these issues are likely to affect abstinence and the recovery programs of the other family members. The therapist encourages the family to keep on course and to push ahead with their individual personal programs of recovery. The emphasis is on the maintenance of therapeutic gains (e.g., abstinence for the patient and a personal program of recovery for all family members).

Of course, issues of abuse, abandonment, or other painful affective topics do emerge during family therapy sessions. The skilled therapist knows how threatening the emergence of this material can be for the patient and family members. At the end of a difficult therapy session the therapist might state, "I know this has been a difficult time for the family. Sometimes this may trigger cravings or a desire to use. Let's talk about how we can address these cravings if they should occur." The individuals might sustain themselves and handle the cravings by increasing the frequency of self-help meetings and sponsor contact. In this way self-help meetings and family psychotherapy work in conjunction with each other to support the family's ongoing process of recovery. For example, here is what happened for one adolescent patient:

> This young man had been dealing with the reality that his parents were on the verge of divorce. Even as the adolescent was progressing through treatment and getting sober, the parents were planning to separate. At the time of the session, the parents were still living together, and the tension was heavy in the air at home. The patient was attempting to deal with his sadness and frustration over the divorce by isolating himself in his room. The patient's mother, a recovering alcoholic with 10 years of sobriety, went to the boy in his room and encouraged him to go to a meeting. The patient and his mother went to the meeting together. By talking in the meeting, the patient gained support and came home feeling more relieved and relaxed. Through this simple experience, the boy realized for the first time that he could relieve his feelings of sadness and frustration without the use of psychoactive drugs. He began to see feelings more like waves that would pass over him rather than like a permanent fixture that needed to be blotted out through pharmacological means.

With experiences such as these, it becomes safer to begin exploring affective material in a more meaningful way. As therapy progresses, abstinence becomes more secure. The therapist can then begin the work of traditional psychodynamic uncovering because the family no longer views this work as a threat to recovery.

In addition to uncovering painful affective material and working through traumatic family events, the family psychotherapist can offer other specific skills to the family members to help them cope with the stresses of living a sober lifestyle. Many of these interventions, such as communication skills and stress reduction mechanisms, originate from behavioral or learning theory models of family psychotherapy such as O'Farrell's (1993) behavioral marital therapy.

Other programs teach similar behavioral skills to enhance marital satisfaction and decrease the probability that the identified patient will return to drinking or drug use. Noel and McCrady (1993) and Sisson and Azrin

(1993) have also developed programs that focus on learning communication and stress reduction techniques that help the early stage recovering person.

Although O'Farrell's (1993) techniques are used in his couples program, many of these techniques can be altered and used in a more traditional individual family psychotherapy setting. The therapist who wishes to work with patients with AOD disorders should become familiar with these techniques as a means of enhancing effectiveness with this population. The therapist who is most effective in working with addicted families is generally not locked into one ideological model (e.g., disease model, social learning model, psychodynamic model) but knows and uses an assortment of tools to achieve the desired outcome.

DEVELOPING RELAPSE PREVENTION STRATEGIES

The final task of the family therapist who works with patients with AOD disorders is to assist the family in formulating and implementing a relapse prevention strategy. On a basic level, a relapse prevention plan addresses how each family member, including the identified patient, intends to address relapse if and when it occurs. On a more complex level, the plan should identify what steps the identified patient and the family members can take to prevent relapse from occurring in the first place. The plan should address not only what to do once the relapse has occurred but also what concrete steps can be undertaken to prevent it.

For the purposes of the plan, the definition of *relapse* is expanded to include not only the use of psychoactive drugs by the identified patient but also the return to dysfunctional behaviors by the individual family members. These dysfunctional behaviors signal a regression of the family toward more primitive, dysfunctional coping strategies. For example, after having worked at a recovery program successfully for a number of months, a wife may find herself returning to controlling behaviors such as searching through her husband's car and possessions to find evidence of whether he has returned to drinking. Sometimes these behaviors reappear at the point at which the identified patient is beginning to make real therapeutic gains. Many family members feel threatened by these gains, especially when the patient begins to behave in a more autonomous manner.

> Perhaps an adolescent girl is beginning to develop new friendships within the recovering community. She wants to go on a weekend camping trip to the mountains. She will go with her new recovering friends, and the trip will be properly supervised by adults. The parents unfortunately associate this type of fun with using behaviors and become increasingly suspicious. "Why does she want to go camping? What are they doing out in the woods? Can they be trusted? Will there be girls and boys together?" As they become increasingly suspicious, the parents move to reassert control. They cancel the plans for the camping trip, thus undermining the adolescent's attempts to bond with other recovering peers.

The family therapist should identify and address these behaviors as relapse behaviors. Although the parents' fears must be validated, it is important to identify for them how they have allowed their fears to propel them into relapse behavior. In this case, however, relapse is defined not as the use of psychoactive drugs but as a regression out of recovery and into dysfunctional, controlling behavior patterns.

Handling Triggers

The relapse plan needs to begin to focus on the dysfunctional behaviors that often precede relapse for the identified patient and for the family members. Often a good place to start with the relapse prevention plan is to discuss triggers for the identified patient. For adult patients the most common relapse triggers include negative affect states. For adolescent patients the most common triggers involve peer interactions. The therapist can assist the patient and family members to identify triggers, the obvious ones being, for example, returning to old using friends, frequenting places where using occurred, and unanticipated situations and events. For example, major life changes, such as moving to another city or changing jobs, are potential triggers.

A move to another city involves establishing a new support network, meeting with a new therapist, and attending new outside support meetings. These situations involve a large amount of planning. Contacting a new therapist prior to the move is an important step. Perhaps the family can make advance contact with existing self-help support groups while visiting the city so that the process of bonding with a new group can begin before the move actually occurs. Changing jobs may mean that the patient's meeting schedule is disrupted. In addition, the new environment may be less conducive to recovery (e.g., coworkers who frequent bars after work). The therapist should also discuss the timing of these changes. Is it wise to undertake a change of jobs early in the recovery process? It is wise to discuss issues like these.

Some triggers cannot be avoided. These include serious illnesses or deaths. Although it is impossible to develop specific plans for unforeseen catastrophes, it is often important to mention that they are a possibility and to underscore the necessity of the patient connecting with his or her sponsor (see Chapter 7), therapists, and other support systems in time of crisis.

Handling Cravings

In addition to discussing triggers, the therapist should openly discuss the nature of cravings and how the patient intends to handle them. Craving is normal for addicts and alcoholics. To deny the existence of craving is to ask the patient to suppress powerful urges and feelings and thus to shut down communication within the family. Although it is scary for family members to hear that the patient is craving, it is an important realization that needs to be acknowledged and validated by the therapist. The relapse plan helps because it gives the therapist and family members specific tasks to do when cravings occur and gives them a sense of mastery over the situation. The patient can call his sponsor or go to a meeting. The family can assist the patient by providing transportation or taking over responsibilities, thus freeing the patient to deal with the cravings in a healthy way.

Another goal of the relapse prevention plan is to specify specific behaviors that the family members can practice that will minimize the possibility of a relapse for each family member. Family members and patients may commit to practicing stress reduction techniques such as exercise, meditation, or breathing exercises on a daily basis. The therapist can remind the family members of the new communication patterns that they have developed and incorporate them into the relapse prevention plan.

Relapse Prevention for Couples

The therapist should encourage the family to commit to handling troubling new situations and issues by reengaging in the therapeutic process. Frequently, sexual issues emerge after some months of sobriety. As these issues emerge, the couple needs to reengage with the therapist to resolve them as part of the relapse plan. After developing a 10-session behavioral marital therapy (BMT) protocol, O'Farrell (1993) discovered that although patients often reported increased marital satisfaction a year later, their rates of relapse did not differ significantly between the BMT group and the control group. After adding a 12-month relapse prevention component to his program, drinking outcomes improved considerably.

O'Farrell's relapse prevention component consists of 15 couples sessions over the course of a year, with a gradually decreasing frequency. The relapse prevention component has three goals. The first goal is to help the couple maintain the gains achieved in the BMT group during the initial phase of the program. The couple is asked to list the specific goals that were achieved and to examine any problems that might arise in regard to maintaining these goals. The couple is encouraged to develop a written plan that involves specific therapeutic interventions, such as continuing with disulfiram, attending Alcoholics Anonymous and Al-Anon meetings, and implementing new coping strategies such as improved communication skills.

The second goal of the relapse prevention phase is to deal with unresolved issues that emerge during the first year of recovery. Difficulty often arises when the identified patient attempts to assume a more assertive or dominant role in the family after having been labeled as the "sick" person for so long (O'Farrell, 1993). Other issues include substance abuse by other family members and sexual issues. Couples are encouraged to apply the communication and coping skills that they were taught during the initial phase of the program.

The third goal of the relapse prevention phase is to develop and rehearse cognitive–behavioral strategies for dealing with relapse. The strategies involve a framework or method for discussing relapse, identification of high-risk situations and early warning signs, plans for preventing drinking, and plans for minimizing the intensity and duration of any relapse. The identified patient and spouse are encouraged to specify what they will do if they encounter high-risk situations and how they will deal with any drinking that might occur.

After the 15 sessions over the course of a year, couples also participate in quarterly follow-up visits either in the clinic or at home for an additional 18 months. As stated previously, the outcomes regarding drinking were significantly improved and marital satisfaction remained high after the implementation of the relapse prevention plan. O'Farrell's program is an example of one specific relapse prevention plan or program within the context of family or couples therapy. More general discussions of relapse prevention and relapse plans can be found in Chapter 8 of this volume, Marlatt and Gordon (1985), and Gorski (1989).

Although a formal relapse prevention plan including contracts and agreements is an essential component of the relapse prevention process, the therapist's attitude and skill in keeping the family focused around sobriety and recovery-related issues are of paramount importance in helping to prevent relapse. Good psychotherapy with patients with AOD disorders, whether in a family, individual, or group context, involves a focus on recovery alternating with a focus on interpersonal and psychodynamic issues. S. Brown (1985) described this process of shifting between an alcohol/drug/ recovery focus and a psychodynamic or cognitive–behavioral focus as *cyclotherapy* (p. 271).

The question that beginning therapists ask is, "When is it safe to shift to a psychodynamic or interpersonally oriented focus and move away from the abstinence or recovery focus?" The skilled therapist who works with patients with AOD disorders realizes that relapse behavior may potentially be just on the horizon no matter the length of sobriety achieved by the patient. As painful affective material is uncovered, the risk of relapse or at least craving may increase. The therapist should be mindful that addiction is a chronic condition that although seemingly dormant for weeks, months, even years, is quite capable of surfacing at any time.

The patient views such questions as "So how are things with your recovery program?" as a sign of caring and an indication that the therapist is sensitive to the ever-present struggle with sobriety. Returning to this line of questioning periodically is always a good idea. Staying in touch with the patient's recovery focus allows the therapist to be sensitive to the ebb and flow of the patient's inner process. It helps to remind patients that they need to maintain this same sensitivity. Of all the specific relapse prevention skills that a therapist can bring to the process, this focus is perhaps the most important.

CONCLUSION

Family therapy techniques have added a new richness and depth to the treatment of substance abuse patients. For years clinicians have stated that returning addicts to dysfunctional families sets them up for relapse. Although they acknowledged the importance of family dynamics for several decades, it was not until the family therapy movement became popular in the 1980s that family therapists developed the structured family therapy programs that support and reinforce this view. Since then, substantial research has indicated that family therapy enhances treatment outcomes in terms of both sobriety and overall life satisfaction for recovering people and family members.

7

Group Therapy and Self-Help Groups in Addiction Treatment

M ost addiction treatment practitioners view group treatment and self-help group participation as the primary elements in treatment. Aside from the practical considerations to be discussed, the emphasis on groups reflects the conviction that social forces are powerful influences on behavior change beyond that which can be achieved by insight or dyadic interaction alone. This focus arose for historical reasons, such as the heritage from Alcoholics Anonymous (AA) and from the therapeutic community (TC) model, in which the group or the community is the agent of change. Clinical experience and longitudinal studies (Bond, Kaskutas, & Weisner, 2003; Moos & Moos, 2006; Timko, Moos, Finney, & Lesar, 2000) have indicated that connection to a subculture that supports recovery is important to produce enduring gains. Although individual work has an important place, it is essential for therapists to understand the significance and purpose of group activities and be prepared to facilitate participation, if not conduct such activities themselves. The existence of well-developed group interventions has permitted the addiction treatment system to handle greater numbers of clients than would be the case if individual sessions were the norm. Indeed, this feature has allowed practitioners to negotiate for extended lengths of stay in outpatient treatment in some managed care or health maintenance organizations, obtaining a duration of treatment more likely to produce positive outcomes.

Although the concept of the community as the change agent is perhaps best articulated by TC proponents (de Leon, 2000), similar elements are evident in self-help groups, recovery groups, and other affiliative activities. Yalom (1995) and Vannicelli (1992) enumerated the therapeutic factors that are also common to other group activities: reducing the sense of isolation, instilling hope, acquiring information, learning by watching others, learning socializing techniques, altering distorted self-concepts, and having an opportunity for a reparative family experience. These forces operate both in treatment and in self-help groups, and the treatment outcome literature has suggested that long-term immersion is associated with a positive outcome (Barthwell & Brown, 2009).

In this chapter, we describe various forms of groups in addiction treatment and discuss their commonalties and differences. We also explore some of the controversial areas of group work, such as phase models and the role of confrontation. We do not provide a comprehensive overview of all aspects of group functioning but select certain issues that are routinely discussed in case conferences and supervision. For more comprehensive coverage, the reader is referred to Vannicelli (1992); Khantzian, Halliday, and McAuliffe (1990); the Center for Substance Abuse Treatment (CSAT) Treatment Improvement Protocol on Group Therapy (Flores & Georgi, 2005); and Flores (2007). We offer recommendations for facilitating the use of self-help groups and describe a process for creating a network of concerned others who can support an individual's recovery process.

GROUPS LED BY PROFESSIONALS

A variety of professionally led groups are available for people in and out of addiction treatment. These include motivational enhancement groups, recovery groups, and harm reduction groups. In this section, we review them from the perspective of the stages of recovery, looking at how they facilitate addressing the tasks of the patient. Newer group activities outside abstinence-oriented models are also described.

Motivational Enhancement Strategies

As it becomes more widely appreciated that untreated alcohol and other drug (AOD) use is expensive, activities designed to enhance motivation are becoming more common. As described in Chapter 3, it is possible to identify a patient's position along a continuum of readiness for change and design interventions accordingly (W. R. Miller, 1999). Those who run programs geared for compliant patients willing to commit to action about their AOD use are recognizing the high costs of untreated AOD users in the larger health care system. They are broadening their outreach to those who are more ambivalent, and they are taking a second look at methods to enhance motivation.

For example, some treatment programs within HMOs have extensive requirements for participation and may rapidly discharge those unable or unwilling to meet program expectations. This difficulty can be analyzed as a mismatch between the program and what the client is willing to accept (Washton & Zweben, 2006); the client is at fault (e.g., "unmotivated, not ready yet"). Reliance on the denial concept to describe client behavior allows clinicians to justify hostile and rejecting behavior that promotes dropout, rather than encouraging them to analyze what happened to alienate the client. The task is to assess the client's readiness for change and strengthen the commitment to change.

It is becoming apparent that those who refuse treatment or drop out early go on to use more costly medical services, as do their family members (McLellan et al., 1995). Therefore, increasing attention is being paid to equipping practitioners who have a relationship with the patient (e.g., primary care physician, therapist) to prepare them to address AOD use. In this context, group activities for the skeptical or unwilling are becoming more common. These groups are referred to in a variety of ways: *transition groups, early intervention groups* (Matrix Center, 1997), *pretreatment groups,* or *step zero groups* (Washton & Stone-Washton, 1981). Their purpose is to provide an opportunity for patients to explore their concerns without pressure to label themselves or commit to action on the program's timetable. Such groups provide an arena for patients to take a closer look at their relationship with whatever mood-altering substances or behaviors are causing them trouble or inconvenience. It is a common clinical trap to attempt to convince the patient he or she is an addict or alcoholic as a means of securing a commitment to abstinence; however, this is by no means necessary in order to begin. In these groups, participants take a new look at their situation, work on achieving greater clarity, explore convictions that change is not possible for them, build a vision of an alternative lifestyle, and take action. In later work, they will have to address the issues that emerge with abstinence, which is typically a theme of recovery groups. Washton and Stone-Washton (1981) recommended eight to 12 sessions to remain a catalyst for movement rather than a substitute.

Recovery Groups

We use the term *recovery groups* to describe the wide variety of abstinence-oriented forms of group therapy that can be found both in institutional and private practice settings. We consider how basic principles of group psychotherapy are adapted to meet the needs of patients using AODs. We initially assume abstinence-based treatment models and then discuss harm-reduction groups that are not primarily abstinence-based.

Phase Models

Larger programs have the option of offering *phase models,* in which participants are grouped according to stages of recovery. For example, the program may offer transition groups for those who are actively using and are on a waiting list for treatment, Phase I groups for those in the process of establishing abstinence, and Phase II and III groups for those in later stages of recovery. This stratification offers the advantages of composing groups of persons struggling with similar issues and providing tangible markers of progress as individuals complete a phase. The groups themselves can be ongoing, with patients leaving and joining according to specific program criteria. For example, a patient can graduate from Phase I after reaching 90 days of continuous abstinence and attending a prescribed number of education groups and self-help meetings. A Phase I group typically focuses on strategies for achieving abstinence and explores other issues in a focused manner as related to that goal. Later stage recovery groups deal with a wider range of issues in more depth, as required by the recovery tasks of such stages: repairing interpersonal relationships and forming new ones, working to resolve trauma issues, learning new ways of managing stress, and so forth. Although relapse issues certainly arise, the Phase II group as a whole does not focus primarily on AOD use but on broader issues. Although phase programs have their advocates, a significant disadvantage is resistance of members to leaving a group with whom they have bonded. Given that this cohesion and bonding is a powerful force for change, it is appropriate to ask whether the tradeoffs of phase programs are worth the disruption, particularly for members who do not easily adapt to new groups.

Mixed-phase group models are more feasible for the private practitioner or small program. In a mixed group model, the group can be open-ended, and members arrive when there is an opening and terminate according to the goals in their individual treatment plan (i.e., they stay as long as participation is productive). Group members in early recovery are exposed to other members as role models with longer term sobriety. Members with sustained abstinence report it is useful to be reminded of the life circumstances of someone who is struggling with using, particularly if this period of their lives seems so remote that they become overconfident and begin taking risks. No matter how long the period of sustained abstinence, the issues of someone who has relapsed are similar to those of the newcomer, with variations depending on the severity of the regression evident in the relapse pattern. Also, people in recovery move at such different tempos that it is difficult to select any particular marker and obtain homogeneity on an issue. Two people, each with a year's sobriety, may have different levels of personal and lifestyle transformation. Inasmuch as there is no empirical evidence that either model is superior to the other, considerations are largely practical: what best meets the needs of the patient population and is possible within the treatment setting.

Screening and Orientation

An interview prior to placing an individual in a group is used to assess appropriateness for the group, elicit the prospective patient's concerns and hopes, and orient him or her to expectations and requirements. An individual who is still actively using may exhibit such sporadic attendance at other treatment activities that it is doubtful he or she is ready to maintain consistent participation in recovery group. Indeed, this is one of the most difficult issues. Dropout from substance abuse treatment is greatest in the first 30 days, and new group members who attend several sessions and disappear have a demoralizing effect on a group. However, it is often the support of savvy group members that helps new members establish abstinence. In the screening process, the group leader should attempt to determine whether the prospective member is capable of consistent attendance. If not, transition groups (in which there is no expectation of stable composition) or individual work can help stabilize a patient and create readiness for other activities.

The screening interview is also the occasion on which to review the specifics of the individual's treatment plan and orient him or her as to how to use the group to achieve personal goals. For example, a woman whose ability to remain abstinent is undermined by her partner's drug use can be encouraged to use the group as a laboratory for practicing assertion and evaluating the nature of the relationship. New members may see the group mainly as a place to obtain help by getting feedback on their issues and may not be aware of other advantages the format offers. It is also common for patients to be concerned about being subjected to aggressive confrontation (discussed later in this chapter). The group leader can reassure the prospective member that the leaders work to ensure there is a healthy feedback process that is not assaultive.

Another important issue to clarify in screening is how the group process in 12-step programs is different from that in a recovery group. Patients who are active in 12-step programs can be a great asset in recovery groups, particularly if they are actively working at the steps. The group leader, however, needs to clarify the distinctions between recovery groups and 12-step meetings. The most important is that the "no crosstalk" rule (i.e., no feedback or interactive discussion by others in the meeting) does not apply to therapy groups; in fact, the feedback process, guided by the leader, is one of the great benefits of a professionally led group. There are other differences, such as the expectation of regular attendance and active participation (this issue is discussed further later in this chapter). Prospective members should be helped to see professional groups as complementary to 12-step groups, not as substitutes for them.

The Abstinence Commitment

It is important that group members have a common understanding that the goal of treatment is abstinence from all intoxicants. Group members can struggle for many months to achieve abstinence and be highly ambivalent about this goal, but if the patient is truly uncommitted to abstinence for extended periods of time, there will be a negative impact on other group members. Resistance and ambivalence should be viewed as the focus of the clinician's work. It is widely accepted among addiction specialists that there is a population in the community that is able to stop using alcohol, tobacco, and illicit drugs with no intervention from professionals. As professionals working in treatment settings, we see a subgroup that, for a variety of reasons, finds it difficult to stop without help; resistance and ambivalence are givens. People need help to deal with their inner and outer obstacles, but there must be a fundamental understanding of the importance of complete abstinence as the goal of treatment. This can be a difficult matter to determine, particularly if the therapist is committed to encouraging the patient to verbalize ambivalence openly. A patient who is floundering but showing signs of progress is different from one who continues to attend but shows no signs of change:

> Janice came to recovery group having recognized that her long period
> of dependence on a variety of prescription drugs was becoming haz-
> ardous as her use escalated. Frightened by recent events, she openly
> and insightfully grappled with her ambivalence about considering
> herself an addict. She successfully made the transition from regular
> to episodic use of opioids (obtained for pain) and benzodiazepines
> (for anxiety) but refused to consider eliminating alcohol ("I don't

drink regularly, and it's not my preferred drug anyway"). Her psychotropic medication could be more finely tuned in the absence of regular drug use, she felt better, and her life had more stability. As this occurred, she realized that improvement made it easier for her to downplay the seriousness of her addictive behavior. Group members had varying reactions to her ambivalence as she verbalized familiar thought patterns that they recognized in themselves and found threatening, and many productive discussions ensued.

If the group is working productively, the members will zero in on the issue of ambivalent commitment to abstinence and often read it more accurately than a nonrecovering professional. At that point, the leader can decide (with input from group members) to remove the individual from the group and work individually until the member's commitment to common goals is more dependable. It is also possible to ask the group member to take a leave of absence until he or she feels committed to abstinence. In the example, the group members considered Janice an integral part of the group and were quite clear they did not want her to leave, despite the apprehension evoked by many of the group discussions of her issues.

Group Structure

Many therapists prefer that group members meet only for therapeutic purposes, and they discourage contact at other times. This is impractical with AOD-using populations, however. Members have often had previous or current contact in settings where they drank and used, at work sites, in homeless shelters, treatment programs, and self-help meetings. The norm of groups of AOD-using patients is for members to provide ongoing help to one another outside meeting times, and a therapist's attempt to discourage such contact is likely to be viewed with surprise and skepticism. It is more useful to review the hazards of such contacts and create a climate in which relationships outside group are discussed freely in the group. Exhibit 7.1 provides an example that can be used in or adapted for particular settings. This handout can be modified to cover fee issues and other program requirements. Prospective group members can be given the handout at screening and asked to sign it when they commit to joining the group.

Exhibit 7.1

Group Rules and Expectations

Our groups are one of the liveliest and most powerful parts of our program, but to keep them working well, we ask certain commitments:

1. Come on time.
2. Do not come intoxicated.
3. Notify your group leader if you will be absent or you know you will be late. Other group members are usually concerned about those missing.
4. Keep the identities of the members in strictest confidence, as well as the content of discussions. You can share anything you like about what you experience in the group, but not about others.
5. Be open to looking at yourself and your behavior and to giving and receiving feedback. It is especially important to discuss any alcohol or drug use in the group.
6. Although contact with other group members outside group can be beneficial, please do not become involved in any relationship outside group that would interfere with your ability to be honest and explore issues in the group. A romantic or sexual relationship with another group member is an obvious example, but it is not the only type of relationship that can be an impediment.
7. A minimum of 3 months' participation is needed to learn to use the group; more to receive full benefits. Please give 1 month's notice if you plan to leave the group.
8. There is a list of group members' names and telephone numbers, because we think you are an important support system for one another. This list must be kept strictly confidential.

I give/do not give (circle one) permission to have my name on the group list given to members. (First names only on the list.)

I have read and agree to the above rules and guidelines:

Name: _____ Date: _____

Note. Compiled by Joan E. Zweben. This form can be used or reproduced without permission from the publisher or the authors. If reproduced, a source citation is appreciated.

It is useful to have an initial check-in process that explicitly refers to the patient's status with respect to AOD use. Check-in is a process that allows both leaders and members to hear briefly from each person about the significant events in their week and allows members to explicitly ask for time to discuss a specific issue. It provides an overview of issues and encourages more reticent members to participate. In a recovery group, check-in should include a statement about whether there has been any AOD use (including prescription drug misuse) since the last session. Like the statement "I am an addict/alcoholic" in 12-step meetings, this is an opportunity to disclose and a process that disrupts denial. Although some patients will lie, this structure creates a confrontation with the self over behavior that otherwise may be more easily minimized. Ries (1996), who deals with severely mentally ill substance abusing clients, also added the following elements to the check-in statement: "When I last was offered a drug"; "When I last offered someone else a drug"; "My psychiatric diagnosis"; and "The medication I am on." This addresses the tendency toward denial in the area of the patient's mental illness and reveals other significant issues in the person's life situation.

Confrontation

Substance abuse treatment is widely viewed as favoring aggressive confrontation. In this practice, challenging comments are given with the intent of heightening awareness and disrupting complacency. This practice originated in Synanon, which at the time it was launched offered the only effective intervention for heroin addiction. Synanon founder Charles Dederich viewed addicts as having a "character armor" that had to be penetrated to launch a meaningful change process (Deitch & Zweben, 1981). Individuals emerging from Synanon formed the leadership in proliferating TCs and also, to a much lesser extent, in developing the 28-day inpatient hospital programs.

In some programs, harsh confrontation was promoted as a dominant feature, which we would argue created more casualties than successes. In addition, the successes occurred despite this practice, because of the presence of other positive elements. The practice was perpetuated by the fact that in the early days, programs were staffed by recovering people with no clinical training, so there were few alternatives available to the counselors, many of whom were troubled by the practice of aggressive confrontation. By the mid-1970s, alternative interventions were being taught in addiction treatment programs, but the stereotype has persisted and is defended by some. TC clients often view confrontation groups as perhaps the most significant treatment component in the TC. In his extensive description of TC methods, George de Leon (2000) stressed the importance of careful planning, training, and clarity about goals. Confrontation, properly planned, implemented, and balanced by other elements such as support, responsible concern, and affirmation, is a useful element of group and individual therapy. It is designed to raise client/patient awareness of attitudes and behaviors toward self, the environment, or others.

Clinical supervisors should keep in mind that many counselors who wish to renounce harsh practices nonetheless repeat them because their early models and experiences have become so ingrained. Both didactic and experiential (e.g., role playing) alternatives are necessary to move counselors beyond reliance on the "tough" style. Individuals exposed to this in the course of their treatment attempts may be decidedly reluctant to enter groups. It is important that the therapist respect their concerns and be vigilant to foster a feedback process that is forthright without being assaultive. Those supervising noncredentialed staff should be aware that basic clinical skills such as active listening and skilled inquiry go a long way toward reducing reliance on heavy confrontation. Motivational interviewing techniques (discussed in Chapter 6) have been enthusiastically welcomed by counselors in need of a broader repertoire.

Dealing With the Intoxicated Patient

A member who comes to group intoxicated can provide a difficult challenge for the therapist, particularly if the patient's state is not apparent until after the group is under way. Such members are often unable to follow what is going on the group, interrupt impulsively, launch conversations while others are talking, and in some cases threaten violence if confronted. If the intoxication is clear at the outset, the patient can be sent home, with provisions made for traveling safely if needed. If the question emerges during the group, the therapist can comment on specific behaviors that are inappropriate and suggest that the patient take a break for a few minutes and return when able to exercise restraint. Although some clinicians take the position that intoxicated persons should be immediately removed from a group, a rigid policy has its disadvantages, particularly if there is no immediate way to verify intoxication. The therapist can base that decision on the patient's ability to cease being disruptive and can ask the patient to be an observer (the practice in AA meetings) and not speak up during that particular session. Because newcomers are more likely to have problems abstaining, this approach is less likely to exacerbate shame and create obstacles to returning to group.

A most difficult problem is the faint smell of alcohol in the room. It is unwise to avoid mention of this because others may have noticed and the leader should not model ignoring an issue that is obvious. Also, recovering persons are much more sensitive to the signs of intoxication than are nonrecovering therapists. It is useful to introduce the issue by commenting on a faint smell that could be alcohol and asking for group members' reactions. "Proving" the existence of a smell is usually impossible without using special detection methods (see Washton & Zweben, 2006), but even in the event that no others detect such an odor, a discussion of whether members would comment openly if they had suspicions is productive for clarifying work norms in the group. Members often worry about "being right" or being too intrusive; therefore, it is necessary to emphasize the value of open discussion of topics that are usually taboo.

The Patient in Individual Therapy

Several arrangements are possible for combined individual and group therapy. The patient in an addiction treatment program may participate in both, if the resources of the program permit. For example, patients in methadone programs are often required by regulation and clinic policy to participate in individual counseling and attend groups as well. Some therapeutic communities also include individual sessions, particularly for those with severe psychiatric conditions. Managed care organizations are often unenthusiastic about providing individual sessions within addiction programs, so insured populations usually have to pay out of pocket if such service is desired. It is not unusual to find individual therapists in the community sending patients to recovery groups run by specialist practitioners or addiction treatment programs:

> Jerry was referred to recovery group for crack cocaine use by his psychodynamically oriented individual therapist. He had recently remarried and at age 45 was eager to break out of his decades-long, highly destructive pattern of binge use. Sexual concerns and activities were a key element in his cocaine use.
>
> The therapists remained in regular communication as Jerry's gradually lengthening periods of sobriety continued to be followed by 3- to 4-day cocaine binges. Discussion of his sexual issues was highly anxiety provoking and stimulated urges to use cocaine but could not be avoided because of the salience of this issue as a trigger in the absence of discussion. He explored this first in individual therapy and was encouraged to bring it to group. On other occasions, the group members appeared to be the lesser threat. Following a relapse, he would sometimes find it easier to overcome his shame with group members who shared his addictive problems, and thus he was able to find his way back to his individual therapist.

Therapist collaboration was a key element in retaining this man in both forms of treatment and in gradually making progress. Such collaboration requires bridging the gap between practitioners of differing orientations and establishing an understanding about communication in routine as well as urgent situations.

Network Therapy

Network therapy is an approach that addresses the all-important task of developing a support system to promote recovery. Formulated by Marc Galanter (2005), a physician specializing in addiction medicine, it brings together family members and relevant others in a team and coaches them on how to help the patient achieve abstinence and a satisfying drug-free adaptation. It gathers those who are part of the patient's natural support system and guides their activity so they can be effective in promoting treatment goals. In contrast to participants in couples or family therapy, members of the network are not the focus of treatment and are not invited to use network meetings to work toward goals for themselves. Similarly, exploring past or current areas of conflict is avoided as potentially disruptive to the main task. The therapist functions as a coach to keep the team focused. Galanter (2005) offered detailed recommendations for forming and working with the network.

Harm Reduction Group Activities

Public health concerns, intensified by the AIDS epidemic, have brought increasing attention to harm reduction strategies. *Harm reduction* is defined as a set of strategies that encourage substance users and service providers to reduce the harm done to drug users, their loved ones, and communities by their licit and illicit drug use. This approach begins from the position that abstinence should not be the only objective of services to drug users because it excludes a large proportion of the people who are involved in long-term drug use. Although abstinence is envisioned as a possibility and, for some, a final goal, commitment to it is not a prerequisite for participating in activities or obtaining services. Proponents note the alienation that occurs when users seek help from abstinence-oriented programs and stress the importance of creating alternatives. In their view, the most effective way of getting people to minimize the harmful effects of their drug use is to provide user-friendly services that attract them into contact and empower them to change their behavior toward a suitable intermediate objective. This approach is increasingly used to address HIV in community settings, particularly because treatment capacity is inadequate even when individuals are motivated to pursue it, and its use in other settings outside the HIV arena have been documented to have a beneficial public health impact as well (Rhodes, 1993; Weibel, 1993). It is also useful for end-stage users for whom abstinence is not realistic.

These groups usually use a psychoeducational model, in which information is shared and participants have an opportunity to explore issues.

They focus on increasing safety in a variety of ways, such as identifying the dangers of particular use patterns (e.g., sharing needles) or sexual practices. Participants list their own hazardous behaviors and discuss ways to reduce their risk. The educational component covers ways in which using alcohol and drugs increases vulnerability to victimization through violence, participating in unsafe sex, accidents, and acting out negative moods (e.g., exacerbating depression). They address how to reduce HIV transmission through using clean needles and practicing safer sex. Reducing the frequency and amount of drugs used is a valid safety strategy, as is attention to using in safe environments.

There are other examples of harm reduction strategies, either as an end in themselves or a stepping-stone to an abstinence-oriented treatment. Ries (1996) described an outpatient program for mentally ill chemical abusers in which the prephase component of the program offered groups illustrating harm reduction principles. Patients in this component were relatively unengaged in treatment and were unstable in either their behavioral or substance-abuse disorder. They were not ready for interactive groups or many structured activities. However, on referral from their case manager, they were allowed to attend Club Med, a 1-hour morning group that met daily, in which they received coffee and snacks and took their medication in front of a staff member. At the end of the session, they received a small amount of spending money. The group encouraged routine daily activity, promoted medication compliance, and provided a structure to budget funds on a daily basis (and thus reduced the amount available at one time to spend on drugs). This low-demand group activity began to stabilize patients and prepare them to take advantage of other treatment opportunities. In summary, harm reduction can be an effective engagement strategy for those who are unwilling to commit to abstinence and can yield public health and safety benefits even without an abstinence commitment.

SELF-HELP GROUPS

Self-help (also called *mutual help*) group participation is widely viewed as a key element in successful recovery because it provides several essential ingredients. These groups provide access to a community that supports the recovery process from which participants can begin to rebuild social networks that are not organized around alcohol and drug use. They also offer a process for personal development that has no financial barriers. The rapid proliferation and wide variety of groups make it possible to find a good match within most urban communities and many rural ones. Our main focus here is on the 12-step system because it is the oldest and largest, but we briefly describe some of the alternative groups as well. We review some of the basic characteristics of self-help groups and suggest strategies for fostering effective utilization.

Self-help groups usually strive to maintain the least amount of hierarchy and structure necessary for smooth functioning and safety of participants. They generally emphasize the voluntary nature of participation (e.g., "a program of attraction") and tolerate a wide range of commitment and participation. Some confusion is evident among professionals and the public as to the similarities and differences between self-help groups and treatment, especially when there are close links between them. For example, 12-step programs are different from treatment programs based on 12-step principles; however, these distinctions are sometimes unclear in discussion and in the literature.

There are important differences between self-help groups and professional treatment, with each having strengths and limitations. At their best, self-help groups offer a powerful sense of belonging (exemplified by the term *fellowship*) that generates hope and enthusiasm, in addition to the beneficial effects of the activities offered. Meetings or members may be available any time of the day or night and may provide forms of support not possible outside residential or inpatient treatment. Professional treatment offers the possibility of much greater accountability and structure. It is possible to track whether and how well individuals participate in a treatment plan usually formulated by an interdisciplinary team. Although various procedures have been devised to monitor attendance at self-help meetings, by the very nature of such meetings, there is minimal or no formal hierarchy and hence no objective means of holding the patient accountable. Treatment programs, employers, and probation officers can mandate attendance, but this gives a false sense of accountability that is in some ways worse than none at all. In addition, many a fine meeting has been disrupted by the negative behavior of those mandated to attend.

If a patient becomes involved with a self-help group, the therapist will see evidence of learning and application of new concepts. Reliable monitoring is usually not possible; hence the therapist is better off investing effort elsewhere. Although self-help groups have a definite structure, they do not necessarily accomplish what the therapist may need at a particular point in time. For example, anyone attending regularly will learn a great deal about alcohol and drugs and about the process of recovery. However, they will not get the kind of systematic presentation that allows clinician and patient to arrive at a meaningful treatment plan on an appropriate time schedule. Family members beginning to attend Al-Anon may go to an entire meeting and never hear the word *alcohol,* although over time they will learn a great deal about alcoholism and be exposed to many coping strategies. Thus, the clinician hoping to build a foundation quickly needs to fill these gaps with other treatment activities, such as education classes. The combination is particularly powerful because a basic conceptual framework usually enables participants to derive much more benefit from self-help meetings.

The clinician's role is to facilitate self-help participation through encouragement, sharing information, and exploring resistance. Attitudes and feelings about attendance are a mirror of feelings about being addicted or in recovery. A focus on the nature of the patient's resistance clarifies the obstacles to attendance. Eliciting the patient's picture of what goes on in meetings often reveals areas of misinformation as well as charged issues. For example, being exposed to others in the group situation challenges denial and intensifies the shame many feel about their addiction. A common initial resistance is "I'm afraid someone will recognize me." Thus, meeting attendance is often a perfect metaphor to talk about these other issues. It is useful to stress that resistance or ambivalence does not preclude benefit. In AA lore, "Bring the body; the mind will follow." It is common for patients to report that it took great effort to overcome the desire to stay home, but once present, they felt better during or after the meeting, even when they disliked being there. Therefore, the therapist seeks a balance of focus between feelings and behavior, understanding that action that is less than wholehearted nonetheless produces benefits.

Practical supports are also important. Stranger anxiety is certainly a major obstacle, and many participate enthusiastically once they have found a group in which they feel at home. Therapist encouragement and facilitation by connecting the patient with others who attend can go a long way to help surmount this obstacle. The camaraderie (reflected in the term *fellowship*), which ultimately becomes a powerful force for change, can be a deterrent at the outset for persons who are shy or sensitive about being rejected or about being the outsider. Firm encouragement to "give it a fair try" and coaching about how to make use of the process often results in a connection that greatly augments the treatment process. As Stephanie Brown noted in response to a query about what to do when a patient says, "I don't want to go": "I never met *anyone* who wanted to go to an AA meeting. But I've met hundreds who managed to find a way to make use of AA" (S. Brown, 1996).

12-Step Programs

The generic name for the programs conducted by AA and its many descendants is *12-step programs*. AA formulated the principles and traditions on which these groups are based. Founded in 1935, AA groups constituted the largest self-help system in the world. Although it is impossible to obtain completely accurate data on membership, AA World Services reports that as of 2007, there were approximately 116,773 groups and more than 2,000,000 members worldwide (Alcoholics Anonymous World Services, 2007a). For this reason they are a major staple of addiction treatment. As discussed in Chapter 6, members indicated that the major factors responsible for them coming to AA were self-motivation, other AA members, the treatment facility, and family influences (in that order; AA World Services, 2007a). This suggests that the partnership between AA and treatment is improving, and the negative attitudes toward professional treatment, including psychotherapy, are diminishing. However, it is important for therapists to understand that a long history of professionals failing to appropriately address alcoholism and addiction left a legacy of deep mistrust, which is unfortunately often well founded. The situation is improving steadily as more and more professionals become proficient at handling addiction issues and more and more 12-step program members recognize the value of addressing their coexisting disorders through psychotherapy, medication, and other professional services.

The group process of 12-step programs shares some characteristics with therapy groups, but there are some important differences. It is useful to consider the strengths and limitations of each approach. The policy of "no cross-talk" emphasizes that helping occurs through learning from the experiences of others and is widely viewed as a safety feature that is important in a leaderless group. Participants are not to inquire, confront, or otherwise disrupt another's "share." This fosters an atmosphere of acceptance and offers some protection against aggressive interrogation and other forms of invasiveness. Therapists are typically troubled by the fact that a person in great distress may not receive an immediate response, but usually support is offered once the meeting is over. The constraint on confrontation may also make it difficult to control members whose behavior is disruptive. However, the no cross-talk feature is widely viewed by members as providing protection and wide latitude to progress at their own pace. The therapy group, by contrast, offers the benefits of interaction and feedback, under the guidance of a trained leader. When 12-step program members come to therapy groups, they may need assistance in distinguishing between the norms of the meetings and those of the therapy group and in understanding that the leader's job is to keep the process productive. Some are so conditioned to avoid comment on what others say that they do not engage in the kinds of interaction that makes therapy groups useful.

The process of "working the steps" is a natural complement to psychotherapy. Members of 12-step groups review the steps and traditions, reflect on how they apply to themselves, and ultimately share with another person, often their sponsor. Some of this work can be done by keeping a journal. This commitment to rigorous self-examination can greatly enhance the psychotherapy process.

Patients and therapists often wonder which 12-step program would be best: AA, Narcotics Anonymous (NA), or some other variant. In general, it is useful to pick a place to begin, looking for meetings composed of people from a similar socioeconomic, gender, or age group, in the neighborhood of home or work. For those starting out, however, there may be an advantage to selecting a group organized around their drug of choice (e.g., Cocaine Anonymous, Marijuana Anonymous). Although most participants have used AODs, the groups vary in how much they tolerate discussion of this. Rapid engagement is useful and patients report being able to identify more readily when they hear "their story" in meetings. They can and should be encouraged to "shop" until they find a "home" meeting, one in which they feel comfortable and are willing to return to regularly. Once they select one or more of such meetings, they can begin to use them to develop social relationships, increasing understanding and support for the process of recovery, and building a support system that is compatible with a satisfying abstinent lifestyle.

Initial resistance frequently centers on the first step, "We admitted we were powerless over alcohol—that our lives had become unmanageable" (AA World Services, 1976, p. 59). Members of various disempowered groups, such as women and minorities, find the concepts of admitting powerlessness to be painfully close to their ongoing life experience and do not see its relevance to healing. The empowering feature of this concept is usually better appreciated after a period of abstinence. The therapist working with this early form of resistance can reframe the issue, emphasizing how the patient gains control over his or her life by abandoning efforts to engage in controlled AOD use. Many patients report that relinquishing the struggle to control AOD use frees enormous energy to devote to other things.

Selecting a sponsor is a key element in successful engagement and fruitful participation. A *sponsor* is an experienced, recovering member who acts as an advisor, guide, or teacher on how to work at a program of recovery (AA World Services, 1983). Although there are no formal rules for selecting a sponsor, newcomers are encouraged to find someone with a year or more of sobriety who "has something you want." It should be someone who appears to be enjoying sobriety and who is not an object of sexual or other interest that would detract from the primary purpose of the relationship. Sponsors can be short or long term; members are encouraged to change them as their needs evolve in recovery. For the therapist, the sponsor relationship can provide a challenge, especially if the sponsor disparages professional treatment. S. Brown (1985) described ways in which therapists and sponsors can develop difficult conflicts, and made recommendations for a productive partnership in which AA involvement, in all its aspects, is complementary to psychotherapy.

Discomfort with the spiritual component of AA is a common form of resistance, which can often be reduced by exploration and provision of information. It is important for the therapist to be comfortable with this dimension of recovery. Inquiry into how the patient understands the spiritual focus often yields misconceptions; it is intended to be non-denominational, with participants identifying their own higher power wherever they find it (AA World Services, 2001). In some regions of the country, groups tend to reflect the religious affiliation of that region (e.g., Christian fundamentalist), and churches, where meetings are often held, may be uncomfortable sites for some. However, in many communities meetings are available in hospitals, community centers, mental health centers, and other settings.

On a psychodynamic level, several experiences can contribute to discomfort with the spiritual dimension. Negative experiences with institutionalized religion in childhood are a common source of resistance. Another is the projection of harsh, punitive features onto God or the higher power, which is then seen as a force to be avoided. Self-esteem issues, such as "I don't deserve anything good," may also be involved. All these issues are amenable to modification. In addition, reminders to "take what you need and leave the rest" can encourage patients to select what is useful, use therapy to air their negative feelings, and otherwise avoid dwelling on elements they dislike.

Two recent review articles summarized the research supporting the effectiveness of AA and examining the key ingredients (Kaskutas, 2009; McCrady & Tonigan, 2009). Both summarized studies on the relationship between long-term AA involvement and abstinence. Consistent involvement

is associated with better outcomes. Participants need to go beyond attendance and actually affiliate. This is usually measured by sharing at meetings,
leading meetings, having a sponsor, working the steps, and doing 12th-step
work (i.e., carrying "the message" to others). Gains in abstinence self-efficacy
and increased social support are also associated with AA benefits.

When evaluating the research, it is important to remember that many
treatment programs encourage or require AA. Thus, they should not be
compared with AA itself because they are not something entirely distinct.
Kaskutas (2009) noted that in both Project MATCH and a well-known
inpatient study (Walsh et al., 1991), the cognitive–behavioral therapy and
motivational enhancement therapy aftercare patients attended more
meetings than the outpatients in the 12-step facilitation arm. This illustrates some of the difficulty of doing research on AA; patients will choose
to go on their own, independent of their treatment provider. Random
assignment does not result in pure research conditions. Thus, it is not
surprising that a variety of research methodologies have been used to
examine the effectiveness of AA and related issues such as key mechanisms
of change.

Newer Self-Help Groups

A variety of discomforts and objections have led to the development of
other self-help groups, offering an advantage for clinicians working with
those unable to make a 12-step connection. The sheer number and variety of 12-step meetings is an asset; however, there are many who do not
use this system and seek alternatives. The clinician encouraging this path
should remain mindful of the need for a readily available support structure. If the patient selects a self-help group that meets only once a week,
other activities will be needed to fill the gaps.

Two alternative groups that have grown in membership in the
past decade are LifeRing and Self-Management and Recovery Training
(SMART) Recovery. LifeRing (http://www.unhooked.com) is an abstinence-
based support group that views the power to get clean and sober as within

the individual. They stress the value of the positive reinforcement of the group process, which includes an exchange of feedback, as being important to strengthening the power within. Most LifeRing groups do not adopt a competitive stance with 12-step groups, and patients are often comfortable attending both. Groups are more concentrated in California but now exist in many other parts of the county. SMART (http://www.smartrecovery.org) supports people who have chosen to abstain or are considering abstaining from any type of addictive behaviors, including activities such as gambling. It draws from motivational enhancement therapy, cognitive–behavioral therapy, and other approaches to teach how to change self-defeating thinking, emotions, and actions and to work toward long-term satisfactions and quality of life. It offers both face-to-face and online meetings.

Cultural Issues

McCrady and Tonigan (2009) reviewed the data on various cultural, racial, and ethnic subgroups and concluded that individuals from minority groups have a more mixed experience in AA. Although they saw value in their experiences, they also reported more negative experiences. Much less work has been done on NA and the other self-help groups, but clinical experience suggests that finding congenial groups in the patient's geographical area has a significant influence over whether the patient makes extensive use of the self-help system.

Therapist Field Trip

Familiarity with self-help meetings in the community increases effectiveness in facilitating participation. Visiting meetings is an excellent way to understand what actually goes on in meetings and increases the therapist's ability to neutralize resistance. The assignment in Exhibit 7.2 is offered to students and new staff members. This "assignment" typically generates strong feelings and often clarifies attitudes about addiction; hence, a forum for discussion is enormously useful.

Exhibit 7.2

Understanding 12-Step Programs and Other Self-Help Groups

A good understanding of 12-step programs (the generic term for all the descendants of Alcoholics Anonymous) is crucial for anyone working in the addiction field. These programs offer a wealth of resources at every stage of the recovery process, with no financial barriers. One of the most important jobs of the therapist or counselor is to help the client make a good connection with these programs and learn to use them effectively. This is a complex task.

To increase your effectiveness, it is important that you have some familiarity with the meetings in your community. Please look up the telephone number of the Central Office (you can start with Alcoholics Anonymous) and select two meetings in your area. These can be Alcoholics Anonymous, Al-Anon, Narcotics Anonymous, Cocaine Anonymous, or anything else you prefer. If you are not in recovery yourself, check to be sure you have selected an "open" meeting (i.e., one that people who do not consider themselves addicts or alcoholics can attend). You can also ask for a nonsmoking meeting. If you are not recovering, you can introduce yourself by first name only, or you can give your name and identify yourself as a guest, therapist, or counselor. Within 24 hours of your visit, please make some notes (journal style) on the following issues:

- What you felt in anticipation of going (e.g., avoidances, resistances).
- What you felt on arriving, throughout the meeting, and afterward.
- Your observations on the group process (both the standard rituals, and things such as introductions and the informal aspects) and its advantages and limitations.

Please distinguish between your feelings, observations, and analyses and include all three.

Exhibit 7.2

Understanding 12-Step Programs and Other Self-Help Groups (continued)

Those who wish to attend Rational Recovery or other self-help groups are encouraged to do so. Staff and students who are in recovery and familiar with meetings should visit a type of meeting with which they are not familiar (e.g., Overeaters Anonymous, Sex and Love Addicts Anonymous).

Note. Compiled by Joan E. Zweben. This handout can be used or reproduced without permission from the publisher or the authors. If reproduced, a source citation is appreciated.

CONCLUSION

In summary, this chapter described a variety of group activities that facilitate recovery. Therapists who are engaged primarily in individual work need to develop an appreciation for the many essential ingredients provided by group activities. Indeed, for the addiction specialist, individual work plays a relatively unimportant role in the overall recovery process, although it can be lifesaving or otherwise crucial at particular points in the process. The most powerful and enduring forces for change are activities in which peers in the patient's community create an expectation and provide assistance in making the lifestyle transition that is needed to promote recovery. To the extent that the therapist assists in fashioning such a support system or connecting the patient to existing support systems, treatment effectiveness will be enhanced.

8

Relapse Prevention

Relapse to alcohol and other drug (AOD) use is the norm, not the exception (Douaihy, Daley, Marlatt, & Spotts, 2009) and can be viewed as part of the natural history of the disorder. In fact, because AOD disorder is a chronic condition, it is similar to disorders such as diabetes, asthma, and hypertension (McLellan, Lewis, O'Brien, & Kleber, 2000). *Relapse prevention* refers to a set of strategies and specific interventions designed to forestall a resumption of AOD use. Although often discussed as a separate component, these strategies and interventions are embedded in good treatment. This chapter focuses on the relapse prevention element, separating it out for the purpose of discussion.

Alan Marlatt is regarded as the father of relapse prevention, and he and his colleagues (e.g., Marlatt & Donovan, 2005) developed a set of interventions based on the premise that the behaviors necessary to initiate abstinence are different from those needed to maintain it. With the availability of a conceptual framework from which intervention strategies flowed, research proliferated and materials were developed for patients with a range of educational levels.

IDENTIFYING RELAPSE PRECIPITANTS

The first step was to understand relapse precipitants. Focusing on events that triggered relapse, their research indicated that most precipitants fell into three categories: negative mood states, such as boredom or depression; interpersonal conflict; and social pressure. Other factors (less dominant) included physical discomfort, pleasant emotions or pleasant times with others, testing personal control, and urges or temptations to drink. A wide variety of assessment tools and patient workbooks exist to help identify and address distinctive relapse patterns.

Previous periods of abstinence ending in relapse provide information about important relapse prevention issues. The therapist needs to verify that the patient was indeed abstinent and did not make exceptions, such as for marijuana ("It's natural" or "It's so mild it doesn't count") or alcohol ("It wasn't a problem before I found cocaine" or "It's legal so not a problem") or prescription drug misuse. The quality of that sobriety, as well as detailed inquiry about what happened to end it, sheds light on untreated coexisting disorders or hidden issues that need to be addressed. For example, long periods of sobriety characterized by persistent dysphoria may indicate untreated depression, a common occurrence among chronic relapsers. Relapse rates decrease once such disorders are properly addressed (Sacks & Ries, 2005).

Careful, detailed inquiry focuses attention on psychological or inter-personal issues that need attention. Conflict in intimate relationships or significant losses are common precipitating factors. Patients also need to be alerted to periodic occurrences that constitute hazards, such as holidays, birthdays, celebrations, and anniversaries (e.g., sobriety dates). Increased stress is often a component. The Alcoholics Anonymous (AA) maxim to be especially watchful when one is hungry, angry, lonely, tired (HALT) is a practical tactic that can guide the development of new coping skills (AA World Services, 1975; Nowinski et al., 1994).

Gorski and colleagues (Gorski, 1988a, 1988b) were among the first to provide materials for recovering people to use in identifying and addressing their own relapse vulnerabilities. He noted that relapse is a state of mind that precedes actual use and offered ways to take inventory of those shifts.

Relapse prevention worksheets, such as those found in the "Matrix Manuals" (Center for Substance Abuse Treatment, 2006a, 2006b, 2006c), can help the therapist become familiar with early warning signs and intervene accordingly. It is common for patients to conceal slips and relapses in an effort to avoid being confronted or disappointing the therapist. A concealed relapse breeds many taboo topics, ultimately causing the therapeutic process to stagnate, so it is crucial for therapists to be attentive and vigorous in efforts to address this issue.

Familiarity with experiential techniques, such as role play, is invaluable. Many of the effective relapse prevention strategies focus on the development of new coping skills for high-risk situations, and active learning strategies are essential. A number of manuals are available for therapists to use in formulating tasks for individual or group sessions or for the patient to use as a workbook. These are listed in Chapter 5. Drink refusal skills are one example of how attention to specific details of each patient's situation can build skills, strengthen self-confidence, and bring psychological and interpersonal issues into focus. Using behavioral strategies may reveal psychodynamic issues because these emerge in the course of the role play and other exercises that otherwise remain hidden or more ambiguous:

> Sam was a construction worker with a high investment in the tough, independent male stance. He was introduced to cocaine at his work site and rapidly began to develop problems. In working on a role play in which he refused cocaine and extricated himself from the situation in which he was offered it, he began to become aware of the extent to which he was influenced by a strong need for his coworkers' approval. He wondered aloud why he so badly wanted to belong to a clique engaged in self-destructive behavior. This evoked memories of a childhood situation in which he abandoned the effort to maintain his excellent school performance when he was recruited into a peer group with antisocial propensities. These issues were tagged for later exploration. He was encouraged to see refusal of cocaine and aloofness from the group as a sign of great strength in a difficult situation.

In thinking about the timing of relapse, it is useful to distinguish between a failure to establish abstinence and a resumption of alcohol or drug use after a period of time. The former may reflect ambivalence about the abstinence commitment or simply the struggle to establish it. For these early stage events, it is often useful for the therapist to focus initially on the motivational status of the patient before focusing on behavioral strategies that might be useful. Adequate discussion of relapse prevention strategies followed by repeated failure to apply them is also a tipoff that motivation, not behavior, is the first issue to consider. Patients may be committed to reducing rather than eliminating drug use and may defend their behavior on the grounds that they have made progress. Faced with a patient who continues to use episodically in the early stages, some clinicians will expend considerable energy on behavioral strategies, becoming frustrated when this does not yield success. Focusing on the ambivalence and working to enhance motivation are likely to be more fruitful. Once progress is made in these areas, behavioral strategies are used more readily. A *slip* is an occasion of use, often seen as accidental, to which the patient responds with concern and remorse and a renewal of effort to achieve abstinence. In this situation, emphasis can be placed on behavioral strategies to promote success.

Circumscribed episodes of use should be distinguished from a resumption of ongoing use. The pattern of recurrence of use can vary from a single recurrence (a slip or lapse) to a time-limited episode (a binge) and a return to the frequency and pattern of use prior to abstinence (a full-blown relapse). Even if a full relapse occurs, it is important to distinguish between individuals who seek help at that point and those who return to the behavior and attitudes characteristic of a drug-abuse lifestyle. The deeper the regression, the more difficult it is to reverse the relapse.

Specific Relapse Factors and Strategies

Research indicates that there are similarities in treatment issues and outcomes for opiate, cocaine, and alcohol users. Greater severity of alcohol and drug use at admission was the main predictor of substance use at follow-up (McLellan et al., 1994). Demographic characteristics and other patient factors did not predict alcohol and drug use following treatment. However, it has long been agreed that psychosocial adjustment factors are related to relapse and are thus a focus of most treatment efforts. Measures generally focus on employment, criminal behavior, medical (including psychiatric) status, and family functioning. Severe psychiatric, employment, and family problems at admission were associated with worse adjustment in these areas after treatment. However, treatment services targeted specifically to those areas were associated with improved social adjustment scores.

McLellan et al. (1997) demonstrated that treatment that is truly individualized and disciplined with respect to providing activities relevant to the individual's areas of difficulty (as identified by their profile on the Addiction Severity Index) improves functioning in areas related to relapse vulnerability. This is referred to as *problem–service matching* (as discussed in Chapter 4, this volume). Left to their own devices, clinicians do not necessarily use readily available intake data to implement an individualized plan. McLellan et al. (1997) demonstrated that even when adequate data are in the chart, clinicians implemented a more focused treatment plan when there was a tailored treatment plan requiring the provision of at least three professional sessions in any of the three areas (psychiatric, family, and/or employment) indicated as problematic at the time of admission. Although all patients improved, those who were not under the specific problem–service matching protocol tended to drop out of treatment earlier, and their outcomes were somewhat less positive. Thus, clinicians in a supervisory role need to attend to the specificity with which the patient's needs are being addressed.

Tradition has granted wide latitude to experienced, licensed clinicians, many of whom are unaccustomed to having their clinical work closely scrutinized. However, this may not produce the best outcome for the patient in addiction treatment. For example, most therapists are not usually highly skilled in the area of vocational counseling, so the patient with strong needs in that area may not even receive a well-chosen referral. Therapists with a preference for individual sessions will reconceptualize family problems to be amenable to intervention in an individual session format. Although this is successful for some, it is less effective to tailor treatment to the preferences, skills, and limitations of the individual therapist rather than to the needs of the patient.

The Outpatient Therapist

If the patient is in outpatient psychodynamically oriented psychotherapy and not involved in an addiction treatment program, a variety of challenges can arise. Indeed, many therapists see recovering people who are long clean and sober and make a profound contribution to the quality of their sobriety. However, such therapists may also miss more subtle warning signs that usually signal problems to an addiction specialist: discontinuation of self-help meeting attendance, regular exercise, or other self-care activities without thought or discussion; a drift into daydreaming about the possibility of controlled use or experimentation with "lightweight" forms of a drug; or a growing rejection of the identity of a recovering person:

> Sara had been a methamphetamine user as an adolescent and had ended her first year in college in an inpatient chemical-dependency program. She completed the program successfully, made a good connection with 12-step groups, and attended regularly for 3 years. After this, she gradually diminished her attendance but remained clean and sober for 7 years. During this time, she entered graduate school, where her performance was stellar. While in graduate school, she ended a difficult long-term relationship and geared up reluctantly to face the "relationship marketplace." During this period, she resumed occasional drinking. Her therapist, impressed by her personal growth and professional accomplishments, did not raise questions about this practice. At a party, after two glasses of wine, an acquaintance offered her cocaine and she accepted.
>
> The therapist was surprised and unnerved by this episode, and sought consultation from an addiction specialist. Careful review of the case revealed other precursors to relapse, such as becoming "too busy" to maintain a regular exercise schedule, falling into the unhealthy eating habits characteristic of her professional group, and becoming critical of people who dwell on their identity as a recovering person.

In the course of discussing these issues, the patient recognized the elements in her relapse drift and reconnected to some of her previous recovery supports.

In a case such as this, the therapist has a variety of options. One is to secure regular consultation from the addiction specialist for a period of time until the patient has again been stabilized. Another is to refer the patient to a recovery group for the kind of exploration and feedback that benefits from the keen eyes of a group of other recovering people. The patient can and should be encouraged to reconnect to 12-step programs that worked well for her in the past, as well as resume the self-care practices that protect sobriety. Therapists and family members may assume an inpatient stay is the best remedy for a relapse, but for this patient, no inpatient treatment is indicated. The extent to which specialized addiction treatment (including a residential stay) is necessary is usually decided on the basis of the duration of the relapse and the extent of the regression to an earlier lifestyle. This assessment is best done in collaboration with an addiction specialist.

It would likely be beneficial for the individual therapist to explore the patient's resistance to the identity of a recovering person. Some therapists concur with the popular criticism that this constitutes a form of self-disparagement, but the desirable outcome is a comfortable integration of one's recovery status and an acceptance that one cannot safely use intoxicants, no matter how much personal progress has been achieved.

Relapse Factors: Specific Drugs

When developing relapse prevention plans, it is useful to look separately at the different drugs, especially at the distinctive features of each substance. Rawson (1995) and his colleagues have examined this issue within an outpatient clinic system. Although relapse prevention strategies are generic to all the drugs, knowledge of some key differences can help the therapist attend to details that might otherwise seem insignificant. For alcohol, the key relapse factors were its widespread availability and social pressure to drink. Consistent with many studies in the literature, negative affect states were also important. Effective strategies included enhancing self-efficacy, developing skills to cope with emotional triggers, teaching techniques from social skills models, managing depression, and focusing on the role of relationships in relapse (Rawson, 1995).

For stimulants such as cocaine or methamphetamine, the distinctive factors identified are drug craving and external cues, sexual behavior as a stimulus, and alcohol use as a common antecedent. Effective relapse prevention strategies included creating structure, using information, identifying triggers, addressing the connection with sexual behavior, and reducing craving. The power of conditioned triggers seems especially great in working with cocaine users, presumably because of the unique manner in which cocaine acts on the pleasure centers of the brain. Thus, a high level of structure and attention to specific triggers is essential, particularly in early recovery (Rawson, 1995).

For opiate users, relapse factors include stressful events or periods of time, pain control, and related medical factors. Relapse prevention strategies include providing tools for dealing with protracted abstinence and relapse, using and complying with narcotic antagonists, teaching stress-reduction techniques, and using behavioral and careful pharmacological measures for managing pain (Rawson, 1995).

For benzodiazepine users, relapse factors include rebound anxiety and/or symptom reemergence. These are difficult to distinguish, particularly because withdrawal from these drugs is accompanied by a rebound that can last for long periods of time. As with any prescription drug abuse or misuse, physician offices or medical settings can be a trigger. Strategies include coping with insomnia, using physical exercise for anxiety reduction, and teaching progressive relaxation and thought-stopping procedures (Rawson, 1995).

The Abstinence Violation Effect

Marlatt and Donovan (2005) made an excellent conceptual and clinical contribution by focusing on the *abstinence violation effect* (AVE), that is, the impact on the individual of having failed to keep a behavioral commitment.

The AVE is assumed to occur when the individual is personally committed to an extended or indefinite period of abstinence and a lapse occurs during this period. The actual AVE is a "cognitive–affective reaction to an initial slip that increases the probability that the lapse will be followed by an increased use of the substance or activity" (Marlatt & Gordon, 1985, p. 179). The greater the intensity of the reaction, the higher the probability of an exacerbation effect following a lapse. For example, it is common for patients to feel so ashamed and discouraged that they conclude, "Well, I've already blown it; might as well go all the way." In Marlatt and Gordon's (1985) terms, however, when the individual perceives the cause of the lapse to include specific factors over which he or she potentially has control, the relapse can more easily be abbreviated.

Within their patient's framework, perceived self-efficacy is of central importance. The patient who concludes that he or she is powerless once a lapse has occurred is more likely to fall into a more serious behavioral regression. This has been a criticism of the 12-step program approach. The emphasis on powerlessness is seen as unhelpful in this situation. (However, this stance actually reflects a lack of understanding of the concept of powerlessness.) Resetting one's sobriety date is another example. For the patient with 20 years' abstinence who relapses, starting again from Day 1 is interpreted as invalidating the achievements of the 2 decades of sobriety. Although these are matters of understanding and interpretation, there is little question that many patients respond negatively to their perceived sense of failure and benefit from having previous accomplishments validated and being empowered to move forward.

It is important for the therapist to help the patient and his or her family or significant others develop a plan to interrupt a relapse:

> Dan complained bitterly to his individual therapist about his wife's return to episodic drinking after a period of extended sobriety. His antenna grew finely tuned to her increasing irritability, insomnia, and distractibility, which he had come to recognize as a harbinger of a drinking episode. When he tried to discuss this with her, she exploded and then cried, telling him she felt he was impossible to please. On the recommendation of his therapist, she agreed to short-term work

with an addiction specialist, who reviewed the situation and helped them to make a plan.

In the case of relapse warning signs, prior to actual drinking and using, agreements on how others can give constructive feedback on what they observe can reduce the defensiveness and friction of such interactions. Similar action plans are useful once a relapse has occurred. Once elements in the buildup have been identified, preventive measures can be incorporated into a relapse prevention plan. Recovering partners or spouses can express their preferences about how constructive feedback can be offered once warning signs are noted. Other strategies include using constructive self-talk (e.g., changing from "I am a failure because I used" to "I can get a grip and build on what I have accomplished"), behaviors that have worked in the past (e.g., exercise regimens), and resumption of self-help group involvement. Reducing the extent to which the patient regresses to engagement in an alcohol- and drug-using lifestyle and increasing the commitment to recovery-related behaviors is the main focus of psychosocial efforts.

Strategies for Early and Ongoing Recovery

In keeping with the conceptual framework of initiation versus maintenance strategies for change, Annis (1982) identified specific strategies for relapse prevention counseling. For those focused on initiating a change in behavior, making use of external supports is emphasized. Examples include avoidance of risk situations, coercion, hospitalization or residential care, protective drugs, involvement of spouse or collaterals, and a directive role on the part of the therapists. In the next phase, after a period of abstinence has been achieved, external aids are gradually withdrawn while activities that promote self-efficacy are emphasized. Annis included graduated real-life exposure to a hierarchy of risk situations, multiple homework tasks within each type of risk situation, gradually reducing the use of all external aids to performance, and design of homework tasks to promote self-attribution of control. Thus, the therapist and patient, working together, identify and prioritize the high-risk situations, and the patient develops coping skills in a step-by-step fashion. In this phase, it is important that the patient not attribute success to a drug, other external constraint, or the therapist, but grow in confidence that he or she has mastered coping skills for the difficult situations.

MEDICATION AS A TOOL

A variety of medications are useful in addressing relapse dangers. Taken alone, they are not usually effective, but combined with a full program of recovery, they can be invaluable. Medications can be used to treat acute withdrawal, facilitate deterrence by causing negative or unpleasant symptoms, block the effects of a drug, block craving, and treat comorbid disorders. Through all these means, medications can be used to address specific difficulties that precipitate relapse.

Treating Withdrawal

Treatment of acute withdrawal is primarily an issue of medical safety and in addition makes the patient more comfortable. Neither of these things in themselves correlates with long-term abstinence, but the detoxification process should be viewed as an opportunity to engage the patient further in treatment and provide a "map" of the journey, making the link to activities that constitute an appropriate next step. Although expectations for the detoxification process should be limited, omitting it can undermine efforts that might otherwise be effective. Abundant clinical experience suggests that failure to provide a medicated withdrawal often results in premature treatment dropout. For example, the high early dropout of heroin addicts from therapeutic communities can be reduced by increasing the accessibility of a methadone detoxification program closely linked with the residential program to prevent attrition near the end, when the detoxification dose gets low. The admission workup for a therapeutic community is typically extensive; hence, losing the patient quickly is a costly proposition. Brief medicated withdrawal in alcoholics permits better treatment participation by improving attention and concentration. In some circumstances, it avoids life-threatening consequences. Thus, medicated withdrawal should be considered as an adjunct in the process of establishing abstinence, an important component in a comprehensive treatment strategy. The Center for Substance Abuse Treatment's Treatment Improvement Protocol (N. S. Miller & Kipnis, 2006) provides detailed descriptions of detoxification protocols for different drugs and discusses their unique issues.

Disulfiram (Antabuse) and Other Deterrents

The use of disulfiram as a deterrent to impulsive drinking is perhaps the practice most widely recognized by those outside the addiction field. It is an alcohol-sensitizing drug that was introduced in 1948 as a treatment for alcoholism (Banys, 1988). Disulfiram inhibits the oxidation of alcohol, causing a buildup of acetaldehyde, a breakdown product of alcohol that causes a toxic reaction. A person who drinks while taking disulfiram may vomit for several hours and may evidence flushing, tachycardia, shortness of breath, sweating, and a fall in blood pressure. It is the specter of profound physical discomfort that provides the deterrent effect. Unlike other medications used in treatment, disulfiram itself has no direct drug effect; it "works" by putting the brakes on impulsivity, and as such it is useful for some patients.

The research literature on disulfiram fails to support the view that its addition to a treatment program improves the long-term abstinence outcome. This is in part because there are many conceptually and methodologically flawed studies, and clinicians support the proposition that there are subgroups of alcoholics for whom it can make an important difference. These subgroups include those who are older, relapse-prone, uninsightful, compulsive, capable of tolerating a treatment relationship and following rules, and/or those who are court ordered to use the drug. Other considerations are patients in early abstinence who are in crisis or are under severe stress and those with established sobriety who can benefit from support for anxiety-provoking explorations in individual or group psychotherapy (Banys, 1988).

Disulfiram should be integrated into a comprehensive program of recovery, with collaboration between the prescribing physician and others involved in the treatment. It is all too common to find that disulfiram has been prescribed by a physician who is not connected to the overall recovery effort and who has given little instruction about how to use it effectively and how to decide when to discontinue it. Therefore, the therapist with a patient on disulfiram is advised to assume the coordinating role in this matter.

If the therapist or patient decides that disulfiram might be useful, collaboration with the prescribing physician is important. If the patient has had a recent contact with the physician, an actual visit may not be required; otherwise, laboratory work is usually done to rule out medical conditions (e.g., severe liver damage) that would contraindicate the use of disulfiram. Physicians will often prescribe it when there is some liver damage because the risks are usually lower than those of drinking until the existing liver damage becomes too great. Patients can be encouraged to obtain a prescription even if they do not fill it, because it may not be possible to obtain disulfiram quickly if a crisis occurs. The therapist should ask the physician to keep him or her informed of any changes and, if possible, to notify the therapist if the patient does not refill the prescription on the timetable that would be expected if the medication were taken as prescribed.

The therapist should also inquire periodically whether the patient is taking the disulfiram, bearing in mind that "taking my Antabuse" can drift into taking it every 3 days, when the patient happens to remember. This is often part of the buildup to a resumption of drinking. Disulfiram is less useful for those who plan their drinking, because they plan to discontinue their disulfiram, more or less consciously. Monitored (observed) disulfiram use may be ordered by the criminal justice system or by employers as a condition of return to work. Examples of less formal practices include a husband taking his disulfiram in front of his wife, who notifies the therapist if days are missed. These practices are discussed in more detail in the section on community reinforcement strategies in Chapter 7.

Many patients report that disulfiram brings enormous relief from the struggle to avoid drinking. "I only have to make the decision once a day, when I take the Antabuse," is a common reaction. Once the routine is established, the therapist should be attentive to whether the patient continues to make the behavior changes needed to achieve reliable abstinence. For some, the disulfiram provides safety, and the patient becomes more passive:

> Mary began taking disulfiram after an episode with drinking that landed her in the emergency room in a life-threatening situation. She had a stormy relationship with her sister, also an alcoholic, who was still drinking. Before a planned visit, she asked her sister on the telephone to remove the alcohol from the refrigerator and other obvious places, and her sister agreed. When she arrived, she discovered an open bottle of wine in the refrigerator. She said to herself, "Oh well, I'm on Antabuse, I don't really need to worry," and she did not raise the issue with her sister. Although she did not drink, she also missed an opportunity to develop the kind of assertion skills she will need to protect herself once she discontinues the medication.

Disulfiram is most useful when the therapist integrates it into the rest of the work, monitoring medication compliance and determining whether the necessary behavior changes are occurring. The decision to go off disulfiram is one that is only given proper attention when the therapist brings it into the treatment. Exhibit 8.1 is a handout for patients that captures the issues. It should be noted that dilsulfiram can also play a role in reducing relapse to cocaine use (Carroll, Nich, Ball, McCance, & Rounsaville, 1998). Patients often use cocaine and alcohol together, and using alcohol can precede a relapse to cocaine use. For some patients, dilsulfiram is effective in interrupting the cycle by stopping the alcohol use. Disulfiram and other medications used for alcohol rehabilitation are discussed in Kranzler, Ciraulo, and Jaffe (2009).

Naltrexone (Trexan, Revia, Vivitrol)

This opioid antagonist (blocker) was first developed for use with heroin addicts and was subsequently discovered to have benefits for alcoholics. It occupies the receptor sites and thus blocks the effects of opiates such that if the person uses heroin he or she does not get high or readdicted. It blocks reinforcement of drug taking (e.g., "No point in spending the money if I'm not going to get anything out of it") and in the same manner protects

Exhibit 8.1

Preparing to Go Off Antabuse

Antabuse is a valuable tool that can help you buy time while changing behavior patterns to support sobriety. Though it can provide security in the short run, it is important not to allow it to substitute for making needed changes.

- Looking back over the period you have been taking Antabuse, what were the hazardous times in which you might have begun drinking had you not been on it? What were the key elements that made you vulnerable?
- What old behavior patterns need to be changed to reduce your vulnerability? Pay particular attention to the areas of assertion and stress reduction. What specific changes do you need to make to be on more solid ground when you go off Antabuse? What criteria do you need to meet in order to set a date?
- What are the difficult times you anticipate during the 90 days following the date you propose for getting off Antabuse? What changes or new supports would you need in order to weather them without Antabuse?
- What would be warning signs that you need to resume Antabuse for at least a short period of time? (Use relapse prevention materials and identify specific signs.) How would you like your spouse or significant other to cooperate in this task? Have specific discussions with him or her to clarify the issues and come to an understanding about constructive actions.
- Elicit input from others about how they decided to go off Antabuse, what worked and did not work, how they would have done things differently, and so forth.

Note: Compiled by Joan E. Zweben. This handout can be used or reproduced without permission from the publisher or the authors. If reproduced, a source citation is appreciated.

the patient from readdiction. Naltrexone has been widely studied in opiate users of various socioeconomic strata and appears to be most useful for medical professionals seeking to retain their licenses, middle class or suburban addicts, and those on probation (Brahen, Henderson, Capone, & Kordal, 1984; Greenstein, Fudala, & O'Brien, 1997). Among others, the dropout rate is high. It is difficult for street heroin addicts or patients on methadone maintenance to complete the detoxification and remain drug-free long enough to be started on naltrexone, and once on naltrexone, they do not continue to take it for long (Greenstein et al., 1997).

The use of naltrexone with alcoholics (called Revia in this context) began in the early 1990s with the publication of several studies indicating decreased relapse rates when used with alcoholics involved in outpatient treatment (O'Malley et al., 1992; Volpicelli, Alterman, Hayashida, & O'Brien, 1992). Subjects in the studies reported significantly less craving and less drinking. Although the neurobiological mechanisms by which naltrexone acts are under investigation, it appears to modify the reinforcing effects of alcohol. Efforts are under way to identify subgroups of patients with alcoholism most likely to benefit, with high levels of craving and somatic symptoms being two indicators (Volpicelli, Clay, Watson, & O'Brien, 1995). It is possible that genetic studies will find markers to identify those who can benefit. O'Malley et al. (1992) investigated the integration of naltrexone and psychosocial therapy in the treatment of both opioid and alcohol dependence, looking at both supportive and coping skills therapy in an effort to determine the best matching strategies. The optimal time frame for treating alcoholics with naltrexone is not presently known.

Vivitrol is a long-acting, injectable form of naltrexone that permits dosing once a month, thus simplifying adherence. Approved for clinical use with alcoholics in 2006, it has shown efficacy in decreasing heavy drinking in alcoholic males and in promoting abstinence and decreasing relapse (Johnson, 2007). However, the studies are few at present, and lack of widespread use makes it difficult to assess Vivitrol's ultimate clinical utility.

These and other issues will be clarified through studies in progress and through longer clinical experience. Several considerations emerge for the practicing clinician. New medications often generate an excitement that may enhance the placebo effect in patients treated by practitioners compared with those in carefully controlled research studies. Thus, they generally appear more effective for the first few years, before the "romance" wears off. Problems (e.g., new side effects) emerge after medications have been in use for a while. Motivational issues of the patient remain to be clarified. The patient who seeks naltrexone rather than disulfiram may prefer to preserve the option of drinking. There is also the danger of feeding the fantasy that the drug will magically make the patient not want to drink, thereby diminishing the patient's commitment to the work of recovery. These things remain to be seen as more experience is gained with this drug. Therefore, it is important for the clinician to stress that medications are only tools, not solutions.

Medication Issues for the Therapist

The use of medication is increasingly a part of integrated treatment. The temptation to use it as a substitute for psychosocial services is increasing as managed care organizations push for quicker, less costly solutions to complex problems. Frequently, however, the best outcome is obtained through the combination of the two. In their comparison of addiction treatment outcome with three medical disorders characterized by frequent relapse (i.e., insulin-dependent diabetes, hypertension, asthma), McLellan et al. (1995) noted that poor medication compliance was a major relapse factor. This is well-known to be the case with psychiatric disorders. In fact, denial may increase as the patient feels better, and this leads to discontinuing the medication.

The psychotherapist is in an excellent position to monitor and encourage medication adherence and to help the patient solve problems if difficulties arise. Many patients are too timid, confused, and distressed to ask their questions or talk openly with their prescribing physician about their concerns. Encouragement to tolerate transient initial side effects is important to promoting an adequate medication trial. The therapist also needs to address the patient's disappointment that most psychotropic medications do not produce the immediate relief to which alcohol and drug users are accustomed. Control issues are often salient: taking the medication as prescribed versus altering the physician's recommendation without discussion. This latter should be seen as a variant of an addictive pattern.

At the same time, recovering people who are highly motivated are keenly sensitive to the meaning of taking any pill to feel better. Side effects (e.g., feeling speedy from Prozac) may trigger cravings and conflict about taking medication. It is important that the psychotherapist is open to exploring these issues and willing to assume an active role in working with the physician while coaching the patient to do the same. It is important for the therapist to remain as pragmatic as possible, basing his or her recommendations on careful observation of the patient's status and changing needs. Some therapists turn to medication only as a last resort, but some conditions (e.g., depression) are more easily modified or arrested if they are addressed early.

MEDICATIONS AS RELAPSE HAZARDS

There are several medications with legitimate uses that elicit concern about increasing relapse vulnerability. Most clinicians have seen patients whose relapse episodes appear to have been precipitated by benzodiazepines used for anxiety or opiates used for pain. Unfortunately, these issues are not simple, and rigid rules interfere with effective treatment for the individual patient.

Benzodiazepines

Most addiction specialists consider certain medications to be potential relapse hazards and believe they need to be carefully managed. *Benzodiazepines* (BZDs) are the sedative–hypnotic medications (also called *tranquilizers*) singled out for special caution in people with a personal or family history of alcoholism. Trade names include Xanax, Librium, Klonopin, Valium, Dalmane, Ativan, Serax, Restoril, and Halcion. A review of human studies indicated that BZDs have reinforcing effects in people with a past or current history of AOD abuse (Griffiths & Roache, 1985). Clinicians and some studies have also concluded that parental alcoholism is a risk factor in BZD abuse (Ciraulo, Barnhill, Ciraulo, Greenblatt, & Shaer, 1989), perhaps because of an underlying genetic factor that produces an altered response to BZDs as well as alcohol.

Patients without substance use disorders who are prescribed BZDs for anxiety disorders use them at low and stable doses, with little physician supervision of their dose levels. They do not escalate their dose, do not exceed the usual dose prescribed for anxiety, and do not develop tolerance to the antianxiety properties even when they use them over a long period of time. In contrast, in patients with a history of alcoholism, BZDs can themselves be used abusively (with escalating doses, to get high) or can precipitate a relapse to alcohol use (BZDs and alcohol are chemical cousins). There are unfortunate examples of patients who told their physician they could not take Valium because they are in recovery, only to be prescribed another BZD instead. Thus, patients who are not sophisticated about members of this drug class can be placed at risk by careless prescribing. Others, however, deliberately seek BZDs or develop an interest in them once on disulfiram. They may obtain some for a specific stressful event and suggest they will not get in trouble with them because "it's nowhere near a similar experience."

Monitoring over time can reveal that the occasions for use of the medication have become more numerous or that the patient has begun to take it before making any attempt to master the difficult situation. Thus, collaboration with the prescribing physician is desirable. In many cases, however, tricyclic antidepressants, some of the selective serotonin reuptake inhibitors, and Buspar, as well as other medications, can be effectively used without the risks of BZDs, and this is the common practice in addiction medicine. Acupuncture is also available in many addiction treatment programs. Although its use is not consistently supported by research, patients consistently report that regular acupuncture soothes anxiety and increases their stress tolerance. Behavioral techniques for management of anxiety are also well documented to be effective (Waldrop, Hartwell, & Brady, 2009). It is when these tools alone are not sufficiently effective that medication should be considered.

There are times when other medication options are exhausted and the patient is still struggling with debilitating anxiety, certainly a major relapse risk. Although many practitioners within the addiction field may insist that BZDs can never be used, others disagree and note that they may sometimes be safely used in abstaining patients who are carefully selected and closely monitored (Frances & Borg 1993; Kosten, Fontana, Sernyak, & Rosenheck, 2000). A review of articles going back to 1966 found little evidence that substance abusers with anxiety disorders are at higher risk of BZD abuse or dependence, and BZDs also do not appear to precipitate relapse (Posternak & Mueller, 2001). Caution about the use of BZDs is certainly appropriate; however, clinicians should avoid the level of dogmatism that precludes problem solving.

Wesson, Smith, and Seymour (1992) noted the reluctance of psychodynamic psychotherapists to use medication for anxiety, out of the conviction that treatment is best focused on understanding and resolving the underlying issues that generate the anxiety. They noted an important pitfall in assuming that everyone's experience of anxiety is more or less the same, thus underestimating how disabling a true anxiety disorder can be. "Pharmacological Calvinism extracts a toll in terms of needless human suffering. Some people who could benefit . . . do not seek medical treatment even when anxiety is disabling and alternatives to medication are not accessible" (Wesson et al., p. 271). The task of the clinician working with someone in recovery, therefore, is to maintain a balanced perspective that challenges the patient to master new coping skills for life's stressors without discouraging medical intervention when it can make the difference between steady progress and repeated relapse.

Pain Management

As the population ages and conditions requiring pain management increase, it is especially important for the therapist to be sensitive to a range of complex issues. Opioids are the most effective analgesics and are popular drugs of abuse as well. Patients with other drug preferences are still at risk because the use of another intoxicant elevates the risk of returning to the primary drug of abuse. At the same time, inadequate pain management for acute illness prolongs physical recovery time and may also be a factor in relapse to alcohol or illicit drugs. In the case of chronic pain, the dilemmas are even more complex because maintenance on opioid drugs may be desirable. In this context, the distinction between physical dependence and addiction is important. Physical dependence is a pharmacological property of opioid drugs defined solely by the occurrence of an abstinence (withdrawal) syndrome following abrupt discontinuation. Addiction includes compulsive, escalating use despite adverse consequences (Portenoy, Payne, & Passik, 2005).

Clinicians (physicians as well as psychologists) are often confused about these distinctions, with important consequences for sensible and humane pain management. Thus, even the patient in recovery is well advised to use adequate pain medication. For former opioid users or patients on methadone, this will mean higher than the usual doses. The elevated risk should be addressed by a review of safety strategies and an increase in recovery-related activities for several months (at least). For example, the patient who no longer attends meetings can be encouraged to resume attendance for a while. A review of other self-care activities (e.g., diet, exercise, sleep) can suggest areas for improvement or temporary enhancement. Some patients can tolerate medical or dental procedures without pain medications, and their anxious desire to do so should be treated with great sensitivity. However, they should be helped to be realistic and to put energy into strategies that have worked in the past, if they find themselves in a situation that proves more difficult than they anticipated and decide they need pain medication.

OTHER FORMS OF ADDICTIVE BEHAVIORS ASSOCIATED WITH RELAPSE

Behaviors as well as medications can elevate the risk of relapse. These behaviors may involve multiple associative triggers that enhance the desire to drink or use drugs.

Reciprocal Relapse Patterns

Eating disorders, gambling, compulsive sexual behavior, spending, and Internet use are areas in which disturbed behavior patterns resemble addiction so closely that the addiction treatment model has been applied to develop intervention strategies. Patient behaviors can display the characteristics of being compulsive, out of control, and persistent, despite adverse consequences. *Diagnostic and Statistical Manual of Mental Disorders* (4th ed., text revision; *DSM–IV–TR;* American Psychiatric Association, 2000), criteria for substance abuse can be applied to these behaviors, and descriptions of the cycle of indulgence and its aftermath certainly seem to have physical "intoxication" and withdrawal phenomena as part of the experience. It is essential to identify these coexisting disturbances because it is common for them to remain hidden and become a precipitant of relapse. Many patients become trapped in a reciprocal relapse pattern in which the compulsive or disturbed behavior precipitates relapse to cocaine (or other drugs) and vice versa (Washton & Zweben, 2006).

Eating Disorders

The relationship between eating disorders and substance abuse is a large and complex topic. The issues most germane to relapse are addressed briefly here. An *eating disorder* is a severe disturbance in eating behavior that is consistently associated with a psychological or behavioral syndrome (American Psychiatric Association, 2000). Bulimia is the most common eating disorder and the one most frequently associated with substance abuse (Holderness, Brooks-Gunn, & Warren, 1994; Wiederman & Pryor, 1996). However, it is important to be attentive to eating behaviors even when they do not meet sufficient criteria to constitute a psychological disorder. Krahn, Kurth, Demitrack, and Drewnowski (1992) studied subthreshold levels of eating abnormalities and substance use and concluded that the relationship between eating disorders and substance abuse (including alcoholism) in clinical populations extends in a continuous graded manner to subthreshold levels of dieting and substance use behaviors. Thus, concerns about dieting can increase susceptibility to relapse, especially in young women.

There are many possible ways eating disorders can be related to substance abuse patterns. They may be present prior to the onset of substance use and may either be obscured by the substance-using behavior or quiescent during this period. They may coexist with alcohol- and drug-using behaviors, serving similar ends. For example, there are striking parallels between a relapse state of mind and the thinking and behaviors associated with an alcohol, drug, or food binge. Binge eating, like alcohol and drugs, can be a way to avoid rather than address emotional stresses and problems. Alcohol can also be used to suppress the shame and panic associated with binging and vomiting, and then its use may escalate in a further reaction to violating abstinence. Women with eating disorders, noted for their low self-esteem, are especially susceptible to cocaine, which makes them feel powerful and indifferent to eating. Cocaine users may be highly invested in the thinness easily achieved and maintained while using. Weight gain during abstinence may pose a serious relapse risk. It is also a risk for patients on antidepressants, many of whom cannot achieve or sustain abstinence unless their depression is effectively addressed. Thus, treating the psychological disorder to achieve abstinence carries a risk of triggering an eating disorder, particularly if the latter has gone unnoticed during the assessment process.

It is more likely that inquiry about eating disorders will be included in the assessment in adolescent treatment programs, but eating problems are widespread in adult women as well. In fact, clinicians have noted that eating disorders may be more common in substance-abusing men than the baseline rates in epidemiological studies would indicate. Clinicians have observed gay males and middle-aged heterosexual males engaging in eating behaviors that qualify as disordered, but they are rarely the subjects of systematic inquiry:

> Steve, who was HIV positive but medically stable, went through several years of stressful events and gradually lost weight, though he remained asymptomatic. His recovery group was alarmed at the deterioration and encouraged him to pursue other options besides the marijuana he lauded for enhancing his appetite. He was accepted into a study using growth hormones to address weight loss in HIV-positive patients and began to gain weight and improve in appearance. At about the point when he again began to look healthy, he panicked about "getting fat and becoming unmarketable" and discontinued the medication.

It is important that basic interventions for eating disorders be integrated into substance abuse treatment if the relapse potential is to be effectively addressed. A variety of assessment tools exist, and medical stabilization is particularly important (Merlo, Stone, & Gold, 2009). Specialized elements (e.g., medical evaluation for problems known to be associated with substance abuse disorders, nutritional stabilization strategies to stop aberrant eating) may need to be provided by an eating disorders program, but substance abuse treatment must integrate assessment and other elements needed for an adequate relapse prevention plan. This involves having a clear understanding of the relationship between disturbed eating behaviors and the substance use pattern. Making food issues a routine part of discussion in educational sessions and therapy groups will go a long way toward ensuring that eating disorders do not become a concealed relapse risk.

Gambling

Pathological gambling is described in the *DSM–IV* as persistent and recurrent gambling behavior that disrupts personal, family, or vocational pursuits, in the absence of a manic episode. With the proliferation of gambling venues, gambling rates have risen in the general population, and the rates are higher in clinical populations (Grant, Odlaug, & Potenza, 2009). Gambling operates as a relapse factor in several different ways. Alcohol flows freely in gambling environments, and cocaine and other drugs, though less conspicuous, are also usually available. Gambling is also a strong conditioned trigger because it is usually associated with alcohol and drug use in those with a substance abuse disorder. Recent research suggests that the neurobiology of gambling and addiction to substances is similar (Potenza, 2008). For these reasons, it is advisable to discourage gambling, even if the patient does not meet criteria for pathological gambling. Patients are often difficult to convince of the importance of abstaining from gambling, but engaging in this pursuit should be viewed as a striking relapse warning sign. Cognitive–behavioral interventions have been under study for some time, but with one exception, the results are inconclusive (Grant et al., 2009).

Compulsive Sexual Behavior

Compulsive sexual behavior does not have its own formal diagnostic category, but it is certainly a concern of addiction specialists. Controversy exists as to whether the behavior is a separate entity or is secondary to other diagnoses (Shoptaw, 2009). This behavior is marked by a repetitive, compelling, or driven quality that persists despite adverse consequences. Travin (1995) offered four models for understanding compulsive sexual behavior: (a) obsessive–compulsive spectrum disorder model, (b) compulsive sexual behaviors as an affect disorder (particularly depression), (c) sexual addiction, and (d) sexual impulsivity. He noted that some compulsive sexual behaviors fit neatly into one of the models, whereas others have features of two or more of them. Treatment can include medication for the features of obsessive–compulsive disorder or an affective disorder. Compulsive sexual behavior is particularly common among stimulant users, though it is also seen in alcoholics and other drug users. It contributes to chronic relapse, treatment failure, and perpetuation of high-risk sexual behaviors that foster the spread of HIV. Undiagnosed and untreated compulsive sexuality is one of the most common preventable relapse factors. Rarely is this issue systematically addressed at intake. Some examples of specific questions areas include (Washton & Zweben, 2009, pp. 65–67):

- Is your desire to have sex stronger? Do you have more vivid sexual fantasies?
- Are you more likely to masturbate or watch pornography?
- Are you more likely to have sex or take drugs with someone you do not know?
- Are you more likely to put yourself in dangerous situations?
- Are you more likely to engage in sex acts that cause you to feel sexually perverted or abnormal?
- When you think of sex, do you automatically think of drugs?

The stimulant–sex connection appears to be much more common among stimulant-dependent males than females and more common among crack smokers than snorters. This addiction does not disappear when stimulant use stops; indeed, sexual feelings and fantasies often trigger craving.

A reciprocal relapse pattern, in which compulsive sexual behavior precip-itates relapse to cocaine and vice versa, is unfortunately common. Patients should be asked to refrain from all sexual activity for the first 30 days of treatment to give time to identify sexual relapse triggers and respond to them safely.

CONCLUSION

Relapse prevention strategies have evolved considerably in the past 10 years and include a variety of well-researched behavioral strategies, which in selected cases can be augmented in their effectiveness by pharmacological adjuncts. It is important to keep the resumption of alcohol and drug use in perspective. Although certainly an appropriate focus of intervention, it has been singled out as a clear indication of treatment failure, doubtless contributing to the public perception that "treatment doesn't work." In fact, when one considers improvement in one or more areas of psychosocial functioning and reduction of AOD use, the majority of those in treatment show positive benefits (Gerstein, 1994; Hubbard et al., 1989; McLellan et al., 1994). In most cases, unless there is a complete regression to an earlier AOD-using lifestyle, other gains will likely remain.

These gains in the areas of reduction of illicit drug use, reduction of crime, improvement in health and psychiatric status, employment, and family functioning are meaningful accomplishments even if complete abstinence cannot be sustained. This does not mean that psychologists should espouse a permissive attitude or send the message that controlled use is an equally valid goal. Many of our patients come to us having devoted decades of their lives to an effort to control their AOD use, to the detriment of their relationships, health, and job performance. But to avoid height-ening the AVE, relapse is best treated as a fact of life, with an emphasis by therapists that patients can restore good functioning relatively quickly with the appropriate commitment and effort.

References

Abram, K. M., & Teplin, L. A. (1991). Co-occurring disorders among mentally ill jail detainees. *American Psychologist, 46,* 1036–1045. doi:10.1037/0003-066X. 46.10.1036

Alcoholics Anonymous World Services. (1975). *Living sober.* New York, NY: Author.

Alcoholics Anonymous World Services. (1976). *Alcoholics anonymous* (3rd ed.). New York, NY: Author.

Alcoholics Anonymous World Services. (1983). *Questions and answers on sponsorship.* New York, NY: Author.

Alcoholics Anonymous World Services. (2001). *Alcoholics anonymous* (4th ed.). New York, NY: Author.

Alcoholics Anonymous World Services. (2007a). *Estimates of AA groups and members.* Retrieved from http://www.aa.org/subpage.cfm?page=74.

Alcoholics Anonymous World Services. (2007b). *Membership survey.* New York, NY: Author.

Allen, J. P. (2003). Assessment of alcohol problems: An overview. In J. P. Allen & V. B. Wilson (Eds.), *Assessing alcohol problems: A guide for clinicians and researchers* (2nd ed., pp. 1–11). Rockville, MD: National Institute on Alcohol Abuse and Alcoholism.

Allen, J. P., & Mattson, M. E. (1993). Psychometric instruments to assist in alcoholism treatment planning. *Journal of Substance Abuse Treatment, 10,* 289–296. doi:10.1016/0740-5472(93)90077-F

Allen, J. P., & Wilson, V. B. (Eds.). (2003). *Assessing alcohol problems: A guide for clinicians and researchers* (2nd ed.; NIH Publication No. 03-37450). Retrieved from http://pubs.niaaa.nih.gov/publications/Assesing%20Alcohol/index.pdf

American Psychiatric Association. (1994). *Diagnostic and statistical manual of mental disorders* (4th ed.). Washington, DC: Author.

American Psychiatric Association. (2000). *Diagnostic and statistical manual of mental disorders* (4th ed., text revision). Washington, DC: American Psychiatric Association.

American Society of Addiction Medicine. (2001). *Patient placement criteria for the treatment of substance-related disorders (PPC 2R)*. Chevy Chase, MD: Author.

Americans With Disabilities Act of 1990, 42 U.S.C.A. § 12101 *et seq.* (West 1993).

Amodeo, M. (1995). The therapist's role in the drinking stage. In S. Brown (Ed.), *Treating alcoholism* (pp. 95–132). San Francisco, CA: Jossey-Bass.

Anglin, M. D., & Hser, Y. I. (1991). Criminal justice and the drug-abusing offender: Policy issues of coerced treatment. *Behavioral Sciences & the Law, 9,* 243–267. doi:10.1002/bsl.2370090304

Annis, H. M. (1982). *Inventory of drinking situations (IDS-100)*. Toronto, Ontario, Canada: Addiction Research Foundation of Ontario.

Ashley, M. (Speaker). (1996). The scientific basis for guidelines on moderate drinking [Cassette recording no. Infomedix J134-ABCD]. Garden Grove, CA: Infomedix.

Baker, T. B., Piper. M. E., McCarthy, D. E., Majeskie, M. R., & Fiore, M. C. (2004). Addiction motivation reformulated: An affective processing model of negative reinforcement. *Psychological Review, 111,* 33–51. doi:10.1037/0033-295X.111.1.33

Ball, J., & Ross, A. (1991). *The effectiveness of methadone maintenance treatment.* New York, NY: Springer-Verlag.

Bandura, A. (1977). *Social learning theory.* Englewood Cliffs, NJ: Prentice Hall.

Bandura, A. (1999). A sociocognitive analysis of substance abuse: An agentic perspective. *Psychological Science, 10,* 214–217.

Banys, P. (1988). The clinical use of disulfiram (Antabuse): A review. *Journal of Psychoactive Drugs, 20,* 243–261.

Barber, J. G., & Crisp, B. R. (1995). The "pressure to change" approach to working with the partners of heavy drinkers. *Addiction, 90,* 269–276. doi:10.1111/j.1360-0443.1995.tb01044.x

Barthwell, A. G., & Brown, L. S. (2009). The treatment of drug addiction: An overview. In R. K. Ries, D. A. Fiellin, S. C. Miller, & R. Saitz (Eds.), *Principles of addiction medicine* (4th ed., pp. 349–359). Philadelphia, PA: Wolters Kluwer Lippincott Willams & Wilkins.

Batki, S. L., & Selwin, P. A. (2000). *Substance abuse treatment for persons with HIV/AIDS.* (Treatment Improvement Protocol Series 37). Rockville, MD: Substance Abuse and Mental Health Services Administration.

Beck, A. T., Wright, F. D., Newman, C. F., & Liese, B. S. (1993). *Cognitive therapy of substance abuse.* New York, NY: Guilford Press.

Bennett, L. A., & Wolin, S. J. (1990). Family culture and alcoholism transmission. In R. L. Collins, K. E. Leonard, & J. S. Searles (Eds.), *Alcohol and the family: Research and clinical perspectives* (pp. 194–219). New York, NY: Guilford Press.

Bierut, L. J., Saccone, N. L., Rice, J. P., Goate, A., Foroud, T., Edenberg, H., . . . Reich, T. (2002). Defining alcohol-related phenotypes in humans. *Alcohol Research & Health, 26,* 208–213.

Blume, S., & Zilberman, M. (2005). Alcohol and women. In J. H. Lowinson, P. Ruiz, R. B. Millman, & J. G. Langrod (Eds.), *Substance abuse: A comprehensive textbook* (4th ed., pp. 1049–1063). Philadelphia, PA: Lippincott Williams & Wilkins.

Bond, J., Kaskutas, L. A., & Weisner, C. (2003). The persistent influence of social networks and alcoholics anonymous on abstinence. *Journal of Studies on Alcohol, 64,* 579–588.

Brahen, L. S., Henderson, R. K., Capone, T., & Kordal, N. (1984). Naltrexone treatment in a jail work–release program. *The Journal of Clinical Psychiatry, 45,* 49–52.

Brown, S. (1985). *Treating the alcoholic: A developmental model of recovery.* New York, NY: Wiley.

Brown, S. (1988). *Treating adult children of alcoholics: A developmental perspective.* New York, NY: Wiley.

Brown, S. (1995a). A developmental model of alcoholism and recovery. In S. Brown (Ed.), *Treating alcoholism* (pp. 27–53). San Francisco, CA: Jossey-Bass.

Brown, S. (Ed.). (1995b). *Treating alcoholism.* San Francisco, CA: Jossey-Bass.

Brown, S. (1996, February). *Psychotherapy and AA.* Lecture presented at the meeting of the Los Angeles County Psychological Association, Los Angeles, CA.

Brown, S., & Lewis, V. (1995). The alcoholic family: A developmental model of recovery. In S. Brown (Ed.), *Treating alcoholism* (pp. 279–315). San Francisco, CA: Jossey-Bass.

Brown, S. A., Christiansen, B. A., & Goldman, M. S. (1987). The Alcohol Expectancy Questionnaire: An instrument for the assessment of adolescent and adult alcohol expectancies. *Journal of Studies on Alcohol, 48,* 483–491.

Brown, S. A., Goldman, M. S., Inn, A., & Anderson, L. R. (1980). Expectations of reinforcement from alcohol: Their domain & relation to drinking patterns. *Journal of Consulting and Clinical Psychology, 48,* 419–426. doi:10.1037/0022-006X.48.4.419

Brown, S. A., Irwin, M., & Schuckit, M. A. (1991). Changes in anxiety in abstinent male alcoholics. *Journal of Studies on Alcohol, 52,* 55–61.

Brown, S. A., & Schuckit, M. (1988). Changes in depression among abstinent alcoholics. *Journal of Studies on Alcohol, 49,* 412–417.

Bukstein, O. G. (1995). *Adolescent substance abuse: Assessment, prevention, and treatment.* New York, NY: Wiley.

Campbell, R. J. (1989). *Psychiatric dictionary* (6th ed.). New York, NY: Oxford University Press.

Carroll, K. M. (1998). *A cognitive–behavioral approach: Treating cocaine addiction* (Vol. Manual 1). Rockville, MD: U.S. Department of Health and Human Services.

Carroll, K. M., Nich, C., Ball, S. A., McCance, E., & Rounsaville, B. (1998). Treatment of cocaine and alcohol dependence with psychotherapy and disulfiram. *Addiction, 93,* 713–727. doi:10.1046/j.1360-0443.1998.9357137.x

Center for Substance Abuse Treatment. (2006a). *Client's handbook: Matrix intensive outpatient treatment for people with stimulant use disorders* (DHHS Publication No. [SMA] 06-4154). Rockville, MD: Substance Abuse and Mental Health Services Administration.

Center for Substance Abuse Treatment. (2006b). *Counselor's family education manual: Matrix intensive outpatient treatment for people with stimulant use disorders* (DHHS Publication No. SMA 06-4153). Rockville, MD: Substance Abuse and Mental Health Services Administration.

Center for Substance Abuse Treatment. (2006c). *Counselor's treatment manual: Matrix intensive outpatient treatment for people with stimulant use disorders* (DHHS Publication No. [SMA] 07-4152). Rockville, MD: Substance Abuse and Mental Health Services Administration.

Childress, A. R. (2006). What can human brain imaging tell us about vulnerability to addiction and to relapse? In W. R. Miller & K. M. Carroll (Eds.), *Rethinking substance abuse: What the science shows, and what we should do about it* (pp. 46–60). New York, NY: Guilford Press.

Childress, A. R., Ehrman, R., Rohsenow, D. R., Robbins, S. J., & O'Brien, C. P. (1992). Classically conditioned factors in drug dependence. In J. H. Lowinson, P. Ruiz, & R. B. Millman (Eds.), *Substance abuse: A comprehensive textbook* (pp. 56–69). New York, NY: Williams & Wilkins.

Childress, A. R., Hole, A. V., Ehrman, R. N., & Robbins, S. J. (1993). Cue reactivity and cue reactivity interventions in drug dependence. In L. S. Onken, J. D. Blaine, & J. J. Boren (Eds.), *Behavioral treatments for drug abuse and dependence* (NIDA Research Monograph 137, pp. 73–94). Washington, DC: U.S. Government Printing Office.

Childress, A. R., McLellan, A. T., & O'Brien, C. P. (1988). Classically conditioned responses in cocaine and opioid dependence: A role in relapse? In B. A. Ray (Ed.), *Learning factors in substance abuse* (NIDA Research Monograph Series No. 84, pp. 25–42). Rockville, MD: National Institute on Drug Abuse.

Childress, A. R., Mozley, D. M., McElgin, W., Fitzgerald, J., Reivich, M., & O'Brien, C. P. (1999). Limbic activation during cue-induced cocaine craving. *The American Journal of Psychiatry, 156*, 11–18.

Ciraulo, D. A., Barnhill, J. G., Ciraulo, A. M., Greenblatt, D. J., & Shaer, R. L. (1989). Parental alcoholism as a risk factor in benzodiazepine abuse: A pilot study. *The American Journal of Psychiatry, 146*, 1333–1335.

Cone, E. J., Fant, R. V., Rohay, J. M., Caplan, Y. H., Ballina, M., Reder, R. F., . . . Haddox, J. D. (2003). Oxycodone involvement in drug abuse deaths: A DAWN-based classification scheme applied to an oxycodone postmortem database containing over 1000 cases. *Journal of Analytical Toxicology, 27*, 57–67; discussion 67.

Cone, E. J., Fant, R. V., Rohay, J. M., Caplan, Y. H., Ballina, M., Reder, R. F., & Haddox, J. D. (2004). Oxycodone involvement in drug abuse deaths. II. Evidence for toxic multiple drug–drug interactions. *Journal of Analytical Toxicology, 28*, 616–624.

Connors, G. J., & Volk, R. J. (2003). Self-report screening for alcohol problems among adults. In J. P. Allen & V. B. Wilson (Eds.), *Assessing alcohol problems: A guide for clinicians and researchers* (2nd ed., pp. 21–35). Rockville, MD: National Institute on Alcohol Abuse and Alcoholism.

Deitch, D. A. (1973). The treatment of drug abuse in the therapeutic community: Historical influences, current considerations, future outlook. In National Commission on Marijuana and Drug Abuse (Ed.), *Drug abuse in America. Problem in perspective: Vol. IV. Treatment and rehabilitation* (pp. 158–175). Washington DC: National Commission on Marijuana and Drug Abuse.

Deitch, D. A., & Zweben, J. E. (1981). Synanon: A pioneering response in drug abuse treatment and a signal for caution. In J. Lowinson & P. Ruiz (Eds.), *Substance abuse: Clinical problems and perspectives* (pp. 209–302). Baltimore, MD: Williams & Wilkins.

de Leon, G. (1993). What psychologists can learn from addiction treatment research. *Psychology of Addictive Behaviors, 7*, 103–109. doi:10.1037/0893-164X.7.2.103

de Leon, G. (1994a). Therapeutic communities. In M. Galanter & H. D. Kleber (Eds.), *Textbook of substance abuse treatment* (pp. 391–414). Washington, DC: American Psychiatric Press.

de Leon, G. (1994b). The therapeutic community: Toward a general theory and model. In F. M. Tims, G. de Leon, & N. Jainchill (Eds.), *Therapeutic community: Advances in research and application* (NIDA Research Monograph No. 144, NIH Publication 94-3633). Rockville, MD: National Institute on Drug Abuse.

de Leon, G. (2000). *The therapeutic community: Theory, model, and method.* New York, NY: Springer.

Dodd, M. (1997). Social model of recovery: Origin, early features, changes, and future. *Journal of Psychoactive Drugs, 29,* 133–139.

Dole, V. (1988). Implication of methadone maintenance for theories of narcotic addiction. *JAMA, 260,* 3025–3029. doi:10.1001/jama.260.20.3025

Donovan, D. M. (2003). Assessment to aid in treatment planning process. In J. P. Allen & V. B. Wilson (Eds.), *Assessing alcohol problems: A guide for clinicians and researchers* (2nd ed., pp. 125–188). Rockville, MD: National Institute on Alcohol Abuse and Alcoholism.

Douaihy, A., Daley, D. C., Marlatt, G. A., & Spotts, C. R. (2009). Relapse prevention: Clinical models and intervention strategies. In R. K. Ries, D. A. Fiellin, S. C. Miller, & R. Saitz (Eds.), *Principles of addiction medicine* (4th ed., pp. 883–898). Philadelphia, PA: Wolters Kluwer Lippincott Williams & Wilkins.

Drug Addiction Treatment Act of 2000, 42 U.S.C.A. § 3502(a) (2000).

Durazzo, T. C., Gazdzinski, S., & Meyerhoff, D. J. (2007). The neurobiological and neurocognitive consequences of chronic cigarette smoking in alcohol use disorders. *Alcohol and Alchoholism, 42,* 174–185. doi:10.1093/alcalc/agm020

Eisenhandler, J., & Drucker, E. (1993). Opiate dependency among the subscribers of a New York area private insurance plan. *JAMA, 269,* 2890–2891. doi:10.1001/jama.269.22.2890

Ellis, A., McInerney, J. F., DiGiuseppe, R., & Yeager, R. J. (1988). *Rational-emotive therapy with alcoholics and substance abusers.* New York, NY: Pergamon Press.

Erickson, C. (2007). *The science of addiction: From neurobiology to treatment.* New York, NY: Norton.

Ewing, J. (1984). Detecting alcoholism: The CAGE questionnaire. *JAMA, 252,* 1905–1907. doi:10.1001/jama.252.14.1905

Field, G. (1989). The effects of intensive treatment on reducing the criminal recidivism of addicted offenders. *Federal Probation, 53,* 51–56.

Field, G. (1998). *Continuity of offender treatment for substance use disorders from institution to community* (Treatment Improvement Protocol Series 30, DHHS Publication No. [SMA] 98-3245). Rockville, MD: Center for Substance Abuse Treatment.

Fiore, M. C., Jaen, C. R., Baker, T. B., Bailey, W. C., & Benowitz, N. L. Curry, S. J., . . . Healton, C. G. (2008). *Treating tobacco use and dependence: 2008 Update.* Rockville, MD: U.S. Department of Health and Human Services.

Flores, P. (2004). *Addiction as an attachment disorder.* Lanham, MD: Jason Aronson.

Flores, P. J. (2007). *Group psychotherapy with addicted populations: An integration of 12-step and psychodynamic theory* (3rd ed.). New York, NY: Routledge.

Flores, P. J., & Georgi, J. M. (2005). *Substance abuse treatment: Group therapy* (Treatment Improvement Protocol Series 41, DHHS Publication No. [SMA]

05-3991). Rockville, MD: Substance Abuse and Mental Health Services Administration.

Flowers, L. K., & Zweben, J. E. (1996). The dream interview method in recovery oriented psychotherapy. *Journal of Substance Abuse Treatment, 13,* 99–105. doi:10.1016/0740-5472(96)00033-5

Flowers, L. K., & Zweben, J. E. (1998). The changing role of "using dreams" in addiction recovery. *Journal of Substance Abuse Treatment, 15,* 193–200. doi:10.1016/S0740-5472(97)00188-8

Frances, R. J., & Borg, L. (1993). The treatment of anxiety in patients with alcoholism. *Journal of Clinical Psychiatry, 54,* 37–43.

Frances, R., Franklin, J., & Borg, L. (1994). Psychodynamics. In M. Galanter & H. D. Kleber (Eds.), *The American Psychiatric Press textbook of substance abuse treatment* (pp. 239–252). Washington, DC: American Psychiatric Press.

Freedman, R., Adler, L. E., Bickford, P., Byerley, W., Coon, H., Cullum, H., . . . Waldo, M. (1994). Schizophrenia and the nicotinic response. *Harvard Review of Psychiatry, 2,* 179–192. doi:10.3109/10673229409017136

Fudala, P. J., & O'Brien, C. P. (2005). Buprenorphine for the treatment of opioid addiction. In J. H. Lowinson, P. Ruiz, R. B. Millman, & J. G. Langrod (Eds.), *Substance abuse: A comprehensive textbook* (4th ed., pp. 634–640). Philadelphia, PA: Lippincott Williams & Wilkins.

Galanter, M. (2005). Network therapy. In J. H. Lowinson, P. Ruiz, R. B. Millman, & J. G. Langrod (Eds.), *Substance abuse: A comprehensive textbook* (4th ed., pp. 733–743). Philadelphia, PA: Lippincott Williams & Wilkins.

Gerard, D. L., & Kornetsky, C. (1954). Adolescent opiate addiction: A case study. *Psychiatric Quarterly, 28,* 367–380. doi:10.1007/BF01567058

Gerstein, D. R. (1994). Outcome research: Drug abuse. In M. Galanter & H. D. Kleber (Eds.), *Textbook of substance abuse treatment* (pp. 45–64). Washington, DC: American Psychiatric Press.

Gerstein, D. R., & Harwood, H. J. (1990). *Treating drug problems* (Vol. 1). Washington, DC: National Academies Press.

Gerstley, L. J., Alterman, A. I., McLellan, A. T., & Woody, G. E. (1990). Antisocial personality disorder in patients with substance abuse disorders: A problematic diagnosis? *The American Journal of Psychiatry, 147,* 173–178.

Glassman, A. H. (1993). Cigarette smoking: Implications for psychiatric illness. *The American Journal of Psychiatry, 150,* 546–553.

Goff, D. C., Henderson, D. C., & Amico, E. (1992). Cigarette smoking in schizophrenia: Relationship to psychopathology and medication side effects. *The American Journal of Psychiatry, 149,* 1189–1194.

Gold, M., & Jacobs, W. S. (2005). Cocaine and crack: Clinical aspects. In J. Lowinson, P. Ruiz, R. B. Millman, & J. G. Langrod (Eds.), *Substance abuse: A com-*

prehensive textbook (4th ed., pp. 218–251). Philadelphia, PA: Lippincott Williams & Wilkins.

Goldsmith, R. J. (1997). The integrated psychology for addiction psychiatry. In N. S. Miller (Ed.), *The principles and practice of addictions in psychiatry* (pp. 3–18). Philadelphia, PA: W. B. Saunders.

Goldstein, R. Z., & Volkow, N. D. (2002). Drug addiction and its underlying neurobiological basis: Neuroimaging evidence for the involvement of the frontal cortex. *The American Journal of Psychiatry, 159,* 1642–1652. doi:10.1176/appi.ajp.159.10.1642

Gorski, T. T. (1988a). *The staying sober workbook: Exercise manual.* Independence, MO: Independence Press.

Gorski, T. T. (1988b). *The staying sober workbook: Instruction manual.* Independence, MO: Independence Press.

Gorski, T. T. (1989). *Passages through recovery: An action plan for preventing relapse.* New York, NY: Harper & Row.

Grant, J. E., Odlaug, B. L., & Potenza, M. N. (2009). Pathologic gambling: Clinical characteristics and treatment. In R. K. Ries, D. A. Fiellin, S. C. Miller, & R. Saitz (Eds.), *Principles of addiction medicine* (4th ed., pp. 509–517). Philadelphia, PA: Wolters Kluwer Lippincott Williams & Wilkins.

Greenfield, S., & Hennessy, G. (2008). Assessment of the patient. In M. Galanter & H. D. Kleber (Eds.), *Textbook of substance abuse treatment* (pp. 55–78). Arlington, VA: American Psychiatric Publishing.

Greenstein, R. A., Fudala, P. J., & O'Brien, C. P. (1997). Alternative pharmacotherapies for opiate addiction. In J. H. Lowinson, P. Ruiz, R. B. Millman, & J. G. Langrod (Eds.), *Substance abuse: A comprehensive textbook* (pp. 415–425). Baltimore, MD: Williams & Wilkins.

Griffiths, R. R., & Roache, J. D. (1985). Abuse liability of benzodiazepines: A review of human studies evaluating subjective and/or reinforcing effects. In D. E. Smith & D. R. Wesson (Eds.), *The benzodiazepines: Current standards for medical practice* (pp. 209–225). Hingham, MA: MTP Press.

Haaken, J. (1990). A critical analysis of the codependence concept. *Psychiatry and Clinical Neurosciences, 53,* 396–406.

Harper, J., & Capdevila, C. (1990). Codependency: A critique. *Journal of Psychoactive Drugs, 22,* 285–292.

Harris, K. M., Griffin, B. A., McCaffrey, D. F., & Morral, A. R. (2008). Inconsistencies in self-reported drug use by adolescents in substance abuse treatment: Implications for outcome and performance measurements. *Journal of Substance Abuse Treatment, 34,* 347–355. doi:10.1016/j.jsat.2007.05.004

Harrison, L. D. (1995). The validity of self-reported data on drug use. *Journal of Drug Issues, 25,* 91–111.

Harrison, P. A., Fulkerson, J. A., & Beebe, T. J. (1998). *DSM–IV* substance use disorder criteria for adolescents: A critical examination based on a statewide school survey. *The American Journal of Psychiatry, 155,* 486–492.

Hester, R. K. (1994). Outcome research: Alcoholism. In M. Galanter & H. D. Kleber (Eds.), *The American Psychiatric Press textbook of substance abuse treatment* (pp. 35–44). Washington, DC: American Psychiatric Publishing.

Hester, R. K. (1995). Behavioral self-control training. In R. K. Hester & W. R. Miller (Eds.), *Handbook of alcoholism treatment approaches: Effective alternatives* (2nd ed., pp. 148–159). Boston, MA: Allyn & Bacon.

Hoffman, N. G., Halikas, J. A., & Mee-Lee, D. (1987). *The Cleveland admission, discharge, and transfer criteria: Model for chemical dependency treatment programs.* Cleveland: Northern Ohio Chemical Dependency Treatment Directors Association.

Hoffman, N. G., Halikas, J. A., Mee-Lee, D., & Weedman, R. D. (1991). *Patient placement criteria for the treatment of psychoactive substance use disorders.* Washington, DC: American Society of Addiction Medicine.

Holderness, C. C., Brooks-Gunn, J., & Warren, M. P. (1994). Comorbidity of eating disorders and substance abuse review of the literature. *International Journal of Eating Disorders, 16,* 1–34. doi:10.1002/1098-108X(199407)16:1<1::AID-EAT2260160102>3.0.CO;2-T

Hubbard, R. L., Marsden, M. E., Rachal, J. V., Harwood, H., Cavanaugh, E. R., & Ginzburg, H. M. (1989). *Drug abuse treatment: A national study of effectiveness.* Chapel Hill: University of North Carolina Press.

Hurt, R. D., Ebbert, J. O., Hays, J. T., & Dale, L. C. (2003). Pharmacologic interventions for tobacco dependence. In A. W. Graham, T. K. Schultz, M. F. Mayo-Smith, R. K. Ries, & B. B. Wilford (Eds.), *Principles of addiction medicine* (3rd ed., pp. 801–814). Chevy Chase, MD: American Society of Addiction Medicine.

Imhof, J., Hirsch, R., & Terenzi, R. E. (1983). Countertransferential and attitudinal considerations in the treatment of drug abuse and addiction. *International Journal of the Addictions, 18,* 491–510.

Institute of Medicine. (1990). *Broadening the base of treatment for alcohol problems.* Washington, DC: National Academies Press.

Jarvik, M. E., & Schneider, N. G. (1992). Nicotine. In J. H. Lowinson, P. Ruiz, R. B. Millman, J. F. Langrod (Eds.), *Substance abuse: A comprehensive textbook.* Baltimore, MD: Williams & Wilkins.

Johnson, B. A. (2007). Naltrexone long-acting formulation in the treatment of alcohol dependence. *Journal of Therapeutics and Clinical Risk Management, 3,* 741–749.

Johnson Institute. (1987). *How to use intervention in your professional practice: A guide for helping professionals who work with chemical dependents and their families.* Minneapolis, MN: Author.

Kadden, R., Carroll, K., Donovan, D., Cooney, N., Monti, P., Abrams, D., . . . Hester, R. (Eds.). (1995). *Cognitive–behavioral coping skills therapy manual: Vol. 3. Project MATCH monograph series* (NIH Publication No. 94-3724). Rockville, MD: U.S. Department of Health and Human Services.

Kadden, R. M., Getter, H., Cooney, N. L., & Litt, M. D. (1989). Matching alcoholics to coping skills or interactional therapies: Posttreatment results. *Journal of Consulting and Clinical Psychology, 57,* 698–704. doi:10.1037/0022-006X.57.6.698

Kahler, C. W., Leventhal, A. M., & Brown, R. A. (2009). Behavioral interventions in smoking cessation. In R. K. Ries, D. A. Fiellin, S. C. Miller, & R. Saitz (Eds.), *Principles of addiction medicine* (4th ed., pp. 803–818). Philadelphia, PA: Wolters Kluwer Lippincott Williams & Wilkins.

Kalivas, P. W., & Volkow, N. D. (2005). The neural basis of addiction: A pathology of motivation and choice. *The American Journal of Psychiatry, 162,* 1403–1413. doi:10.1176/appi.ajp.162.8.1403

Kandel, D. B. (1975, November 28). Stages in adolescent involvement in drug use. *Science, 90,* 912–914. doi:10.1126/science.1188374

Kaskutas, L. A. (2009). Alcoholics Anonymous effectiveness: Faith meets science. *Journal of Addictive Diseases, 28,* 145–157. doi:10.1080/10550880902772464

Kaskutas, L. A., & Oberste, E. (2002). *MAA*EZ: Making Alcoholics Anonymous easier.* Berkeley, CA: Public Health Institute.

Kaufman, E. (1994). Family therapy: Other drugs. In M. Galanter & H. D. Kleber (Eds.), *Textbook of substance abuse treatment* (pp. 331–348). Washington, DC: American Psychiatric Press.

Kelly, J. F., Finney, J. W., & Moos, R. (2005). Substance use disorder patients who are mandated to treatment: Characteristics, treatment process, and 1- and 5-year outcomes. *Journal of Substance Abuse Treatment, 28,* 213–223. doi:10.1016/j.jsat.2004.10.014

Khantzian, E. J. (1981). Some treatment implications of the ego and self-disturbances in alcoholism. In M. H. Bean & N. E. Zinberg (Eds.), *Dynamic approaches to the understanding and treatment of alcoholism* (pp. 163–193). New York, NY: Macmillan.

Khantzian, E. J. (1982). Psychopathology, psychodynamics, and alcoholism. In M. Pattison & E. Kaufman (Eds.), *Encyclopedic handbook of alcoholism* (pp. 581–597). New York, NY: Gardner Press.

Khantzian, E. J. (1985). The self-medication hypothesis of addictive disorders: Focus on heroin and cocaine dependence. *The American Journal of Psychiatry, 142,* 1259–1264.

Khantzian, E. J. (1997). The self-medication hypothesis of substance use disorders: A reconsideration and recent applications. *Harvard Review of Psychiatry, 4*, 231–244. doi:10.3109/10673229709030550

Khantzian, E. J., Halliday, K. S., & McAuliffe, W. E. (1990). *Addiction and the vulnerable self: Modified dynamic group therapy for substance abusers.* New York, NY: Guilford Press.

Knight, K., Hiller, M. L., Simpson, D. D., & Broome, K. M. (1998). The validity of self-reported cocaine use in a criminal justice treatment sample. *The American Journal of Drug and Alcohol Abuse, 24*, 647–660. doi:10.3109/00952999809019614

Kohut, H. (1977). Preface. In J. D. Blaine & A. D. Julius (Eds.), *Psychodynamics of drug dependence* (NIDA Research Monograph 12). Washington, DC: U.S. Government Printing Office.

Kosten, T. R., Fontana, A., Sernyak, M. J., & Rosenheck, R. (2000). Benzodiazepine use in posttraumatic stress disorder among veterans with substance abuse. *Journal of Nervous and Mental Disease, 188*, 454–459. doi:10.1097/00005053-200007000-00010

Kosten, T. R., & Kleber, H. D. (1988). Differential diagnosis of psychiatric comorbidity in substance abusers. *Journal of Substance Abuse Treatment, 5*, 201–206. doi:10.1016/0740-5472(88)90042-6

Kosten, T. R., Rounsaville, B. J., & Kleber, H. D. (1982). *DSM–III* personality disorders in opiate addicts. *Comprehensive Psychiatry, 23*, 572–581. doi:10.1016/0010-440X(82)90050-5

Kozlowski, L., & Wilkinson, D. (1987). Use and misuse of the concept of craving by alcohol, tobacco, and drug researchers. *Addiction, 82*, 31–36. doi:10.1111/J.1360-0443.1987.tb01430.x

Krahn, D., Kurth, C., Demitrack, M., & Drewnowski, A. (1992). The relationship of dieting severity and bulimic behaviors to alcohol and other drug use in young women. *Journal of Substance Abuse, 4*, 341–353. doi:10.1016/0899-3289(92)90041-U

Kranzler, H. R., Ciraulo, D. A., & Jaffe, J. H. (2009). Medications for use in alcohol rehabilitation. In R. K. Ries, D. A. Fiellin, S. C. Miller, & R. Saitz (Eds.), *Principles of addiction medicine* (4th ed., pp. 631–643). Philadelphia, PA: Wolters Kluwer Lippincott Williams & Wilkins.

Kurtz, E. (1979). *Not-God: A history of Alcoholics Anonymous.* Center City, MN: Hazelden.

Landau, J., & Garrett, J. (2006). *Invitational intervention: A step-by-step guide for clinicians helping families engage resistant substance abusers in treatment.* New York, NY: Haworth Press.

Landau, J., Garrett, J., Shea, R. R., Stanton, M. D., Brinkman-Sull, D., & Baciewicz, G. (2000). Strength in numbers: The ARISE method for mobilizing family and network to engage substance abusers in treatment. *The American Journal of Drug and Alcohol Abuse, 26,* 379–398. doi:10.1081/ADA-100100251

Leshner, A. I. (2001). Addiction is a brain disease. *Issues in Science and Technology, 17*(3), 75–80.

Liftik, J. (1995). Assessment. In S. Brown (Ed.), *Treating alcoholism* (pp. 57–93). San Francisco, CA: Jossey-Bass.

Litt, M. D., Babor, T. F., DelBoca, F. K., Kadden, R. M., & Cooney, N. L. (1992). Types of alcoholics II: Application of an empirically derived typology to treatment matching. *Archives of General Psychiatry, 49,* 609–614.

Madras, B. K., Compton, W. M., Avula, D., Stegbauer, T., Stein, J. B., & Clark, H. W. (2009). Screening, brief interventions, referral to treatment (SBIRT) for illicit drug and alcohol use at multiple health care sites: Comparison at intake and 6 months later. *Drug and Alcohol Dependence, 99,* 280–295. doi:10.1016/j.drugalcdep.2008.08.003

Magill, M., & Ray, L. A. (2009). Cognitive–behavioral treatment with adult alcohol and illicit drug users: A meta-analysis of randomized controlled trials. *Journal of Studies on Alcohol and Drugs, 70,* 516–527.

Magura, S., & Kang, S. Y. (1997). The validity of self-reported cocaine use in two high-risk populations. In L. Harrison & A. Hughes (Eds.), *The validity of self-reported drug use: Improving the accuracy of survey estimates* (NIDA Research Monograph 167, pp. 227–246). Rockville, MD: National Institute on Drug Abuse.

Maisto, S. A., Connors, G. J., & Allen, J. P. (1995). Contrasting self-report screens for alcohol problems: A review. *Alcoholism, Clinical and Experimental Research, 19,* 1510–1516. doi:10.1111/j.1530-0277.1995.tb01015.x

Maisto, S. A., McKay, J. R., & Tiffany, S. T. (2003). Diagnosis. In J. P. Allen & V. B. Wilson (Eds.), *Assessing alcohol problems: A guide for clinicians and researchers* (2nd ed., pp. 55–73). Rockville, MD: National Institute on Alcohol Abuse and Alcoholism.

Marlatt, G. A. (1985). Relapse prevention: A general overview. In G. A. Marlatt & J. R. Gordon (Eds.), *Relapse prevention: Maintenance strategies in the treatment of addictive behaviors* (pp. 3–16). New York, NY: Guilford Press.

Marlatt, G. A., & Donovan, D. M. (Eds.). (2005). *Relapse prevention: Maintenance strategies in the treatment of addictive behaviors* (2nd ed.). New York, NY: Guilford Press.

Marlatt, G. A., & Gordon, J. R. (Eds.). (1985). *Relapse prevention: Maintenance strategies in the treatment of addictive behaviors.* New York, NY: Guilford Press.

Marlatt, G. A., & Rohsenow, D. R. (1980). Cognitive processes in alcohol use: Expectancy and the balanced placebo design. In N. K. Mello (Ed.), *Advances in substance abuse: Behavioral and biological research, a research annual* (Vol. 1, pp. 159–199). Greenwich, CT: JAI Press.

Martin, C. S., Kaczynski, N. A., Maisto, S. A., Bukstein, O. M., & Moss, H. B. (1995). Patterns of *DSM–IV* alcohol abuse and dependence symptoms in adolescent drinkers. *Journal of Studies on Alcohol, 56,* 672–680.

Martin, J., Zweben, J. E., & Payte, J. T. (2009). Opioid maintenance treatment. In R. K. Ries, S. C. Miller, D. A. Fiellin, & R. Saitz (Eds.), *Principles of addiction medicine* (4th ed., pp. 671–687). Philadelphia, PA: Wolters Kluwer Lippincott Williams & Wilkins.

Matrix Center. (1997). *Matrix model of early intervention.* Los Angeles, CA: Matrix Center.

McCrady, B. S. (1994). Alcoholics anonymous and behavior therapy: Can habits be treated as diseases? Can diseases be treated as habits? *Journal of Consulting and Clinical Psychology, 62,* 1159–1166. doi:10.1037/0022-006X.62.6.1159

McCrady, B. S., & Epstein, E. E. (1996). Theoretical bases of family approaches to substance abuse treatment. In F. Rotgers, D. Keller, & J. Morgenstern (Eds.), *Treating substance abuse: Theory and technique* (pp. 117–142). New York, NY: Guilford Press.

McCrady, B. S., Epstein, E. E., & Sell, R. D. (2003). Theoretical bases of family approaches to substance abuse treatment. In F. Rotgers, J. Morgenstern, & S. Walters (Eds.), *Treating substance abuse: Theory and technique* (pp. 112–139). New York, NY: Guilford Press.

McCrady, B. S., & Tonigan, J. S. (2009). Recent research into 12-step programs. In R. K. Ries, D. A. Fiellin, S. C. Miller, & R. Saits (Eds.), *Principles of addiction medicine* (4th ed., pp. 923–937). Philadelphia, PA: Wolters Kluwer Lippincott Williams & Wilkins.

McElrath, D. (1997). The Minnesota model. *Journal of Psychoactive Drugs, 29,* 141–144.

McFarland, B. H., Faulkner, L. R., Bloom, J. D., Hallaux, R., & Bray, J. D. (1989). Chronic mental illness and the criminal justice system. *Hospital and Community Psychiatry, 40,* 718–723.

McLellan, A. T. (1983). Patient characteristics associated with outcome. In J. Cooper, F. Altman, B. S. Brown, & D. Czechowicz (Eds.), *Research on the treatment of narcotic addiction* (pp. 500–529). Rockville, MD: U.S. Department of Health and Human Services.

McLellan, A. T., & Alterman, A. I. (1991). Patient–treatment matching: A conceptual and methodological review with suggestions for future research. In R. Pickens, C. G. Leukefeld, & C. R. Schuster (Eds.), *Improving drug abuse treatment* (Research Monograph No. 106, pp. 114–135). Rockville, MD: U.S. Department of Health and Human Services.

McLellan, A. T., Alterman, A. I., Cacciola, J., Metzger, D., & O'Brien, C. P. (1992). A new measure of substance abuse treatment: Initial studies of the treatment services review. *Journal of Nervous and Mental Disease, 180,* 101–110.

McLellan, A. T., Alterman, A. I., Metzger, D. S., Grissom, G. R., Woody, G. E., Luborsky, L., & O'Brien, C. P. (1994). Similarity of outcome predictors across opiate, cocaine, and alcohol treatments: Role of treatment services. *Journal of Consulting and Clinical Psychology, 62,* 1141–1158. doi:10.1037/0022-006X.62.6.1141

McLellan, A. T., Grisson, G. R., Zanis, D., Randall, M., Brill, P., & O'Brien, C. P. (1997). Problem–service matching in addiction treatment. *Archives of General Psychiatry, 54,* 730–735.

McLellan, A. T., Kushner, H., Metzger, D., Peters, R., Smith, I., Grissom, G., . . . Argeriou, M. (1992). The fifth edition of the Addiction Severity Index. *Journal of Substance Abuse Treatment, 9,* 199–213. doi:10.1016/0740-5472(92)90062-S

McLellan, A. T., Lewis, D. C., O'Brien, C. P., & Kleber, H. D. (2000). Drug dependence, a chronic medical illness: Implications for treatment, insurance, and outcomes evaluation. *JAMA, 284,* 1689–1695. doi:10.1001/jama.284.13.1689

McLellan, A. T., Luborsky, L., O'Brien, C. P., & Woody, G. E. (1980). An improved diagnostic instrument for substance abuse patients: The Addiction Severity Index. *Journal of Nervous and Mental Disease, 168,* 26–33. doi:10.1097/00005053-198001000-00006

McLellan, A. T., Metzger, D. S., Alterman, A. I., Woody, G. E., Durrell, J., & O'Brien, C. P. (1995). Is addiction treatment "worth it"? Public health expectations, policy-based comparisons. In D. Lewis (Ed.), *The Macy Conference on Medical Education* (pp. 165–212). New York, NY: The Macy Press.

Mee-Lee, D., & Schuman, G. D. (2009). The ASAM patient placement criteria and matching patients to treatment. In R. K. Ries, D. A. Fiellin, S. C. Miller, & R. Saitz (Eds.), *Principles of addiction medicine* (4th ed., pp. 387–399). Philadelphia, PA: Wolters Kluwer Lippincott Williams & Wilkins.

Mee-Lee, D., Shulman, G. D., Fishman, M., Gastfriend, D. R., & Grifith, J. H. (2001). *Patient placement criteria for the treatment of substance-related disorders* (2nd ed.). Chevy Chase, MD: American Society of Addiction Medicine.

Merlo, L. J., Stone, A. M., & Gold, M. S. (2009). Co-occurring addiction and eating disorders. In R. K. Ries, D. A. Fiellin, S. C. Miller, & R. Saitz (Eds.), *Principles of addiction medicine* (4th ed., pp. 1263–1274). Philadelphia, PA: Wolters Kluwer Lippincott Williams & Wilkins.

Milkman, H., & Frosch, W. A. (1973). On the preferential abuse of heroin and amphetamine. *Journal of Nervous and Mental Disease, 156,* 242–248. doi:10.1097/00005053-197304000-00004

Miller, N. S. (1995). *Addiction psychiatry: Current diagnosis and treatment.* New York, NY: Wiley-Liss.

Miller, N. S., & Kipnis, S. S. (2006). *Detoxification and substance abuse treatment* (Treatment Improvement Protocol Series 45, DHHS Publication No. [SMA] 06-4131). Rockville, MD: Substance Abuse and Mental Health Services Administration.

Miller, W. R. (1999). *Enhancing motivation for change in substance abuse treatment* (Treatment Improvement Protocol Series 35, DHHS Publication No. [SMA] 99-3354). Rockville, MD: U.S. Department of Health and Human Services.

Miller, W. R., & Baca, L. M. (1983). Two-year follow-up of bibliotherapy and therapist-directed controlled drinking training for problem drinkers. *Behavior Therapy, 14,* 441–448. doi:10.1016/S0005-7894(83)80107-5

Miller, W. R., & Hester, R. K. (1986). Inpatient alcohol treatment: Who benefits? *American Psychologist, 41,* 794–805. doi:10.1037/0003-066X.41.7.794

Miller, W. R., & Hester, R. K. (1995). Treatment for alcohol problems: Toward an informed eclecticism. In R. K. Hester & W. R. Miller (Eds.), *Handbook of alcoholism treatment approaches: Effective alternatives* (2nd ed., pp. 1–11). Boston, MA: Allyn & Bacon.

Miller, W. R., & Page, A. C. (1991). Warm turkey: Other routes to abstinence. *Journal of Substance Abuse Treatment, 8,* 227–232. doi:10.1016/0740-5472(91)90043-A

Miller, W. R., & Rollnick, S. (1991). *Motivational interviewing: Preparing people to change addictive behavior.* New York, NY: Guilford Press.

Miller, W. R., Zweben, A., DiClemente, C. C., & Rychtarik, R. G. (1994). Motivational enhancement therapy manual. (NIAAA Project MATCH Monograph Series No.2). Rockville, MD: U.S. Department of Health and Human Services.

Miller, W. R., Zweben, J. E., & Johnson, W. (2005). Evidence-based treatment: Why, what, where, when, and how? *Journal of Substance Abuse Treatment, 29,* 267–276. doi:10.1016/j.jsat.2005.08.003

Monti, P. M., Kadden, R. M., Rohsenow, D. J., Cooney, N. L., & Abrams, D. B. (2002). *Treating alcohol dependence: A coping skills training guide* (2nd ed.). New York, NY: Guilford Press.

Monti, P. M., Rohsenow, D. J., Abrams, D. B., & Binkoff, J. A. (1988). Social learning approaches to alcohol relapse: Selected illustrations and implications. In B. A. Ray (Ed.), *Learning factors in substance abuse* (NIDA Research Monograph 84, pp.141–159). Washington DC: U.S. Government Printing Office.

Moos, R. H., Finney, J. W., & Cronkite, R. C. (1990). *Alcoholism treatment: Context, process, and outcome.* Oxford, England: Oxford University Press.

Moos, R. H., & Moos, B. S. (2006). Participation in treatment and Alcoholics Anonymous: A 16-year follow-up of initially untreated individuals. *Journal of Clinical Psychology, 62,* 735–750. doi:10.1002/jclp.20259

Morgan, D., Grant, K. A., Gage, H. D., Mach, R. H., Kaplan, J. R., Prioleau, O., . . . Nader, M. A. (2002). Social dominance in monkeys: Dopamine D2 receptors and cocaine self-administration. *Nature Neuroscience, 5,* 169–174. doi:10.1038/nn798

Murphy, S., & Irwin, J. (1992). "Living with the dirty secret": Problems of disclosure for methadone maintenance clients. *Journal of Psychoactive Drugs, 24,* 257–264.

Najavits, L. M. (2002). *Seeking safety: A treatment manual for PTSD and substance abuse.* New York, NY: Guilford Press.

National Institute on Alcohol Abuse and Alcoholism. (1993). *Alcohol and health: Eighth special report to the U.S. Congress* (DHHS Publication No. ADM-281-91-0003). Rockville, MD: Author.

National Institute on Alcohol Abuse and Alcoholism. (2000). *Alcohol and health: Tenth special report to the U.S. Congress* (DHHS Publication No. ADM-281-88-0002). Rockville, MD: Author.

National Institute on Drug Abuse. (2007). *Drugs, brains, and behavior: The science of addiction* (NIH Publication No. 07-5605). Bethesda, MD: National Institutes of Health.

National Institute on Drug Abuse. (2009). *Principles of drug addiction treatment: A research-based guide* (NIH Publication No. 09-4180). Retrieved from http://www.nida.nih.gov/PODAT/PODATIndex.html

Nelson, C. E. (1985). The styles of enabling behavior. In D. E. Smith & D. R. Wesson (Eds.), *Treating the cocaine user* (pp.49–72). Center City, MN: Hazelden.

Noam, G. G., & Houlihan, J. (1990). Developmental dimensions of *DSM–III* diagnoses in adolescent psychiatric patients. *American Journal of Orthopsychiatry, 60,* 371–378. doi:10.1037/h0079171

Noel, N. E., & McCrady, B. S. (1993). Alcohol-focused spouse involvement with behavioral marital therapy. In T. J. O'Farrell (Ed.), *Treating alcohol problems: Marital and family interventions* (pp. 210–235). New York, NY: Guilford Press.

Nowinski, J., Baker, S., & Carroll, K. (1994). *Twelve-step facilitation therapy manual* (Vol. 1). Rockville, MD: U.S. Department of Health and Human Services.

O'Bryant, R. G., & Peterson, N. W. (1990). Social setting detoxification. In S. Shaw & T. Borkman (Eds.), *Social model alcohol recovery: An environmental approach* (pp. 23–30). Burbank, CA: Bridge Focus.

O'Farrell, T. J. (1993). A behavioral marital therapy couples group program for alcoholics and their spouses. In T. J. O'Farrell (Ed.), *Treating alcohol problems: Marital and family interventions* (pp. 170–209). New York, NY: Guilford Press.

O'Farrell, T. J., Choquette, K. A., Cutter, H. S., & Birchler, G. R. (1997). Sexual satisfaction and dysfunction in marriages of male alcoholics: Comparison with nonalcoholic maritally conflicted and nonconflicted couples. *Journal of Studies on Alcohol, 58,* 91–99.

O'Farrell, T. J., & Cowles, K. S. (1989). Marital and family therapy. In R. K. Hester & W. R. Miller (Eds.), *Alcoholism treatment approaches: Effective alternatives* (pp. 183–205). New York, NY: Pergamon Press.

O'Farrell, T. J., & Fals-Stewart, W. (2006). *Behavioral couples therapy for alcoholism and drug abuse.* New York, NY: Guilford Press.

O'Farrell, T. J., Hooley, J., Fals-Stewart, W., & Cutter, H. S. G. (1998). Expressed emotion and relapse in alcoholic patients. *Journal of Consulting and Clinical Psychology, 66,* 744–752. doi:10.1037/0022-006X.66.5.744

Office of National Drug Control Policy. (2010). *2010 national drug control policy.* Washington, DC: Author.

O'Malley, S. S., Jaffe, A. J., Chang, G., Schottenfeld, R., Meyer, R., & Rousaville, B. (1992). Naltrexone and coping skills therapy for alcohol dependence. *Archives of General Psychiatry, 49,* 881–887.

Orford, J., Guthrie, S., Nicholls, P., Oppenheimer, E., Egert, S., & Hensman, C. (1975). Self-reported coping behavior of wives of alcoholics and its association with drinking outcome. *Journal of Studies on Alcohol, 36,* 1254–1267.

Papp, M., Klimek, V., & Willner, P. (1994). Parallel changes in dopamine D2 receptor binding in limbic forebrain associated with chronic mild stress-induced anhedonia and its reversal by imipramine. *Psychopharmacology, 115,* 441–446. doi:10.1007/BF02245566

Peters, R. H., & Wexler, H. K. (2005). *Substance abuse treatment for adults in the criminal justice system* (Treatment Improvement Protocol Series 44, DHHS Publication No. [SMA] 05-4056). Rockville, MD: Substance Abuse and Mental Health Services Administration.

Phillips, P. E., Stuber, G. D., Heien, M. L., Wightman, R. M., & Carelli, R. M. (2003, April 10). Subsecond dopamine release promotes cocaine seeking. *Nature, 422,* 614–618. doi:10.1038/nature01476

Portenoy, R. K., Payne, R., & Passik, S. D. (2005). Acute and chronic pain. In J. H. Lowinson, P. Ruiz, R. B. Millman, & J. G. Langrod (Eds.), *Substance abuse: A comprehensive textbook* (pp. 863–903). Philadelphia, PA: Lippincott Williams & Wilkins.

Posternak, M. A., & Mueller, T. I. (2001). Assessing the risks and benefits of benzodiazepines for anxiety disorders in patients with a history of substance abuse or dependence. *The American Journal on Addictions, 10,* 48–68. doi:10.1080/105504901750160484

Primm, B. (1990). *Office for Treatment Improvement: Mission, goals, and program summary.* Rockville, MD: U.S. Department of Health and Human Services.

Potenza, M. N. (2008). The neurobiology of pathological gambling and drug addiction: An overview and new findings. *Philosophical Transactions of the Royal Society B, 363,* 3181–3189. doi:10.1098/rstb.2008.0100

Prochaska, J. O., & DiClemente, C. C. (1986). Toward a comprehensive model of change. In W. R. Miller & N. Heather (Eds.), *Treating addictive behaviors: Processes of change* (pp. 3–27). New York, NY: Plenum Press.

Project MATCH Research Group. (1997). Matching alcoholism treatments to client heterogeneity: Project MATCH posttreatment drinking outcomes. *Journal of Studies on Alcohol, 58,* 7–29.

Rawson, R. A. (1990–1991). Chemical dependency treatment: The integration of the alcoholism and drug addiction/use treatment systems. *International Journal of the Addictions, 25,* 1515–1536.

Rawson, R. A. (1994, April). Relapse prevention models. In J. E. Zweben & R. Rawson (Co-chairs), *Psychological models of outpatient substance abuse treatment: Recovery oriented psychotherapy and relapse prevention models.* Workshop conducted at the meeting of the American Society of Addiction Medicine, New York, NY.

Rawson, R. A. (1995, April). *Psychological models of outpatient treatment: Relapse prevention models.* Workshop conducted at the meeting of the American Society of Addiction Medicine, Chicago, IL.

Rector, N. A., Zuroff, D. A., & Segal, Z. V. (1999). Cognitive change and the therapeutic alliance: The role of technical and nontechnical factors in cognitive therapy. *Psychotherapy: Theory, Research, & Practice, 36,* 320–328. doi:10.1037/h0087739

Regier, D. A., Farmer, M. E., Rae, D. S., Locke, B. Z., Keith, S. J., Judd, L. L., & Goodwin, F. K. (1990). Comorbidity of mental disorders with alcohol and other drug abuse. *JAMA, 264,* 2511–2518. doi:10.1001/jama.264.19.2511

Rettig, R. A., & Yarmolinsky, A. (1995). *Federal regulation of methadone treatment.* Washington, DC: National Academies Press.

Rhodes, F. (1993). *The behavioral counseling model for injection drug users: Intervention model.* Rockville, MD: National Institute on Drug Abuse.

Ries, R. (1993). Clinical treatment matching models for dually diagnosed patients. *The Psychiatric Clinics of North America, 16,* 167–175.

Ries, R. (1994). *Assessment and treatment of patients with coexisting mental illness and alcohol and other drug abuse* (Treatment Improvement Protocol Series 9,

REFERENCES

DHHS Publication No. [SMA] 95-3061). Rockville, MD: Substance Abuse and Mental Health Services Administration.

Ries, R. K. (1996, March). *Group therapy interventions.* Paper presented at the Second Annual Conference on Dual Disorders, San Francisco, CA.

Robbins, M. S., Szapocznik, J., Alexander, J. F., & Miller, J. (1998). Family systems therapy with children and adolescents. In T. H. Ollendick (Ed.), *Comprehensive clinical psychology: Vol. 5. Children and adolescents: Clinical formulation and treatment* (pp. 149–180). Oxford, England: Elsevier Science.

Robbins, S. J., Ehrman, R. N., Childress, A. R., Cornish, J. W., & O'Brien, C. P. (2000). Mood state and recent cocaine use are not associated with levels of cocaine cue reactivity. *Drug and Alcohol Dependence, 59,* 33–42. doi:10.1016/S0376-8716(99)00103-9

Robbins, S. J., Ehrman, R. N., Childress, A. R., & O'Brien, C. P. (1999). Comparing levels of cocaine cue reactivity in male and female outpatients. *Drug and Alcohol Dependence, 53,* 223–230. doi:10.1016/S0376-8716(98)00135-5

Robert Wood Johnson Foundation. (2001). *Substance abuse: The nation's number one health problem.* Princeton, NJ: Author.

Robinson, T. E., & Berridge, K. C. (1993). The neural basis of drug craving: An incentive-sensitization theory of addiction. *Brain Research Reviews, 18,* 247–291. doi:10.1016/0165-0173(93)90013-P

Rotgers, F. (1996). Behavioral theory of substance abuse treatment: Bringing science to bear on practice. In F. Rotgers, D. Keller, & J. Morgenstern (Eds.), *Treating substance abuse: Theory and technique* (pp. 174–201). New York, NY: Guilford Press.

Rotunda, R. J., & O'Farrell, T. J. (1997). Marital and family therapy of alcohol use disorders: Bridging the gap between research and practice. *Professional Psychology, Research and Practice, 28,* 246–252. doi:10.1037/0735-7028.28.3.246

Rounsaville, B. J., Carroll, K. M., & Beck, S. E. (2009). Individual Psychotherapy. In R. K. Ries, D. A. Fiellin, S. C. Miller, & R. Saitz (Eds.), *Principles of addiction medicine* (4th ed., pp. 769–785). Philadelphia, PA: Wolters Kluwer Lippincott Williams & Wilkins.

Russell, M. (1994). New assessment tools for drinking in pregnancy: T-ACE, TWEAK, and others. *Alcohol Health and Research World, 18,* 55–61.

Sacks, S., & Ries, R. K. (2005). *Substance abuse treatment for persons with co-occurring disorders* (Treatment Improvement Protocol Series 42). Rockville, MD: Substance Abuse and Mental Health Services Administration.

Saunders, J. B., Aasland, O. G., Babor, T. F., de la Fuente, J. R. & Grant, M. (1993). Development of the Alcohol Use Disorders Screening Test (AUDIT). WHO collaborative project on early detection of persons with harmful alcohol consumption. II. *Addiction, 88,* 791–804.

Sayette, M. A., Shiffman, S., Tiffany, S. T., Niaura, R. S., Martin, C. S., & Shadel, W. G. (2000). The measurement of drug craving. *Addiction, 95,* S189–S210.

Schottenfeld, R. S., & Pantalon, M. V. (1999). Assessment of the patient. In M. Galanter & H. D. Kleber (Eds.), *The American Psychiatric Press textbook of substance abuse treatment* (2nd ed., pp. 109–119). Washington, DC: American Psychiatric Press.

Schuckit, M. A. (1989). *Drugs and alcohol abuse: A clinical guide to diagnosis and treatment* (3rd ed.). New York, NY: Plenum Press.

Schuckit, M. A. (1994). Goals of treatment. In M. Galanter & H. D. Kleber (Eds.), *The American Psychiatric Press textbook of substance abuse treatment* (pp. 3–10). Washington, DC: American Psychiatric Press.

Schuckit, M. A. (2005). *Drug and alcohol abuse.* New York, NY: Springer-Verlag.

Schultz, W. (1998). Predictive reward signal of dopamine neurons. *Journal of Neurophysiology, 80,* 1–27.

Selzer, M. L. (1971). The Michigan Alcoholism Screening Test: The quest for a new diagnostic instrument. *American Journal of Psychiatry, 127,* 1653–1658.

Sharon, E., Krebs, C., Turner, W., Desai, N., Binus, G., Penk, W., & Gastfriend, D. R. (2004). Predictive validity of the ASAM patient placement criteria for hospital utilization. *Journal of Addictive Diseases, 22,* 79–93. doi:10.1300/J069v22S01_06

Shedler, J., & Block, J. (1990). Adolescent drug use and psychological health: A longitudinal inquiry. *American Psychologist, 45,* 612–630. doi:10.1037/0003-066X.45.5.612

Shoham, V., Rohrbaugh, M. J., Stickle, T. R., & Jacob, T. (1998). Demand–withdraw couple interaction moderates retention in cognitive–behavioral versus family-systems treatments for alcoholism. *Journal of Family Psychology, 12,* 557–577. doi:10.1037/0893-3200.12.4.557

Shoptaw, S. J. (2009). Sexual addiction. In R. K. Ries, D. A. Fiellin, S. C. Miller, & R. Saitz (Eds.), *Principles of addiction medicine* (4th ed., pp. 519–530). Philadelphia, PA: Wolters Kluwer Lippincott, Williams & Wilkins.

Sisson, R. W., & Azrin, N. H. (1993). Community reinforcement training for families: A method to get alcoholics into treatment. In T. J. O'Farrell (Ed.), *Treating alcohol problems: Marital and family interventions* (pp. 34–53). New York, NY: Guilford Press.

Smith, J. E., & Meyers, R. J. (2004). *Motivating substance abusers to enter treatment: Working with family members.* New York, NY: Guilford Press.

Sobell, M. B., & Sobell, L. C. (1978). *Behavioral treatment of alcohol problems.* New York, NY: Plenum Press.

Sobell, M. B., & Sobell, L. C. (1993). *Problem drinkers: Guided self-change treatment.* New York, NY: Guilford Press.

Stanton, M. D., & Heath, A. W. (2005). Family/couples approaches to treatment engagement and therapy. In J. E. Lowinson, P. Ruiz, R. B. Millman, & J. G. Langrod (Eds.), *Substance abuse: A comprehensive textbook* (4th ed., pp. 680–689). Philadelphia, PA: Lippincott Williams & Wilkins.

Steinbauer, J. R., Cantor, S. B., Holzer, C. E., & Volk, R. J. (1998). Ethnic and sex bias in primary care screening tests for alcohol use disorders. *Annals of Internal Medicine, 129,* 353–362.

Steinglass, P. (1979). The alcoholic family in the interaction laboratory. *Journal of Nervous and Mental Disease, 167,* 428–436. doi:10.1097/00005053-197907000-00006

Steinglass, P. (1981). The alcoholic family at home: Patterns of interaction in dry, wet, and transitional stages of alcoholism. *Archives of General Psychiatry, 38,* 578–584.

Steinglass, P., Bennett, L. A., Wolin, S. J., & Reiss, D. (1987). *The alcoholic family.* New York, NY: Basic Books.

Stiles, W. B., Agnew-Davies, R., Hardy, G. E., Barkham, M. E., & Shapiro, D. A. (1998). Relations of alliance with psychotherapy outcome: Findings in the second Sheffield Psychotherapy Project. *Journal of Consulting and Clinical Psychology, 66,* 791–802. doi:10.1037/0022-006X.66.5.791

Stine, S. M., Greenwald, M. K., & Kosten, T. R. (2003). Pharmacologic interventions for opioid addiction. In A. W. Graham, T. K. Schultz, M. F. Mayo-Smith, R. K. Ries, & B. B. Wilford (Eds.), *Principles of addiction medicine* (3rd ed., pp. 735–750). Chevy Chase, MD: American Society of Addiction Medicine.

Stine, S. M., & Kostem, T. R. (2009). Ultrarapid opiate detoxification. In R. K. Ries, D. A. Fiellin, S. C. Miller, & R. Saitz (Eds.), *Principles of addiction medicine* (4th ed., pp. 604–606). Philadelphia, PA: Wolters Kluwer Lippincott Williams & Wilkins.

Substance Abuse and Mental Health Services Administration, Office of Applied Studies. (2008). *National Survey of Substance Abuse Treatment Services (N-SSATS): 2007. Data on substance abuse treatment facilities* (DHHS Publication No. [SMA] 08-4348). Rockville, MD: Author.

Sutton, M. A., & Beninger, R. J. (1999). Psychopharmacology of conditioned reward: Evidence for a rewarding signal at D1-like dopamine receptors. *Psychopharmacology, 144,* 95–110. doi:10.1007/s002130050982

Szapocznik, J., Hervis, O., & Schwartz, S. (2003). *Therapy manuals for drug addiction: Brief strategic family therapy for adolescent drug abuse.* Bethesda, MD: National Institute on Drug Abuse.

Thanos, P. K., Volkow, N. D., Freimuth, P., Umegaki, H., Ikari, H., Roth, G., . . . Hitzemann, R. (2001). Overexpression of dopamine D2 receptors reduces alcohol self-administration. *Journal of Neurochemistry, 78,* 1094–1103. doi:10.1046/j.1471-4159.2001.00492.x

Thombs, D. L. (1994). *Introduction to addictive behaviors.* New York, NY: Guilford Press.

Tiffany, S. T., Carter, B. L., & Singleton, E. G. (2002). Challenges in the manipulation, assessment and interpretation of craving relevant variables. *Addiction, 95,* 177–187.

Tiffany, S. T., & Conklin, C. A. (2000). A cognitive processing model of alcohol craving and compulsive alcohol use. *Addiction, 95,* S145–S153.

Timko, C., Moos, R. H., Finney, J. W., & Lesar, M. D. (2000). Long-term outcomes of alcohol use disorders: Comparing untreated individuals with those in Alcoholics Anonymous and formal treatment. *Journal of Studies on Alcohol, 61,* 529–540.

Travin, S. (1995). Compulsive sexual behaviors. *The Psychiatric Clinics of North America, 18,* 155–169.

Travin, S., & Protter, B. (1982). Mad or bad? Some clinical considerations in the misdiagnosis of schizophrenia as antisocial personality disorder. *The American Journal of Psychiatry, 139,* 1335–1338.

U.S. Department of Health and Human Services. (2007). *The Surgeon General's call to action to prevent and reduce underage drinking: A guide to action for families.* Washington, DC: Author.

Vaillant, G. E. (1981). Dangers of psychotherapy in the treatment of alcoholism. In M. H. Bean & N. E. Zinberg (Eds.), *Dynamic approaches to the understanding and treatment of alcoholism* (pp. 36–54). New York, NY: Free Press.

Vaillant, G. E. (1983). *The natural history of alcoholism.* Cambridge, MA: Harvard University Press.

Vannicelli, M. (1992). *Removing the roadblocks: Group psychotherapy with substance abusers and family members.* New York, NY: Guilford Press.

Vigdal, G. L. (1995). *Planning for alcohol and other drug abuse treatment for adults in the criminal justice system* (Treatment Improvement Protocol Series 17). Rockville, MD: U.S. Department of Health and Human Services.

Volkow, N. D., Fowler, J. S., & Wang, G. J. (2003). The addicted human brain: Insights from imaging studies. *The Journal of Clinical Investigation, 111,* 1444–1451.

Volkow, N., & Li, T. K. (2005). The neuroscience of addiction. *Nature Neuroscience, 11,* 1429–1430. doi:10.1038/nn1105-1429

Volkow, N. D., Wang, G. J., Fowler, J. S., Thanos, P. P., Logan, J., Gatley, S. J., . . . Pappas, N. (2002). Brain DA D2 receptors predict reinforcing effects of stimulants in humans: Replication study. *Synapse, 46,* 79–82. doi:10.1002/syn.10137

Volkow, N. D., Wang, G. J., Telang, F., Fowler, J. S., Logan, J., Childress, A. R., . . . Wong, C. (2008). Dopamine increases in striatum do not elicit craving in cocaine abusers unless they are coupled with cocaine cues. *NeuroImage, 39,* 1266–1273. doi:10.1016/j.neuroimage.2007.09.059

Volpicelli, J. R., Alterman, A. I., Hayashida, M., & O'Brien, C. P. (1992). Naltrexone in the treatment of alcohol dependence. *Archives of General Psychiatry, 49,* 876–880.

Volpicelli, J. R., Clay, K. L., Watson, N. T., & O'Brien, C. P. (1995). Naltrexone in the treatment of alcoholism: Predicting response to naltrexone. *The Journal of Clinical Psychiatry, 56*(Suppl. 7), 39–44.

Waldrop, A. E., Hartwell, K. J., & Brady, K. T. (2009). Co-occurring addiction and anxiety disorders. In R. K. Ries, D. A. Fiellin, S. C. Miller, & R. Saitz (Eds.), *Principles of addiction medicine* (4th ed., pp. 1183–1192). Philadelphia, PA: Wolters Kluwer Lippincott Williams & Wilkins.

Wallace, J. (1986). Smoke gets in our eyes: Professional denial of smoking. *Journal of Substance Abuse Treatment, 3,* 67–68. doi:10.1016/0740-5472(86)90054-1

Wallace, J. (1989). *Writings: The alcoholism papers.* Newport, RI: Edgehill.

Wallace, J. (1996). Theory of 12-step-oriented treatment. In F. Rotgers, D. Keller, & J. Morgenstern (Eds.), *Treating substance abuse: Theory and technique* (pp. 117–137). New York, NY: Guilford Press.

Walsh, D. C., Hingson, R. W., Merigan, D. M., Levenson, S. M., Cupples, L. A., Hereen, T., . . . Kelly, C. A. (1991). A randomized trial of treatment options for alcohol-abusing workers. *The New England Journal of Medicine, 325,* 775–782. doi:10.1056/NEJM199109123251105

Wampold, B. E., & Serlin, R. C. (2000). The consequences of ignoring a nested factor on measures of effect size in analysis of variance. *Psychological Methods, 5,* 425–433. doi:10.1037/1082-989X.5.4.425

Washton, A. M. (1995). Clinical assessment of psychoactive substance use. In A. M. Washton (Ed.), *Psychotherapy and substance abuse: A practitioner's handbook* (pp. 23–24). New York, NY: Guilford Press.

Washton, A. M., & Stone-Washton, N. (1981). *Step zero: Getting to recovery.* Center City, MN: Hazelden.

Washton, A. M., & Zweben, J. E. (2006). *Treating alcohol and drug problems in psychotherapy practice: Doing what works.* New York, NY: Guilford Press.

Washton, A., & Zweben, J. E. (2009). *Cocaine and methamphetamine addiction: Treatment, recovery, and relapse prevention.* New York, NY: Norton.

Weibel, W. (1993). *The indigenous leader outreach model: Intervention model* (NIDA Publication No. 93-3581). Rockville, MD: National Institute on Drug Abuse; U.S. Department of Health and Human Services.

Weider, H., & Kaplan, E. H. (1969). Drug use in adolescents: Psychodynamic meaning and pharmacogenic effect. *The Psychoanalytic Study of the Child, 24,* 399–431.

Wesson, D. (1995). *Detoxification for alcohol and other drugs* (Treatment Improvement Protocol Series 19, DHHS Publication No. [SMA] 95-3046). Rockville, MD: Department of Health and Human Services.

Wesson, D. R., Smith, D. E., & Seymour, R. (1992). Sedative–hypnotics and tricyclics. In J. H. Lowinson, P. Ruiz, R. B. Millman, & J. G. Langrod (Eds.), *Substance abuse: A comprehensive textbook* (2nd ed., pp. 271–278). Baltimore, MD: Williams & Wilkins.

Wexler, H. K., DeLeon, G., Thomas, G., Kressel, D., & Peters, J. (1999). Amity Prison TC evaluation: Reincarceration outcomes. *Criminal Justice and Behavior, 26,* 147–167. doi:10.1177/0093854899026002001

Wexler, H., Falkin, G. P., & Lipton, D. S. (1992). Outcome evaluation of a prison therapeutic community for substance abuse treatment. In C. G. Leukefeld & F. M. Tims (Eds.), *Drug abuse treatment in prisons and jails* (pp. 156–175). Rockville, MD: National Institute on Drug Abuse.

White, W. (1998). *Slaying the dragon: The history of addiction treatment and recovery in America.* Bloomington, IL: Chestnut Health Systems.

White, W. L. (2008). *Recovery management and recovery-oriented systems of care: Scientific rationale and promising practices.* Pittsburg, PA: Northeast Addiction Technology Transfer Center, Great Lakes Addiction Technology Transfer Center, Philadelphia Department of Behavioral Health and Mental Retardation Services.

Wiederman, M. W., & Pryor, T. (1996). Substance use and impulsive behaviors among adolescents with eating disorders. *Addictive Behaviors, 21,* 269–272. doi:10.1016/0306-4603(95)00062-3

Winters, K. C. (2003). Assessment of alcohol and other drug use behaviors among adolescents. In J. P. Allen & V. B. Wilson (Eds.), *Assessing alcohol problems: A guide for clinicians and researchers* (2nd ed., pp. 101–123). Rockville, MD: National Institute on Alcohol Abuse and Alcoholism.

Winters, K. C., Stinchfield, R. D., Henly, G. A., & Schwartz, R. H. (1990–1991). Validity of adolescent self-report of alcohol and other drug involvement. *International Journal of the Addictions, 25,* 1379–1395.

Wright, A., Clay, T., & Weir, G. (1990). Description of the Los Angeles County community model alcohol recovery program: The community recovery center. In S. Shaw & T. Borkman (Eds.), *Social model alcohol recovery: An environmental approach* (pp. 75–86). Burbank, CA: Bridge Focus.

Wunsch, M. J., Boyd, C., & McMasters, M. G. (2009). Nonmedical use of prescription medications. In R. K. Ries, S. C. Miller, D. A. Fiellin, & R. Saitz (Eds.),

Principles of addiction medicine (4th ed., pp. 453–463). Philadelphia, PA: Wolters Kluwer Lippincott Williams & Wilkins.

Yalom, I. (1995). *The theory and practice of group psychotherapy.* New York, NY: Basic Books.

Yamaguchi, K., & Kandel, D. B. (1984). Patterns of drug use from adolescence to young adulthood: III. Predictors of progression. *American Journal of Public Health, 74,* 673–681.

Zweben, J. E. (1989). Recovery oriented psychotherapy: Patient resistances and therapist dilemmas. *Journal of Substance Abuse Treatment, 6,* 123–132. doi:10.1016/0740-5472(89)90040-8

Zweben, J. E., & Clark, H. W. (1990–1991). Unrecognized substance misuse: Clinical hazards and legal vulnerabilities. *International Journal of the Addictions, 25,* 1431–1451.

Zweben, J. E., & Payte, J. T. (1990). Methadone maintenance in the treatment of opioid dependence: A current perspective. *The Western Journal of Medicine, 152,* 588–599.

Index

AA. *See* Alcoholics Anonymous

Abram, K. M., 106–107

Abstinence

    behavioral contract for, 154–155

    commitment to. *See* Commitment
        to abstinence

    coping strategies for, 139

    in diagnosis, 19

    with disulfiram treatment, 210

    in identification of relapse precipi-
        tants, 200

    in individual psychotherapy,
        129–137

    patient experimenting with, 125

    and psychodynamic model,
        123–124

    in psychosocial interventions,
        130–133, 136–137

    in services to drug users, 186–187

    as stabilization, 152–156

    as therapeutic orientation, 5–9

    as treatment goal, 21–22, 130

    treatment model based on, 6–8

    weight gain during, 221

    withdrawal and detoxification,
        133–136

Abstinence violation effect (AVE),
    206–208

Action stage (readiness for change),
    79

Adaptive mechanism(s)

    alcohol and other drug use as,
        41–42, 46

    in family systems, 48

    and negative reinforcement, 57–58

    neuroadaptation as, 30, 35–36, 57

Addiction

    and cigarette smoking, 100–101

    conceptualization of, 96

    continuum of, 5, 31

    defined, 5, 9

    and dopamine, 32–34

    heroin. *See* Heroin addiction

    individual psychotherapy for, 103

    models and theories of. *See* Models
        and theories of addiction

    neurobiology of, 222

    outpatient treatment for, 103

    philosophical approaches to,
        15–16

    physical dependence vs., 219

    physical vs. psychological, 31

    and psychiatric disorders, 19–20

    as stigmatizing label, 125

Addiction Research Foundation, 91

Addiction Severity Index, 73, 113

Addiction specialists, 10

Addictive behaviors, 219–224

Addicts, 9

Adolescents

assessment of, 68, 74–76

formal interventions for, 147–148

inhalant users, 69–70, 74

and modeling behavior, 37

parents' denial of AOD abuse in,
149–152

and positive expectancies about
AOD use, 54–55

Affective material, 164–166

Affect tolerance, 143

Agency for Health Care Research and
Quality, 101

Aggressive confrontation, 182–183

AIDS epidemic, 96, 186

Al-Anon, 189, 196

Alcohol and other drug (AOD) use,
13. *See also specific headings*

absence of warning signs with, 3

and benzodiazepines, 216–217

biopsychosocial model of, 54–56

check-in process for group therapy, 182

coexistence of psychiatric disorders with, 68–70

conditioned responses to, 39–40

continuum of, 5, 31

and controlled use, 6–7, 16–17,
57–58

costs of not treating, 175–176

in criminal justice populations,
106–107

cue reactivity in, 39–40

denial of. *See* Denial

loss of control with, 61–63

medical costs of, 108–109,
175–176

and modeling behavior, 36–37

in outpatient therapy settings,
22–24

self-reports of, 75–76

withdrawal from. *See* Withdrawal

Alcohol dependence

and cocaine use, 132–133

disulfiram treatment for, 210–212

and eating disorders, 221

relapse factors for, 205–206

and smoking cessation, 100–101

withdrawal symptoms with, 134

Alcoholics, 9

Alcoholics Anonymous (AA)

as coerced treatment, 106

and "crossing the wall," 5

disease model in, 15, 28

effective elements of, 193–194

as evidence-based practice, 90

in family disease model, 51–52

as group intervention, 173

HALT maxim of, 200

and individual psychotherapy,
103, 119

origins of, 14

referrals to, 192

required participation in, 194

resistance to participation in, 190

spiritual component of, 193

and therapeutic communities, 85,
88

therapist knowledge of, 195, 196

as 12-step program, 190–191

Alcoholism

and benzodiazepines, 216–217

defined, 5, 9

family interaction patterns with,
49–51

genetics of, 28–29

naltrexone treatment for, 214

as stigmatizing label, 125

Alcohol recovery homes, 92

Alcohol Use Disorders Identification
Test (AUDIT), 71–72

Alco strips, 74

Ambiguity, 142–143

Ambivalence, 179–180, 202
American College of Professional Psychology, 18
American Psychological Association (APA), 18
American Society of Addiction Medicine (ASAM), 93–94, 111, 115–116, 135
Americans with Disabilities Act, 97
Amodeo, M., 20
Anhedonia, 133
Annis, H. M., 208
Antabuse (disulfiram), 210–213
Antisocial personality disorder (APD), 106, 107
Anxiety disorders, 217–218
AOD use. *See* Alcohol and other drug use
APA (American Psychological Association), 18
APD (antisocial personality disorder), 106, 107
Arguments, 126–127
ARISE (A Relational Intervention Sequence for Engagement), 146, 148
ASAM. *See* American Society of Addiction Medicine
Assessment, 59–81
  of adolescents, 68, 74–76
  clinical diagnostic interviews for, 60–70
  and commitment to abstinence, 127
  of eating disorders, 222
  feedback in, 76–80
  measures for, 70–74
  process of, 59–60
  professional caution with, 80
  screening and measures for, 70–74
  of self-efficacy, 73
  treatment goals in, 76–80
Attachment, 43–45, 125

Attitudes, 68
AUDIT (Alcohol Use Disorders Identification Test), 71–72
AVE (abstinence violation effect), 206–208
Azrin, N. H., 166

Babor, T. F., 69
Baker, S., 138
Bandura, A., 37
Barbiturates, 66, 134
Barriers, financial, 188
Beck, A. T., 40, 138
Behavior(s)
  addictive, 219–224
  compulsive sexual, 223–224
  as conditioned responses, 39–40
  dysfunctional, 167–169
  of family members, 68
  learned, 15–17
  modeling of, 36–37
  and motivation, 202
  regression in, 155–156
  in resistance, 127
Behavioral contracting, 154–155
Behavioral management therapy (BMT), 50
Behavioral marital therapy (BMT), 170
Behavioral skills, 166–167
Behavioral therapies, 101
Bennett, L. A., 49
Benzodiazepines (BZDs)
  addiction to, 96
  factors in relapse, 206
  as relapse hazard, 216–218
  withdrawal from, 66, 134
Biobehavioral disorders, 27–28
Biochemical factors, 53–54
Biogenetic theories, 45
Biopsychosocial model, 52–58, 115–116
Birchler, G. R., 51
Bloom, J. D., 106

BMT (behavioral management therapy), 50
BMT (behavioral marital therapy), 170
Bodily processes, 133–134
Borderline personality disorder, 19
Boundaries, 47
Brain disease, 5
Brain structure
    fundamental changes in, 6, 34–36
    neuroimaging studies of, 29–30
    permanent changes in, 95
    physical changes in, 28
Bray, J. D., 106
Breathalyzers, 74
Broome, K. M., 76
Brown, S., 62, 121, 139, 156, 161–162, 164, 171, 190, 193
Bulimia, 220
Buprenorphine, 99–100
Bupropion (Zyban), 101
Burnout, 21
Buspar, 217
BZDs. *See* Benzodiazepines

Carroll, K. M., 138
CATOR (Chemical Abuse/Addiction Treatment Outcome Registry), 89
Center for Substance Abuse Treatment (CSAT), 93, 114, 138, 210
Change, readiness for, 73, 78–79
Chantix (varenicline), 101
Character pathology, 19–20
Check-in process, 182
Chemical Abuse/Addiction Treatment Outcome Registry (CATOR), 89
Chemical dependency, 89
Chief enabler role, 48
Childress, A. R., 32, 39
Choquette, K. A., 51
Cigarette smoking, 100–103
Civil Addict Program, 104–105
Clark, H. W., 19

Clinical diagnostic interview, 60–70
    coexisting psychiatric disorders in, 68–70
    degree of patient loss of control in, 61–63
    developmental and family history in, 66–68
    DSM–IV for, 63–65
    functional impairment in, 65
    physical and sexual abuse in, 70
    substance use profile in, 67–68
Clinicians, 10
Cocaine
    and anhedonia, 133
    cravings for, 66, 136–137
    disorders induced by, 69
    drug screening for, 74
    and eating disorders, 221
    and other intoxicants, 132–133
    relapse factors for, 206
    withdrawal from, 66, 134
Cocaine Anonymous, 196
Codependence (codependency)
    AOD abuse as, 51–52
    in families, 161–164
    misuse of concept of, 119–120
Coerced treatment, 105–106
Coexisting disorders
    in clinical diagnostic interview, 68–70
    in relapse patterns, 220–224
    treatment models for, 111
    and treatment setting, 4
COGA (Collaborative Study on the Genetics of Alcoholism), 29
A Cognitive–Behavioral Approach (K. M. Carroll), 138
Cognitive–Behavioral Coping Skills Therapy Manual (R. M. Kadden), 138
Cognitive–behavioral strategies
    and AOD abuse treatment models, 40

for AOD interventions, 123, 124
for coping skills, 137–138
for establishing abstinence,
130–131
for pathological gambling, 222
for relapse prevention, 171
Cognitive–behavioral–systemic
framework, 50
Cognitive factors, 121
Cognitive Therapy of Substance Abuse
(A. T. Beck), 138
Collaboration
with benzodiazepine treatment,
217
with disulfiram treatment,
210–211
with group therapy, 184–185
networks for, 117–118
with other professionals and
systems, 107–108
Collaborative Study on the Genetics
of Alcoholism (COGA), 29
College of Professional Psychology, 22
Commitment to abstinence
ambivalence about, 179–180, 202
in assessment, 127
failure to keep, 206–207
in group therapy, 179–180
in individual psychotherapy,
124–126
and psychosocial interventions,
130–133
and recovery, 176
Communication, 86, 166–167
Communities, therapeutic.
See Therapeutic communities
Community corrections programs, 105
Community recovery centers, 92
Community Reinforcement and Family Training (CRAFT), 146, 148
Comorbid disorders
in clinical diagnostic interviews,
68–70

in criminal justice populations,
106–107
of psychiatric disorders, 101–102
and treatment setting, 4
Compliance, 215–216
Comprehensive care models, 114
Compulsive sexual behavior, 223–224
Conditioned response(s)
in biopsychosocial model, 55–56
for cocaine users, 206
and cue reactivity, 39–40
in establishing abstinence, 131–132
gambling as, 222
Confrontation
in group therapy, 182–183
in therapeutic communities, 87
as therapeutic style, 61
in 12-step groups, 191
Connors, G. J., 71
Contemplation stage (readiness for
change), 79
Control, loss of, 61–63
Controlled AOD use, 6–7, 16–17,
57–58
Co-occurring disorders, 111
Cooney, N. L., 69
Coping mechanisms, 155–156
Coping skills
for abstinence, 139
cognitive–behavioral strategies for,
137–138
in family therapy, 164–167
HALT maxim for, 200
for relapse prevention, 201
and self-efficacy, 56
Counselor's Family Education Manual
(Center for Substance Abuse
Treatment), 138
Counselor's Treatment Manual
(Center for Substance Abuse
Treatment), 138
Countertransference, 20
Cowles, K. S., 50

CRAFT (Community Reinforcement and Family Training), 146, 148
Cravings
    in abstinence, 156
    biochemical, 53–54
    for cocaine, 66, 136–137
    defined, 35
    psychosocial interventions for, 136–137
    strategies for, 169–170
Criminal justice system, 103–107
Crises, 62, 155–156
Cronkite, R. C., 50
CSAT. See Center for Substance Abuse Treatment
Cue reactivity, 39–40, 55–56
Cultural issues, 195
Cutter, H. S., 51
Cyclotherapy, 171–172

Daytop, 85
Day treatment, 94
Deaths, 169
Dederich, Charles, 84, 182
Defensiveness, 149, 153–154
DelBoca, F. K., 69
de Leon, G., 85, 183
Demand–withdraw interaction, 50
Demitrack, M., 220
Denial
    and attachment, 44–45
    and awareness, 64–65
    cognitive factors in, 121
    as concept, 120–123
    and education, 132–133
    and loss of control, 62
    in parents of adolescents, 149–152
Dependence. See also Alcohol dependence; Codependence (codependency); Substance dependence
    behavioral indicators of, 63
    defined, 5, 9
    and gateway drugs, 75

Dependency, chemical, 89
Depression, 101–102, 200
Detachment, 51–52, 161–162
Detoxification
    determining need for, 65–66
    process of, 133–136, 209–210
    social model programs for, 91–92
Detoxification and Substance Abuse Treatment (N. S. Miller & S. S. Kipnis), 134
Developmental delay, 75
Developmental history, 66–68, 143–144
Developmental needs, 43
Diagnosis(-es)
    and abstinence, 19
    dual, 111
    instruments for, 72
    misdiagnosis, 22
    multiple, 111
Diagnostic and Statistical Manual of Mental Disorders (4th ed.; DSM–IV)
    abuse vs. dependence in, 9
    for appropriate referrals, 60
    and assessment of adolescents, 75
    and clinical diagnostic interview, 63–65
    definition of dependence in, 5
    and negative consequences, 57
    and organizing role of abuse, 63–64
    pathological gambling in, 222
    and relapse patterns, 220
Diagnostic instruments, 72
DiClemente, C. C., 73, 78–79
Discrepancy, 126
Disease model, 28–36
    in Alcoholics Anonymous, 14
    and attachment, 44
    and common misconceptions, 31
    euphoric recalls in, 140–141

nature of addiction in, 15
neuroimaging studies in, 29–30
and relapse research, 31–34
research evidence for, 28–29
Disempowered groups, 192
Dissemination Library of the Clinical
Trials Network, 138
Disulfiram (Antabuse), 210–213
Division 50 (American Psychological
Association), 18
Dole, V., 94, 95
Donovan, D. M., 206
Dopamine
activation of, 35
and addiction, 32–34
in cue reactivity, 55
triggers for release of, 39
Dreams, 136–137
Drewnowski, A., 220
Drink refusal skills, 201
Dropout, 178
Drug abuse. See Substance abuse
Drug Addiction Treatment Act, 99
Drug courts, 104–105
Drug dreams, 136–137
Drug experimentation, 74–75
Drug replacement therapy, 96
Drug use. See also Alcohol and other
drug (AOD) use
distinctive features of specific
drugs, 205–206
past history of, 66
"rewards" of, 128
substitution of other intoxicants,
141
transmission of HIV through,
186–187
DSM–IV. See Diagnostic and Statistical
Manual of Mental Disorders
(4th ed.)
Dual diagnosis, 111
Duration of treatment, 111–112
Dysfunctional behaviors, 167–169

Early intervention groups, 175
Eating disorders, 220–222
EBCBS (Empire Blue Cross and Blue
Shield), 98
Education
about harmful drug use practices,
186–187
and denial, 120–121
and establishing abstinence, 132–133
in family therapy, 156–160
Ego theory, 41
Ellis, A., 40
Emit Process, 74
Emotional functioning, 75
Emotions, 127, 142–143
Empathy, 60–61, 126
Empire Blue Cross and Blue Shield
(EBCBS), 98
Enabling, 47–48, 118–119. See also
Codependence (codependency)
Engagement, 146–148, 192–193
Enhancing Motivation for Change in
Substance Abuse Treatment
(W. R. Miller), 138
Environmental approaches, 90–93
Environmental cues, 32, 55–56
Episodic relapses, 202
Epstein, E. E., 49–50
Erickson, C., 32, 57
Ethnic subgroups, 195
Euphoria, 37, 140–141
Expectancies, 38, 54–55
Expectations, 181
Experiential techniques, 201
Experimentation, drug, 74–75
"Experiment with abstinence," 125
Expressed emotion, 51
External cues, 39
External supports, 208

Fals-Stewart, W., 51
Family behavioral model, 49–51
Family disease model, 51–52

Family hero role, 48
Family members
    affiliation of, with patient,
        149–152
    alcohol and other drug use by, 128
    assessment of adolescents by, 68
    in formal interventions, 146–148
    in relapse prevention, 207–208
    self-help groups for, 157–158
    substance dependence in, 67
    support/sabotage from, 67–68
Family models, 46–52, 87
Family systems
    affective material in, 165
    analysis of, 160–164
    boundaries in, 47
    history of, 66–68
    model of, 46–49
    roles in, 47–48
    rules in, 165
Family therapy
    affiliation of family members in,
        149–152
    coping strategies in, 164–167
    education in, 156–160
    engagement of patient in, 146–148
    family systems analysis in, 160–164
    relapse prevention in, 167–172
    stabilization of patient in, 152–156
Fantasies, of using, 136–137, 140–141
Faulkner, L. R., 106
Fears, 127–128, 158, 163–164
Feedback, 76–80, 179
Fellowship, 188, 190
Financial barriers, 188
Finney, J. W., 50
Flashback experiences, 69
Flores, P. J., 43–45
Flowers, L. K., 137
Food and Drug Administration, 99
Formal interventions, 146–148
Frosch, W. A., 42
Functional impairment, 61, 65

Galanter, M., 185, 186
Gambling, 222
Gateway drugs, 74–75
Genetic vulnerabilities, 27–29, 34
Gerard, D. L., 42
Gerstley, L. J., 107
Gestalt therapy, 143
Getter, H., 69
Glassman, A. H., 102
Gorski, T. T., 41, 171, 200–201
Griffin, B. A., 76
Group members, 180
Group therapy, 173–187. *See also*
    Self-help groups
    abstinence commitment in,
        179–180
    combined with individual
        psychotherapy, 184–185
    confrontation in, 182–183
    group structure in, 180–182,
        188–189
    harm reduction activities for,
        186–187
    individual psychotherapy combined
        with, 184–185
    intoxicated patients in, 183–184
    motivational enhancement
        strategies in, 175–176
    network therapy as, 185–186
    orientation for, 178–179
    recovery groups, 176–177
    screening for, 178–179
    12-step programs vs., 191

Habilitation, 84, 85
Habits, 159–160
Halfway houses, 91
Hallaux, R., 106
Hallucinogenic drugs, 69, 74
HALT (hunger, anger, loneliness, or
    tiredness), 200
Harm reduction, 5–9, 186–187
Harris, K. M., 76

Harsh confrontation, 182–183
Hazelden Foundation, 87–88
Health maintenance organizations (HMOs), 175
Heroin addiction
    methadone maintenance treatment for, 94–100
    naltrexone treatment for, 212, 214–215
    relapse, 97–98
    therapeutic communities for treatment of, 209–210
    treatment settings for, 84–85
Hervis, O., 149
Hierarchy, 188
Hiller, M. L., 76
Hirsch, R., 20
HIV, 96, 186–187
HMOs (health maintenance organizations), 175
Homeostasis, 46–48
Hooley, J., 51
Hospital-based treatment, 88
"Housing first" model, 7
Hunger, anger, loneliness, or tiredness (HALT), 200

Identity, 139–140
Ideology, 118–123
Imhof, J., 20, 21
Impairment
    in behavioral functioning, 63–64
    functional, 61, 65
    with methadone treatment, 97
    self-regulatory, 142–143
Impulsivity, 210
Indigent populations, 83–84, 98
Individualized treatment, 203
Individual psychotherapy, 117–144
    abstinence in, 129–137
    for addiction, 103
    cognitive–behavioral therapy for, 137–138

    commitment to abstinence in, 124–126
    confrontational style of, 61
    group therapy combined with, 184–185
    ideological issues in, 118–123
    insight-oriented, 123–124
    as integrated treatment, 112
    and managed care organizations, 185
    moderation management strategies in, 17
    motivational enhancement strategies in, 126–129
    as parallel treatment, 112
    recovery issues in, 139–144
    relapse in, 21–22
    as sequential treatment, 112
Inhalants, 69–70, 74
Inpatient treatment. See Residential/ inpatient treatment
Insight-oriented psychotherapy, 123–124
Institute of Medicine, 104
Instruments, 71–73
Insurance companies, 89
Integrated models
    biopsychosocial model as, 52–58
    defined, 110
    disulfiram treatment in, 212
    professional collaboration in, 108
    of treatment, 109–112
Intensive outpatient, 93–94
Interaction patterns, 149–152
Internal cues, 39–40
Interpersonal issues, 200
Interventions
    cognitive–behavioral strategies for, 123, 124
    early, 175
    formal, 146–148
    psychosocial, 99–100, 130–133, 136–137
    therapeutic communities as, 173, 174

Interviews, 178. *See also* Clinical diagnostic interview
Intoxicated patients, 183–184
Intrapsychic conflicts, 43–44
Invitational intervention, 148

Jacob, T., 50
Johnson Institute method, 146, 148
"Joining," 149–152
Juvenile justice system, 76

Kadden, R., 69, 138
Kalivas, P. W., 32
Kaplan, E. H., 42
Kaskutas, L. A., 138, 194
Kaufman, E., 152
Khantzian, E. J., 42, 45, 142
Knight, K., 76
Kohut, H., 43
Kornetsky, C., 42
Krahn, D., 220
Kurth, C., 220
Kurtz, E., 44

Labeling, 61
Lasker Award, 95
Learned behaviors, 15–17
Learning theory, 36–41
Leshner, A. I., 5, 30, 31, 34, 53–54
Level I intensive outpatient treatment, 94
Level II intensive outpatient treatment, 94
Lewis, V., 161–162, 164
LifeRing, 194–195
Litt, M. D., 69
Live-in programs. *See* Residential/inpatient treatment
Long-term residential programs. *See* Residential/inpatient treatment
Loss of control, 61–63
Lost child role, 48
LSD, 74

MAA*EZ: Making AA Easy (L. A. Kaskutas & E. Oberste), 138
Maintenance stage (readiness for change), 79
Maisto, S. A., 72
Managed care organizations
and individual psychotherapy, 185
medication treatment in, 215
and treatment modalities, 90
Marijuana
disorders induced by, 69
drug screening for, 74, 76
withdrawal, 134
Marital couples. *See also* Spouses
conflict resolution in, 130
interaction patterns in, 49–51
relapse prevention for, 170–172
Marlatt, G. A., 16, 41, 171, 199, 206, 207
Mascot role, 48
Matching, of treatment, 80, 112–116, 203
"Matrix Manuals," 201
McCaffrey, D. F., 76
McCrady, B. S., 49–50, 166, 195
McElrath, D., 88, 89
McFarland, B. H., 106
McKay, J. R., 72
McLellan, A. T., 203, 215
MDS (mesolimbic dopamine system), 30, 35
Measures, 70–74
Medical costs, 108–109, 175–176
Medical detoxification. *See* Detoxification
Medical screening, 134
Medication, 209–219. *See also* Self-medication
methadone as, 94–95
physician knowledge of, 135
as relapse hazard, 216–219
for smoking cessation, 101
therapist issues with, 215–216
for withdrawal symptoms, 209–215

Men, 221
Mesolimbic dopamine system (MDS), 30, 35
Methadone maintenance treatment (MMT), 94–100
Methamphetamines, 206
Middle class, 98, 214
Milkman, H., 42
Miller, W. R., 16, 49, 79, 126, 138
Mimesis, 152
Minnesota model, 28, 87–90
Misconceptions, 149–151
Misinformation, 120–121
Mixed-phase group models, 177
MMT (methadone maintenance treatment), 94–100
Modalities, 84–103
Modeling behavior, 36–37
Models and theories of addiction, 27–58
    biopsychosocial model, 52–58, 115–116
    disease model. See Disease model
    family models, 46–52, 87
    learning theory models, 36–41
    psychoanalytic theory, 13–14, 41–46
Moderation management approaches, 8
Moos, R. H., 50
Moralistic view, 13, 21
Morral, A. R., 76
Motivation
    and dopamine activation, 32
    enhancement of, 79–80, 138
    in group therapy, 175–176
    in individual psychotherapy, 126–129
    and positive/negative reinforcement, 37
    in relapse prevention, 202
Multiple diagnoses, 111
Mutual help groups, 187

Naltrexone (Trexan, Revia, Vivitrol), 135, 212, 214–215
Narcotics Anonymous (NA), 103, 192, 195, 196
National Drug Control Strategy, 108–109
National Institute on Alcohol Abuse and Alcoholism (NIAAA), 14, 114
National Institute on Drug Abuse (NIDA), 5, 14, 30, 112, 138
Negative consequences
    connection between AOD use and, 64–65
    feedback for patient about, 76–78
    and loss of control, 57
    memory of, 140
    rationalization of, 62–63
    and therapist as enabler, 119
Negative reinforcement, 37, 57–58
Network therapy, 185–186
Neuroadaptation, 30, 35–36, 57
Neurobiology, 222
Neuroimaging studies, 29–30, 32–33
Neurotransmitter systems, 53–54
NIAAA (National Institute on Alcohol Abuse and Alcoholism), 14
Nicotine dependence, 101
NIDA. See National Institute on Drug Abuse
"No crosstalk" rule, 178–179, 191
Noel, N. E., 166
Nonjudgmental attitude, 60–61
Norms, 191
Nowinski, J., 138
Nyswander, Marie, 94

Oakland, California, 7
Oberste, E., 138
Object relations theory, 41
O'Farrell, T. J., 16, 50, 51, 153, 166, 167, 170, 171
O'Malley, S. S., 214
Open communication, 86

Opiates (opioids)
  disorders induced by, 69
  maintenance treatment for,
    94–100
  naltrexone treatment for, 212,
    214–215
  for pain management, 218–219
  relapse factors with, 206
  ultrarapid detoxification from,
    134–135
  withdrawal from, 66, 134
Orford, J., 50
Orientation, 86, 178–179
Outpatient treatment, 93–103
  abstinence-oriented approach in, 8
  and criminal justice system, 104–105
  harm reduction strategies for, 187
  intensive, 93–94
  opioid maintenance treatment as,
    94–100
  partial hospitalization, 93–94
  psychotherapy as, 103
  smoking cessation programs,
    100–103
  therapists for, 204–205
Overdose, 99
Oxycodone (OxyContin), 99

Pain management, 218–219
Parallel treatment, 109–112
Paranoid states, 69
Parents, 150–152
Partial hospitalization, 93–94
Past history, 66
Patient(s)
  in family therapy, 146–148
  intoxicated, 183–184
  loss of control in, 61–63
  placement criteria for, 111, 115–116
  specific needs of, 203–204
  stabilization of, in family therapy,
    152–156
  therapist collusion with, 80

Patient placement criteria (PPC), 111,
    115–116
Patterns, 159–160, 202, 219–220
Peer groups, 54–55
Phase models, 176–177
Phenotypes, 29
Phoenix House, 85
Physical abuse, 70
Physical addiction, 31
Physical dependence
  absence of, 63
  addiction vs., 219
  and substance dependence, 5–6
Physicians, 10, 135, 211
Placebo studies, 38
Positive reinforcement, 37
Powerlessness, 192, 207
PPC (patient placement criteria), 111,
    115–116
Practitioners, 10
Precipitants of relapse
  and abstinence violation effect,
    206–208
  factors in, 202–206
  identification of, 200–202
  other intoxicants as, 141–142
  prevention strategies, 202–206
  recovery strategies, 208–209
Precontemplation stage (readiness for
    change), 79
Preparation stage (readiness for
    change), 79
Prescription drug abuse, 98–100
Pressure to Change (PTC), 146, 148
Pretreatment groups, 175
Primary disorders, 6
Primary treatment, 86–87
Principles of Drug Addiction Treatment
    (NIDA), 112
Private practitioners, 59–60, 117, 119
"Problem drinking," 16–17
Problem recognition, 73
Problem–service matching, 113, 203

Problem solving, 161
Prochaska, J. O., 73, 78–79
Professionals
    defined, 10
    self-help groups vs., 188–190
Project MATCH, 18, 194
Protracted abstinence syndrome,
    133–134
Psychiatric disorders
    and addiction, 19–20
    of attachment, 43–44
    coexisting. See Coexisting disorders
    in criminal justice populations,
        106–107
    in disease model, 28
    misdiagnosis of, 22
    sequential treatment for, 110
    and smoking cessation, 101–102
Psychoactive drugs, 159, 167
Psychoanalytic theory, 13–14, 41–46
Psychodynamic approach
    to addiction, 13–14
    for discomfort with spiritual
        dimension, 193
    as intervention strategy, 123–124
    to medication for anxiety, 218
Psychoeducation, 132–133, 186–187.
        See also Education
Psychological addiction, 31
Psychologists, 15–18, 21
Psychopharmacology, 66
Psychosis, 69
Psychosocial interventions, 99–100,
    130–133, 136–137
Psychotherapy. See Individual
    psychotherapy
PTC (Pressure to Change), 146, 148
Public health, 7, 186–187
Public sector programs, 114

Questionnaires, 71

Racial subgroups, 195
Rationalizations, 62–63

Rawson, R. A., 205
Reactivity, to cues, 39–40
Readiness for change, 73, 78–79
Recidivism, 104
Reciprocal determinism, 36
Reciprocal relapse patterns, 219–224
"Recovering person" identity,
    139–140
Recovery
    and abstinence, 176
    in Alcoholics Anonymous, 14
    community recovery centers for,
        92
    defined, 8–9
    in individual psychotherapy,
        139–144
    process of, 156–160
    and relapse precipitants, 208–209
    skills for, 138
Recovery checklist, 130–131
Recovery groups, 176–177
Recovery-oriented models, 123–124
Reentry process, 87
Referral, 5, 59–60
Rehabilitation
    habilitation vs., 84, 85
    28-day programs for, 89–90, 93
Reimbursement policies, 89
Reinforcement, 37
Relapse
    in disease model, 31–34
    fears about, 158
    intoxicants as precipitants of,
        141–142
    measures for risk of, 73
    of methadone users, 97–98
    rates of, 199
    research on propensity for, 31–34
Relapse prevention, 199–224
    and addictive behaviors, 219–224
    affective material in, 164–165
    defined, 167, 199
    in family therapy, 167–172

Relapse prevention (*continued*)
  in individual psychotherapy,
    21–22
  medication for, 209–219
  plan for, 158–159
  precipitants of, 200–209
Relationships, 86
Religious approach, 13, 85
Research evidence, 8–9
  for disease model, 28–29
  for psychoanalytic theories, 45
  on relapse propensity, 31–34
Residential/inpatient treatment,
    84–93
  abstinence-oriented approach in, 8
  detoxification in, 134
  environmental approaches for,
    90–93
  Minnesota model of, 87–90
  social model of, 90–93
  therapeutic communities, 84–87
Resistance
  in group therapy, 179
  to self-help groups, 189–190, 192
  to spiritual component, 193
  therapist response to, 127
  to 12-step programs, 137
Responses, conditioned. *See* Conditioned response(s)
Revia (naltrexone), 212, 214–215
Ries, R., 109, 187
Rituals, 161–162
Rohrbaugh, M. J., 50
Role play, 183, 201
Roles, family, 47–48
Rollnick, S., 16
Rotunda, R. J., 50
Routines, 161–162
Rules, 46–47, 151, 181

Safety net, 160
SBIRT (screening, brief intervention,
  referral to treatment), 72

Scapegoat role, 48
Schizophrenia, 69, 70, 102
Schwartz, S., 149
Screening
  in assessment, 70–74
  for group therapy placement,
    178–179
  instruments for, 71–72
  medical, 134
  for multiple drug use, 135
  urine testing, 73–74
Screening, brief intervention, referral
  to treatment (SBIRT), 72
Sedative–hypnotic medications, 216
Seeking Safety (L. M. Najavits), 129,
  138
Seizures, 66, 134
Selective serotonin reuptake
  inhibitors, 217
Self-care, 143
Self-development, 143
Self-efficacy
  in abstinence violation effect, 207
  activities for, 208–209
  assessment of, 73
  in biopsychosocial model, 56
  in learning theory model, 38–39
  therapist support of, 127
Self-esteem, 143
Self-help groups, 187–197
  in addiction treatment, 173–174
  as alternative to 12-step programs,
    194–195
  cultural issues with, 195
  elements of, 187–188
  for family members, 157–158
  professional treatment vs., 188–190
  therapist knowledge of, 195–197
  in treatment recommendations, 78
  12-step programs as, 190–194
Self-identity, 139–140
Self-Management and Recovery
  Training (SMART), 194, 195

Self-medication
  hypothesis of, 41–43
  for physical/sexual abuse, 70
  and resistance to abstinence,
    128–129
Self-regulation, 142–143
Self-reports, 75–76
Sell, R. D., 50
Sequential treatment, 109–112
Serious illness, 169
Settings, 4, 84–103
Sexual abuse, 70
Sexual behavior, compulsive,
  223–224
Sexual issues, 170
Seymour, R., 218
Shame, 21, 61
Shoham, V., 50
Side effects, 215–216
Significant others. See Spouses
Simpson, D. D., 76
Sisson, R. W., 166
Slip, 202
SLT (social learning theory), 36
SMART (Self-Management
    and Recovery Training),
    194, 195
Smith, D. E., 218
"Smoke Gets in Our Eyes"
    (J. Wallace), 100
Smoking cessation, 100–103
Smoking Cessation Guidelines, 101
"Sobering centers," 91
Sobriety, 46, 155, 157, 200. See also
    Abstinence
"Sobriety sampling," 125
Social and community model
    approaches, 90
Social functioning, 75
Social learning theory (SLT), 36
Social model, 90–93
Social networks, 142
Sociocultural theories, 45

Socioeconomic class, 98, 214
Solvent inhalation, 69–70, 74
Specific drugs, 205–206
Spiritual component, 193
Sponsors, 157, 192–193
Spouses. See also Marital couples
  AOD use by, 128
  and codependence, 51–52
  interaction patterns of, 49–51
  in relapse prevention, 207–208
Standardization, 112–113
Steinglass, P., 47
Step zero groups, 176
Stickle, T. R., 50
Stigmatization
  with AOD abuse labels, 125
  and codependency, 120
  with detoxification programs, 91
  with methadone maintenance
    treatment, 95–96, 99
  with multiple diagnoses, 111
  of opiate users, 98
  of recovering persons, 140
Stimulant users, 223–224
Stranger anxiety, 190
Stress, 200
Stress reduction, 166–167
Subcultures, 173
Substance abuse
  and antisocial personality
    disorder, 107
  and benzodiazepine use, 218
  criteria for, 63–64
  defined, 9
  detection of, 59–60
  and eating disorders, 220–222
  family behaviors that perpetuate,
    160–163
  organizing role of, 63–64
  therapeutic model for treatment
    of, 85–87
Substance Abuse and Mental Health
  Services Administration, 72

Substance abuse field, 13–25
  changes in, 13–15
  difficulties of working with
      patients in, 18–22
  psychologists in, 15–18
  rewards of working with patients
      in, 22–24
Substance dependence
  behavioral indicators of, 63
  and controlled use, 17–18
  in families, 67
  family members' attitudes toward,
      67–68
  learning theory on, 41
  and physical dependence, 5–6
Substance-induced disorders, 69–70
Suicide, 69
Support system
  external, 208
  family members as, 67–68
  network therapy for, 185–186
  in ongoing recovery, 142
  practical, 190
  self-help groups as, 187–188
  in social model programs, 92
  subculture of, for recovery, 173
Synanon, 84, 87, 182
Szapocznik, J., 149

TCs. See Therapeutic communities
Teplin, L. A., 106–107
Terenzi, R. E., 20
Terminology, 9–10
Theories. See Models and theories of
      addiction
Therapeutic communities (TCs)
  confrontation in, 182–183
  as group intervention, 173, 174
  for incarcerated patients, 104, 106
  as residential/inpatient treatment,
      84–87
Therapist(s)
  approach to patient drug testing,
      73–74

cautions for, 80, 216–219
  defined, 10
  with group therapies, 183
  medication issues for, 215–216
  outpatient, 204–205
  patient mistrust of, 190–191
  and patient motivation, 127–129
  as professional enablers, 119
  and self-help groups, 189–190,
      195–197
  use of denial label by, 122–123
Therapy. See Individual psychother-
      apy
Thinking disorders, 121
Thought-stopping techniques, 131
Tiffany, S. T., 72
Time frames, 139
Timing, 164–165, 202
Tolerance, affect, 143
Tonigan, J. S., 195
Toxicology screens, 135
Tranquilizers, 216
Transition groups, 175, 178
Traumatic experiences, 129, 143–144
Travin, S., 223
Treating Alcoholism (S. Brown), 156
Treating the Alcoholic (S. Brown), 156
Treatment, 83–116
  and abstinence, 6–8
  attachment model in, 44–45
  Center for Substance Abuse Treat-
      ment model for, 114
  coerced, 105–106
  in criminal justice system, 103–107
  duration of, 111–112
  formulation of plan for, 112–113
  group therapy for. See Group
      therapy
  individualized, 203
  integrated model of, 109–112
  matching of, 80, 112–116, 203
  modalities of, 84–103
  outpatient, 93–103

parallel model of, 109–112
patient placement criteria for,
115–116
problem–service matching in, 113
recommendations for, 78
residential/inpatient, 84–93
selection of, 107–109
self-help groups for. *See* Self-help
groups
sequential model of, 109–112
settings for, 84–103
Treatment goal(s)
abstinence as, 21–22, 130
in assessment, 76–80
behavioral contracting for,
154–155
in behavioral management
therapy, 50
in behavioral marital therapy, 170
controlled drinking as, 16–17
in group therapy, 179–180
of separate treatment systems, 108
and stages of readiness for change,
78–79
Treatment Improvement Protocol,
210
Treatment plan
failure to comply with, 159
formulation of, 112–113
instruments for, 72–73
screening in, 178
structure of, 136
Treatment settings, 4
in environmental approaches,
90–93
for heroin addiction, 84–85
for indigent populations, 83–84
in Minnesota model, 87–90
for outpatient treatment, 93–103
in therapeutic communities,
84–87
Trexan (naltrexone), 212, 214–215
Tricyclic antidepressants, 217

Trigger(s)
for cocaine users, 206
gambling as, 222
identification of, 131–132
for release of dopamine, 39
sexual, 223–224
strategies for, 168–169
Trust, 158
TWEAK, 71
12-step program(s)
Alcoholics Anonymous as, 14,
190–191
alternatives to AA, 194–195
in attachment model, 44–45
and behavioral models, 16
as evidence-based practice, 90
in family disease model, 51–52
group structure in, 188–189
and learning models, 16
process of, 178–179
in recovery process, 157
selection of, 192
self-efficacy in, 207
as self-help group, 190–194
and therapeutic communities
model, 88
therapist knowledge of, 195–197
in treatment plan, 137
*Twelve Step Facilitation Therapy
Manual* (J. Nowinski, S. Baker,
& K. Carroll), 138
28-day rehabilitation programs,
89–90, 93, 182

Unresolved issues, 170–171
Urine drug screens, 73–74
Use-to-addiction continuum, 5, 31

Vannicelli, M., 174
Varenicline (Chantix), 101
Vivitrol (naltrexone), 212, 214–215
Volk, R. J., 71
Volkow, N., 5, 32

Wallace, J., 100
Warning signs, 159–160, 201,
    204–205
Washton, A. M., 61, 64
Weider, H., 42
Wesson, D. R., 218
Willmar State Hospital, 87–88
Wilson, Bill, 14, 28
Withdrawal
    from alcohol, 134
    from barbiturates, 66, 134
    from benzodiazepines, 66, 134
    from cocaine, 66, 134
    educating the patient about, 133
    effects of, 133–136

fear of, 127–128
    medical issues with, 66
    medication for treatment of,
        209–215
    from opiates, 66, 134
    prevention effects of methadone,
        95
Wolin, S. J., 49
Working class, 98
"Working the steps," 191

Yalom, I., 174

Zweben, J. E., 19, 137, 181, 197
Zyban (bupropion), 101

About the Authors

Robert D. Margolis, PhD, is a licensed clinical psychologist and has specialized in adolescent addiction and substance abuse since 1977. He is the founder and executive director of Solutions Intensive Outpatient Program, a treatment program for adolescents in Roswell, Georgia. Dr. Margolis was director of psychological services at the Ridgeview Institute from 1984 to 1997.

Dr. Margolis received his undergraduate degree from Duke University and his doctorate in clinical psychology from Georgia State University. He completed an American Psychological Association (APA)–approved full-time predoctoral clinical psychology internship from Duke University's Department of Psychiatry/Division of Medical Psychology. He holds the APA College Certificate of Proficiency in the Treatment of Alcohol and Other Psychoactive Substance Use Disorders. He is a fellow of APA's Division 50 (Addictions). He has served as an APA consultant on addiction-related matters and has appeared in numerous television documentaries on alcohol and drug abuse problems. Dr. Margolis has authored more than 15 articles and several book chapters on substance abuse and dependence. In 1997, he coauthored the first edition of this book with Joan E. Zweben.

Joan E. Zweben, PhD, is the founder and executive director of the 14th Street Clinic and Medical Group (1979–2007) and the East Bay Community Recovery Project (1989–present) in Oakland, California. The East Bay

Community Recovery Project has been providing medical and psychosocial services to alcohol and other drug-dependent patients and their families and is a training site for graduate students and interns in the San Francisco Bay area. Through these organizations, she has collaborated with researchers locally and nationally since 1981 and has been on the national steering committee of the National Institute on Drug Abuse's Clinical Trials Network since 2002. Dr. Zweben received her undergraduate degree from Brandeis University and her doctorate in clinical psychology from the University of Michigan. She is licensed in California, holds the American Psychological Association (APA) College Certificate of Proficiency in the Treatment of Alcohol and Other Psychoactive Substance Use Disorders, and is a fellow of APA's Division 50 (Addictions). Dr. Zweben is the author of four books and more than 60 articles and book chapters and is the editor of 15 monographs on treating addiction. She is active in training professionals from a variety of disciplines who work in mental health or addiction treatment settings. She is also health sciences clinical professor of psychiatry in the School of Medicine at the University of California, San Francisco.